Advanced Applied
PSYCHOLOGY

Advanced Applied PSYCHOLOGY

Psychology Applied to Crime, Society and Industry

Volume-2

Ram Nath Sharma
Rachana Sharma

ATLANTIC
PUBLISHERS & DISTRIBUTORS (P) LTD

Published by

ATLANTIC

PUBLISHERS & DISTRIBUTORS (P) LTD

7/22, Ansari Road, Darya Ganj, New Delhi-110002
Phones : +91-11-40775252, 40775214, 23273880, 23275880
Fax: +91-11-23285873
Web: www.atlanticbooks.com
E-mail: orders@atlanticbooks.com

Printed & bound in India by Atlantic Print Services

PREFACE

Advanced Applied Psychology is the most important branch of Psychology encompassing applications of psychological knowledge in all areas of psychology. Though several books are available on Applied Psychology, there is hardly any book covering the entire spectrum of psychology applied to various areas of life. This book entitled *Advanced Applied Psychology* has been designed to fill up this gap. Published in two volumes, its Vol. I deals with Psychology Applied to Education, Human Development and Psychological Disorders, while Vol. II covers Psychology Applied to Crime, Society and Industry. Within the scope of these two volumes the book covers the courses of all the Indian Universities for undergraduate and postgraduate degrees in Psychology.

Written in simple language, with examples drawn from Indian life, presenting authentic material with latest data and explaining the subject matter through central, side and running headings, this book is a must on the desk of every teacher and student of psychology. The book will also be a major source of information for professional practitioners and researchers in the domain of psychology.

I am thankful to Dr. K.R. Gupta, Chairman of M/s Atlantic Publishers and Distributors, New Delhi, for publishing the book.

Suggestions, if any, for the improvement of the book in the next edition, will be gratefully acknowledged.

RAM NATH SHARMA
RACHANA SHARMA

CONTENTS

CONTENTS

Part I

Psychology of Criminal Behaviour

1

Psychology of Crime and Punishment

Crime is antisocial behaviour which a group rejects and to which it attaches penalties. In this way all those activities for which society lays down punishments are crimes. Those activities to which no punishments are attached may be sinful but they would not be criminal. But some thinkers have deemed it comprehensively. In the words of C. Darrow, "Crime is an act forbidden by the law of the land and for which penalty is prescribed."[1] This constitutes a definition of crime from the social viewpoint. From the legal viewpoint, violation of law constitutes crime. In the words of Barnes and Teeters, "The term crime technically means a form of antisocial behaviour that has violated public sentiment to such an extent as to be forbidden by statute."[2] This definition does not include those antisocial activities which are not prohibited by law. Actually, criminality should attach both to antisocial activities and to activities forbidden by law. Though no punishment is prescribed for antisocial activities, the public opinion always condemns them.[3] According to Garofalo, even the actions contradictory of the prevalent conceptions of pity and truth should be considered criminal.[4] To quote Elliott and Merill, "A crime *ipso facto* implies a disturbance in a social relationship and a social definition as to what such a disturbance is."[5]

1. Darrow, C., *Crime — Its Causes and Punishment* (1934).
2. Barnes and Teeters, *New Horizons in Criminology,* Prentice Hall (1959), p. 70.
3. Sutherland, E.H., *Principles of Criminology,* J.B. Lippincott Co., New York (1959), p. 14.
4. Garofalo, R., *Criminology,* Little Brown (Boston).
5. Elliott and Merill, *Social Disorganisation,* Harper and Brothers, New York (1950), p. 91.

CAUSES OF CRIME

The main causes of crime are : (1) Social, (2) Economic, (3) Physical and developmental, (4) Geographical and (5) Political.

Social Causes of Crime

The main social causes of crime are as follows :

1. Broken family. The broken family is the most dominant factor in the social causes of crime. Nowadays family disorganisation may be seen in India. The control previously exercised by the family over the individual is now lacking. In urban areas, the members of a family may be seen pursuing their individual paths. With lifting of family control there are no restrictions to the criminal tendencies of children. Now that the natural relations between parents and children are devoid of love, both young boys and girls are prone to criminal activity. Even in the villages the adolescents and young man and women do not respect their elders, and they want to lead a carefree, unrestricted, individual life. Due to all these causes, sex crimes are increasing. One major cause of adultery, abortion, miscarriage, prostitution and juvenile delinquency is the undesirable domestic conditions.

2. Absence of social control. A second social cause of crime in India is the absence of social control. Previously, the caste panchayat in the village kept control over the behaviour and conduct of the members of the caste. It was extremely difficult to conceal crime in the village and when any crime was revealed the caste panchayat, meted it with very stern punishments, going to the limit of exterminating the guilty person from the caste. This tended to control and check crime effectively. Today, these social organisations no longer exist. They have been deprived of all their authority. Secondly, with better facilities of transport being available, the criminal men commit the crime and abscond from the village to the town or to the village from the town. In urban areas no one cares about caste organisations. Nowadays in big cities, even doing favour to neighbourers is a defunct practice because few have intimacy with their neighbour and social relationships have become impersonal. An individual may commit a crime and conceal his identity in the city mob. In this way, the disappearance of the control of caste organisation is another cause of crime in India.

3. Defective education. Modern education in India is very defective. It does not develop the character of students in right direction. Instead, it has led to an increase in selfishness, disorderliness and impotence. Ethical and religious education has no place in the modern education system. Besides this, even after completing his education, an individual does not become capable of earning his livelihood and many well educated people remain unemployed for many years. Late employment leads to late marriage. All these causes tend to aggravate criminal activity.

4. Cinema. According to Blumen and Hansen, cinemas indirectly influence the male criminals. Cinema arouses criminal tendencies in men by teaching crime techniques, by exhibiting many kinds of crimes, by stimulating the desire for wealth and comforts, by showing ways and means of appropriating them illegally, by arousing the feeling of bravado, toughness and adventure, by arousing profound sexual urges, by stimulating day dreams of criminal jobs. In much, the same way it directs or urges many young and inexperienced women to illegitimate relations and crimes by setting alight the sexual desire, the desire for exhibition, love-making, independence, variety, etc. Thus cinema has helped in the increase of crime in India.

5. Newspapers. Besides cinemas, newspapers also have a hand in increasing criminal activity. Newspapers increase criminal activity by publicising methods of crime through news items, by printing many news items relating to crime, by making crime a general subject, by printing news of major crimes and showing their advantages, by circulating the names of criminals, by highlighting causes which tend to increase crime, and by warning and alerting criminals by publicising police methods. The recent wave of dacoities in India was to some extent indirectly assisted by newspapers.

6. Use of alcohol. The consumption of alcohol also is one of the major causes of crime in India. Drinking is more prevalent among those who have a low standard of life and it is also from among them that the largest number of criminals are coming. There are large numbers of crimes committed under the influence of alcoholic stimulants. Drinking affects not only the drinker and makes him a criminal but it also has a deleterious influence on his entire family and inclines men, women and children towards crime. In this way drinking increases crime both apparently as well as indirectly.

7. Prohibition of widow remarriage. In India widow remarriage is now legally accepted as valid but it is still looked down upon in society. Consequently, many young widows do not remarry for the rest of their lives. Such a decision however does not annihilate their sexual passions and these rather lie dormant in a corner of the mind and wait for a suitable opportunity. Even if the widow is religious and saintly she is pursued by men and is lured to the path of evil and sin by many threats and coaxes. In this way, there is an increase in adultery, miscarriage, abortion, infanticide, etc. When their sinful practices are made public many women commit suicide.

8. Defects of the marriage and dowry system. In India the dowry system also is among the social causes of crime. On the one hand the dowry system urges the fathers of girls to earn money through illegitimate means for their daughter's marriage, it on the other hand leads to suicide by many young girls who cannot bear to see the degraded condition of their parents; the dowry system has further encouraged late marriages, both in girls and in boys. In extreme cases, the lack of wealth compels a girl to remain unmarried throughout her life or at the most she is married to an old man or to an unsuitable partner. All these also tend to increase sex crime in society. Very often the parents do not care to ask the girl or boy for opinion and sometimes even proceed against it. This also results in suicide and other crimes.

9. Religion. Religion has also been one of the causes of crime in India. This does not mean that religion itself encourages crimes but encouragement has come from the different sects which encourage the difference of opinion between people on matters of religion and hatred for other religions. In a general way, of course, communal riots and crimes, such as looting, murder and so on, perpetrated in order to increase the followers of one's own religion and to injure another religion have always been happening in India, but the crimes committed during communal riots in the name of religion, when the country was partitioned in 1947 are unequalled in the history of the world. Helpless women were denuded and taken in procession through the main roads all the times being whipped. Their breasts were cut off, they were violated and mutilated, their children's hearts were cut out in front of their eyes. The most heinous crimes that may be discovered in the history of criminal activity have been perpetrated in India.

10. Changes in social values. There has been a tremendous change in social values in recent times in India. Nowadays, new notions such as materialism, individualism, rationalism, craze for wealth, absence of sex restrictions, etc., are becoming very widespread in the country. This has led to a disregard of ancient social values and new values have been reinstated in their stead. There is no one common opinion of any kind in them. This disordered state of values also inspires crime because any individual can manage to produce an argument to justify even that which is improper.

The preceding exposition on the social causes of crime in India brings to light the extent to which defects of such social institutions as family, caste, religion, marriage, etc., contribute to criminal activity. This does not mean that crime has no geographical, economic, political and other causes, but it is intended merely to show the important part played by social organisation in crime.

Economic Causes

The main economic causes of crimes are the following :

1. Poverty. In India one sees extreme poverty. Poverty is a major cause of crime, since a hungry man can do literally anything in order to appease his hunger. One comes across instances where a criminal commits a crime immediately on his release from prison in order that he may be imprisoned again where he is assured of a square meal. Outside the prison he has no such assurance. Dr. Haikerwal has investigated that in the period 1917–27 thefts increased in number when the prices of wheat went up, and decreased when wheat prices fell. In this way, a close relation is found to exist between the number of crimes and the prices of foodgrains in India. It was found in the case of a study conducted upon the prostitutes of

Kanpur that one major cause of prostitution is poverty. Poor girls are easily entranced by men who violate them, take away their virginity and put them on the market. One even comes across news of suicides and murders of families due to poverty.

2. Unemployment. Unemployment, much like poverty, is a major cause of crime in India. Many young men commit suicide when they are frustrated by extreme poverty and continued unemployment. Many others turn to thieving, pick-pocketing, robbery, etc. Among the people who are seen creating disturbances, causing violence, etc., the majority are the unemployed. Most gangsters do not work. Gangsterism is their only occupation.

3. Industrialisation. Industrialisation is also an important cause of crime in India. It has destroyed the family life of millions of labourers. They work very hard for eight to ten hours in the day during which they have to suffer many inconveniences and for this they have to live in towns far away from their families. Continued existence of this type leads them to indulge in drinking alcohol and prostitution, and this encourages other crimes. In India, the most prospering centres of prostitution are important industrial towns which, at the same time, foster crimes such as murder, assault, disturbance, robbery, etc. Industrialisation has encouraged crime also due to another reason. Housing becomes a problem in an industrial town when the population increases beyond limits. In some towns thousands of families live in houses having no more than one room each. In such conditions the married members have no privacy and children and unmarried members witness happenings which they should not see. This has a bad influence upon them and sex crimes increase. These increase tendencies to other crimes which then take place. In industrial towns many thousands of labourers and other men are compelled to live alone; this tends to unbalance the ratio of men to women, which consequently encourages sex crimes. Many girls from rural areas are deceived with promises of employment and brought to towns where they are forced to adopt prostitution.

4. Urbanisation. Urbanisation is the result of industrialisation and other causes. Hence, all the crimes caused by industrialisation are also caused by urbanisation. In cities the society fails to exercise control over the individual who loses his identity in the mob after having committed a crime. There is no such facility, however, redoubtable, in the village. In towns there are better opportunities for pick-pocketing and practising deception in a crowd. There is absence of healthy recreation in the town and hence the cinemas are overcrowded. Gambling dens, indecent movies and wine shops provide means of spurious recreation. This encourages crime.

It is evident from the foregoing account of the socio-economic causes of crime in India that here the main causes of crime are social and economic. Absence of reliable statistics makes it difficult to say definitely that the causes of crime here are hardly psychological. But what can be said is that since life in India still lacks some of the velocity and crowdedness of Western life, the psychological causes of crime in India do not compare favourably with their counterparts in America and other Western countries.

Physical and Developmental Causes

Physical defects also turn a man into a criminal because due to these deformities he lags behind his fellow beings in many respects and it is in order to remove this difference that he turns to criminal activity. For example, the most dangerous criminals have usually been found to be extremely ugly. On examining prisoners imprisoned in the Parkhurst prison, Charles Goring found most of them to be inferior, from the physical viewpoint, to the common individual. Mental defects are just as causative of crime as are physical defects. Among them feeble-mindedness has in particular been found to be a cause of crime. The proportion of feeble-minded criminals among 948 criminals who had committed crimes of various sorts and were studied by Goring was as follows :

Those who set fire to a heap of wheat	52.9 per cent
Those who set fire to other forms of property	16.7 per cent
Those who robbed and murdered	15.6 per cent
Those who committed unnatural sex crimes	14.3 per cent
Those who were dacoits	10.0 per cent

Gillin calculated that 12 per cent of all prisoners are afflicted with mental diseases. Besides feeble-mindedness, individuals are also led to crime by epilepsy and emotional disturbances. In a study of 1,000 young men of Chicago who had repeated their crimes, 7 per cent were afflicted with epilepsy. The reason why crimes originate in physical and mental afflictions is that such people are the objects of social derision and mockery because of their impeded and disease-hampered progress, and this social degradation spurs them to engage in antisocial activities. A person who, being very ugly, fails to win a woman's love, tries to gain ascendancy over her by the power of money, which he amasses by illegitimate means or by sheer dint of physical power and rapacious activity.

Heredity, according to some criminologists, is one main cause of crime. This view is no longer regarded as scientific but there can be no doubt that lineage and descent have some influence upon crime. Early sexual maturity, mental defects and nervous instability, etc., are abnormalities an individual inherits, which help in making him a criminal. In a study in Chicago, Healy went into the family history of 668 out of 1,000 juvenile delinquents and found that in 245 out of the 668, the families were afflicted by one or another mental defect. In 125 cases their ancestors were also found to be criminals. 61 per cent of 823 families which were sampled were found to be suffering from some affliction. But these statistics show the influence of environment at the same time as they indicate the effect of heredity. Some people become criminals due to the influence of psychoses. In this way people indulge in criminal activity in order to make up for mental and physical shortcoming. Elliott and Merrill express this by saying that an individual's criminal tendency may be the reaction aiming at remedying shortcomings.

Besides physical defects, factors concerning physical development may also sometimes be causes of crime. As a general rule it can be said that it is between the ages of 17 to 24 that the greatest number of crimes are committed. In old age rape and other sexual crimes increase in number. Murderous crimes are usually committed by young men. Embezzlement, fraud, vagrancy, alcoholic excess and murder, etc., are peculiar to middle age. Girls who mature early are more prone to become involved in clandestine affairs. In adolescence the aggressive tendency grows.

Geographical Causes

Many geographical causes also stimulate crime. According to criminologists the geographical factors influence crimes indirectly. Lombroso has collected evidence and shown that crimes of rape are more common in plains than in the mountains or plateaus. In Italy where malaria is to be found in excess of every other disease, the crimes most common are those that are against the individual. According to some criminologists, in hot countries one finds more crimes against the person while in cold countries more crimes are committed against property. Lacassagne had formulated a calendar on the basis of seasonal fluctuations in crime. According to this the greatest number of cases of infanticide take place in January, February, March and April, of homicide and fatal assaults in July, of patricide in January and October, of rape upon minors in May, July, August and most of all in December, of rape upon young women in June and January. All criminologists do not agree to such a view of the influences of seasons and climates upon criminal activity but the least that can be said is that crimes are susceptible to climatic and seasonal variations in the same degree in which human relationships and tendencies are influenced by them.

Political Causes

Many political causes also encourage crime. Nowadays many criminals go scot-free with proper legal advice because there is opportunity to prove truth false and falsehood true. This encourages them to engage in further criminal activity. On the other hand, innocent persons who are prosecuted and convicted in their place also become criminals as a reaction. The ill-treatment to which the prison-inmates are subjected also hardens the softest of criminal. Crimes are further encouraged by the inefficiency, immorality and corruption of the police department. People connected with political groups unobtrusively assist criminals and make use of them to inflict injury upon and to defame members of opposing groups.

MEANS TO PREVENT CRIMES

Roughly speaking, the way to prevent crime is to counteract the various causes that have been mentioned above. Many new suggestions are being made in this connection. Some important means are :

1. Probation. Probation is the postponement, on certain conditions laid down by the prosecuting authority, of the punishment due to a criminal by law. These individuals are kept in the guardianship of a probation officer instead of being imprisoned. According to the Probation Act, 1938 of U.P., first offenders below the age of 24 who have committed crimes not punishable by death or life imprisonment may be placed on probation. The decision to place a criminal on probation is taken after due consideration of such factors as his age, his way of life, his conduct, physical and mental condition and others. All criminals placed on probation live under the probation officer's care. Mostly, it is the minor offender or the juvenile delinquent who is released on probation.

The probation officer performs the following functions for curing the criminal :

(a) To keep criminals in his personal care.

(b) To try to improve and reform criminals.

(c) To compile the life histories of criminals and to try to trace their tendencies through them.

(d) To send relevant information to courts regarding the criminals.

(e) To render assistance to criminals in getting employment.

(f) Solution of family problems of criminals such as solving domestic strife and contracting marriage of their daughters, etc.

(g) To make efforts to make them good citizens by every conceivable method.

(h) To send the criminals to prison once again if they show no signs of improvement.

In this way, the probation officer is both the assistant as well as the saviour of the criminals and tries to put them on the right track by convincing and cautioning them.

2. Parole. Parole is also a means of reforming criminals. Under probation the criminal is given over to the protection of the probation officer without being punished but a criminal is placed on parole after he has served a short prison sentence. He is also placed under the parole officer. The parole officer maintains contact with the criminal, keeps an eye on him and tries to reform him. Probation is more popular than parole.

3. Reformatories. In 1916 the Elmira Reformatory was established in New York, U.S.A. Since then this method of reforming criminals has been gaining favour in all civilized countries. Reformatories are of the following two kinds :

(a) **Juvenile Reformatories.** The oldest of this kind of reformatory is in India. In this efforts are made to reform criminals, to educate them and to make them successful citizens. Previously only those who had been given a life sentence were confined in them but now criminals serving shorter prison sentences are also allowed.

(b) **Adult Reformatories.** Only adults who commit some specific kinds of common crimes are confined to these reformatories. They receive education in military discipline, physical exercise, religions, the principles of citizenship, etc. There are very few reformatories of this kind in India at present. Their success depends mainly on those who run them.

4. Borstal schools. Another means of reforming juvenile offenders is the Borstal school. Only criminals between the ages of 16 and 21 are kept in these schools. There are many institutions of this kind in different States of India. Here the juvenile delinquents are educated and efforts are made to turn them into good citizens by providing adequate care.

5. Prison. Prison is a universally accepted means of preventing crime but nowadays efforts are being made to reform rather than to punish criminals in jail. Recently, a model prison has been constructed at Lucknow, U.P. where the inmates are provided with all the opportunities to develop their personalities and effort is made to make them able citizens. An important experiment had been made in this direction in U.P., known as Sampoornanand Camp. In 1954, 2,000 criminals were employed to build a dam across the river Chandraprabha in Banaras district. There was no police to look after them. The warden of the prison was their guide. The criminals lived in tents on open ground like ordinary labourers. All arrangements and facilities such as canteen, hospital, reading room, radio, library, cinema, etc., were provided for them. Teachers and welfare officers educated them. They were paid wages, a part of which was retained to be given to them on release in order to enable them to start some business. This experiment was a complete success and it shed new light on the problem of preventing crimes.

Actually, these means are to reform criminals and to prevent them from subsequent criminal activity. These cannot prevent also those factors which must be eliminated from the social, economic and political life of the community in which crimes orginate. Till then criminals are punished for their offences. In this connection it shall be relevant to discuss various theories of punishment.

THEORIES OF PUNISHMENT

Of the various theories of punishment, the following three are the most important and typical — retributive, preventive and reformative :

Retributive Theory

According to the retributive theory, the purpose of punishment is to seek revenge. It is the theory described in the Old Testament as an eye for an eye and a tooth for a tooth. According to the German philosopher Kant, the offender should not be punished for the reason that it is the means to his or another's benefit but for the simple reason that he has committed a crime. A court of law repays to one only that which he has acquired. He has done crime and it is logical that the reward of his crime, the equivalent of his destructive value, be given to him. The punishment which the society confers upon him, does not deprive him of his right but gives to him that which he has earned and deserves. According to Hegel and Aristotle, punishment is the negative reward of the criminal, who acquires it by infringing the moral law. It is his award which he must receive. For this reason, when some offenders escape with lighter punishment than the merit of their crimes, they try to reap the reward of their misdeeds by penance. According to Bradley, "We pay the penalty because we owe it and for no other reason; and if punishment is inflicted for any other reason whatsoever, than because it is merited by wrong, it is a gross immorality, a crying injustice; punishment is inflicted for the sake of punishment." In this view punishment is the reward of the violation of moral law. In the words of Sir James Stephen, "Criminal procedure is to resentment what marriage is to affection." Thus, the purpose of punishment is to vindicate the superiority of moral law. By punishing the person who has perpetrated the crime the authority of moral law is vindicated. Bosanquet has enumerated two features of this theory :

1. In it personal revenge and punishment coalesce.
2. It has been recognised in this theory that punishment is quantitatively equal to the crime.

Both of these features are defective. Mill and Leslie Stephen have laid great emphasis upon the element of revenge in punishment. The retributive theory has two forms — rigorist and liberal. According to the rigorist retributive theory, the criminal should be punished severely for a serious crime. The liberal retributive theory also includes the consideration of the circumstances of the crime.

But even the liberal form of the retributive theory is not satisfactory. It is not essential that the criminal will, after having been punished, realise his mistake in violating the moral law and feel remorse for his misdemeanour. Mackenzie has said, "If the aim of punishment is to vindicate the authority of the law, this will be partly done in so far as the offender is reformed and in so far as similar acts are prevented. And indeed neither reformation nor prevention is likely to be effected by punishment unless it is recognised that the punishment is a vindication of the law." But this can be possible only when the criminal himself decides the punishment and is prepared to repent for his wrong violation. It cannot be expected, when the punishment has been administered by the state or by any foreign agency, that the criminal will repent. In practice it has been seen that a criminal becomes even worse after punishment. Actually, too, the retributive theory is not practical; it does not remove the causes of crime. Prevention of crimes or transformation of the criminal can be achieved only by preventing crimes or transforming the criminal and not by punishment. John Dewey has said quite correctly that, "We are not relieved of the responsibility for the consequences of our procedure by the fact that the offender is guilty". It is more important to remove those economic, social, mental and physical causes which spur on the ordinary and the more numerous type of offender, though it is not herein implied that punishment is unnecessary in every circumstances because it sometimes does become unavoidably necessary to mete out punishment.

Preventive Theory

According to the preventive theory, the aim behind punishment is to set an example to others and to prevent them from criminal tendencies. In this way, the object of punishment is prevention. The theory is expressed by the judge's formula, "You are not punished for stealing sheep, but in order that the sheep may not be stolen". This theory does not invalidate even capital punishment because though there is no question of improvement in the criminal, other people derive a lesson not to indulge in homicide.

The major defect of this theory is that it uses the offender as means and not as an end. This does not effect any improvement in the culprit. He is made the means of the improvement of others. This theory is incorrect from the practical viewpoint. Actually everyone cannot become a criminal. People who know how to respect laws are in no need of any such exemplary exhibitions. On the other hand, those who have criminal tendencies can be prevented from crime by necessary preventions and the removal of conditions constituting the breeding ground of crime. To punish a man in order to convey a lesson to others is improper and inhuman. This theory is more defective than even the retributive theory.

Reformative Theory

According to the reformative theory, the aim of punishment is the improvement of the offender himself. Modern age seems generally to favour and apply this theory. In this theory, the behaviour directed at the criminal shows him the consideration due to an individual and not conduct analogous to treatment of objects and means. An offender is punished for his own benefit. This theory concurs with the modern humanitarian trend in thought. This theory has been supported from many viewpoints. Some of the major ones are the following :

1. Criminal Anthropology. The modern criminal anthropology propounds that crime is a disease, a pathological state or the state of inherited or acquired degeneration. Thus, it is necessary to treat criminal instead of punishing him. Hospitals, lunatic asylums and welfare homes are better adapted to the execution of projects to decrease crime than prisons. Crime is not the result of a wilful violation of moral law. The most usual causes of crime are mental defects. For example, kleptomania forces the patient to steal.

The major shortcoming of this theory of criminal anthropology is that it assumes the causes of a limited number of crimes to be the causes of all crimes. If some person steals due to kleptomania he should undoubtedly be interned in a hospital rather than jail but the number of kleptomanias is negligible among the number of thieves. All crimes cannot be attributed to diseased conditions. Criminals who resort to illegal means due to mental or physical deformities form only a few small minority in the realm of criminals. Thus people who commit crimes due to reasons other than these should be curbed by other methods.

2. Criminal Sociology. Criminal sociology emphasises the responsibility of social circumstances in crime. Thus, it is more efficacious to induce improvements in social and economic conditions, to remove inequalities and immoralities, than to punish the criminal. Crimes can be stopped not by punishment but by the organisation of human society on the basis of justice and equality.

The opinion of criminal sociology is as partial as is the opinion of criminal anthropology. Social equality is, of course, the cause of some crimes and can be credited as such. But the causes of all crimes cannot be analysed in this way. Many people commit crimes while fully conscious of the fact. And, especially the crimes of white-collar criminals cannot be included in the explanation offered by criminal sociology.

3. Psychoanalysis. Psychoanalysts join hands with criminal anthropologists and sociologists in supporting the reformative theory. According to Freud and his followers, crimes are caused by repressed complexes and tendencies of sex and jealousy caused by desires and frustrated sexual passions. Thus, education and psychoanalytic treatment are needed for preventing crimes instead of punishment. Crime is a mental or neural disease which can be eliminated by searching out repressed unconscious complexes and transporting them to the conscious level, finding their causes and effecting their sublimation through means acceptable to society.

The psychoanalytic suggestions, too, hold true only in relation to particular criminals. Actually, this opinion is not universally true as well as the case with criminal anthropology and criminal sociology.

Reformation Theory is Superior to Others

The reformative theory is effective in all such conditions in which the criminal commits the crime in ignorance and compelled by circumstances or where this criminal tendency is attributable to a mental or physical defect. But the reform of a criminal who wilfully violates moral laws is not so easy a proposition. Thus, for some criminals it becomes unavoidable to arrange for punishment. It can be said that the reformative theory is the most superior among the theories of punishment because it is compatible with the modern humanitarian ideals and seeks to eliminate the cause of, and prevent, crime but it cannot be applied to all crimes. Some crimes are more conducive to the preventive theory.

QUESTIONS FOR EXERCISE

1. What is crime? Discuss the main causes of crime.
2. What are the causes of criminals behaviour? How does psychology help in crime prevention?
3. Criminals are made not born. Elucidate.
4. Write short note on Theories of punishment.

2

Psychology of Juvenile Delinquents

In modern civilised countries a criminal is not looked upon as a sinner or a bad person, but rather as a mentally diseased individual or one who has been victimised by circumstances. There was a time when even small children were severely punished if they committed some crime. But as psychologists proceeded to draw the attention of the civilised world to the causes of juvenile delinquency, the tradition of punishing children lost favour to be replaced by efforts at improving and rehabilitating them. Nowadays, in every nation efforts are made to correct the juvenile delinquent rather than to punish him. To make the deviant once again a healthy and responsible citizen of society, efforts are made through reformatory schools, probation and other measures.

WHAT IS JUVENILE DELINQUENCY

Legal Definition of Juvenile Delinquency

Legal definition of juvenile delinquency does not conform to its psychological definition, as, from the legal viewpoint, a juvenile delinquent is a person between the ages of 15 and 17 who indulges in antisocial activity. In the U.S.A., the Ohio Code defines juvenile delinquency in some such manner as this, "a juvenile delinquent is one who breaks the law, is a vagrant, persists in disobeying orders, whose behaviour endangers his own moral life as well as the moral life of others or one who tries to marry without the consent of his parents." It may as well be pointed out that the age of the so-called juvenile delinquent has not been similarly determined in all countries. It varies from country to country, but is within the usual limits of 16 and 20. Normally, it is the 17-year old adolescent who qualifies for this term, but in India, according to the prevalent laws, the maximum age of a juvenile delinquent is fixed at 16. Laws pertaining to this subject have been passed in U.P., M.P., Maharashtra, Tamil Nadu, Mysore, Delhi, West Bengal, Orissa and Punjab. In those States in which the juvenile Acts have not been passed, the Reformatory Act of 1897 prevails. In these the maximum age of a juvenile delinquent has been determined at 15. In Maharashtra and Madhya Pradesh it is 16. According to the Reformatory Act, the term Youthful Offender will be appended to any individual below 15 who has been sentenced to life imprisonment or has been convicted of some crime.

Psychological Definition of Juvenile Delinquency

Differing from the legal definition of the controversial term, psychologists lay much emphasis upon the causes of juvenile delinquency in defining it. From the legal viewpoint all those who are not apprehended are not criminals but from the psychological viewpoint all such offenders also are criminal. Consequently, the psychological definition of juvenile delinquency is more comprehensive than its legal definition. According to the psychologists, any and every child, of either sex, between the ages of 15 and 18, who commits a crime, irrespective of the fact that he is apprehended or not, is a juvenile delinquent. In this manner juvenile delinquent is one who forcibly possesses the property of another, or causes it damages, indulges in antisocial activity, creates danger to another's life or hinders the activities of others. Hence, a child who throws stones at a car and runs away, one who sets fire without cause, creates dangers for the life of another just for the fun of it, are all juvenile delinquents, from the psychological viewpoint.

Defining juvenile delinquency, Dr. Sethna has written : "Juvenile delinquency involves wrong doing by a child or a young person who is under an age specified by the law (for the time being in force) of the place concerned." Newmeyer puts the same idea in these words, "A delinquent is a person under age who is guilty of antisocial act and whose misconduct is an infraction of law."

DIFFERENCE BETWEEN CRIME AND JUVENILE DELINQUENCY

1. **Difference of age.** The above description of juvenile

delinquency makes it apparent that the main difference between a juvenile delinquent and a criminal is one of age, but both indulge in antisocial activities. Workings of both are subversive and hindering of social relationships. According to Dr. Haikerwal, from the social viewpoint, crime or juvenile delinquency is a form of conduct that acts as an obstacle in the system of human relationships which are believed by society to be its fundamental condition. In this way, if a criminal is below a certain specified age, he will be designated a juvenile delinquent.

2. Difference of actions. But sometimes criminal and juvenile delinquents differ not only in respect of their ages but also in respect of the crimes that they commit. And in this connection, some actions that young men and children do lead them to be regarded as juvenile delinquents even though their activities are not actually crimes. A classification as wide as juvenile delinquent can include the vagrant, cruel, obstinate or young boys who keep the company of thieves, dacoits, other vagrants and prostitutes, those who keep away from the house for long periods of time without the permission of their parents and those who roam in the lonely streets late at night. It should be remembered here that such activities are, strictly speaking, not illegal or infringing any legal statute. Hence, the juvenile delinquent who chooses to act in these ways cannot be included in the same class as ordinary criminals. Another thing that sometimes happens is that the unemployed, unhoused and wandering child may be included in the category of juvenile delinquents along with the beggar, the farce being carried so far as to present the young person before a court and to try to mend his ways.

3. Difference of characteristics. Kohen has distinguished criminals from juvenile delinquents on the basis of the following distinguishing characteristics :

(a) A juvenile's mischief is lacking in utility as he does things that do not benefit him in the least, such as roaming about in the streets without cause. On the other hand, the criminal acts with intent to gain something. A juvenile is sometimes even unaware of the objective of his own actions.

(b) Sometimes a juvenile commits a crime with only an intention to enjoy himself and indulge his sense of humour. It finds expression in practical joking like breaking car glasses, putting boulders on railway tracks or pushing people into a pond of water just for the fun of it. A criminal does not find this a suitable mode of manifesting his sense of humour.

(c) The juvenile delinquent does not commit a crime on a preplanned and well organised basis, being more apt to do things on the spur of the moment. A hardened criminal is more inclined to plan his moves and organise crime with a certain show of skill.

Briefly, criminals and juvenile delinquents are to be distinguished by their difference of age, kinds of work, objective of activities, mode of working. Yet, normally it is the difference in age alone that is considered the sole basis of making distinction between the two classes.

METHODS OF DISCOVERING JUVENILE DELINQUENCY

Before plunging into a detailed study of the causes of juvenile delinquency, it is essential to become acquainted with the methods of discovering them as this will indicate the intrusion of psychology into the subject, as also its scientific bias. Three kinds of methods have usually been employed to delve into the causes of juvenile delinquency : (1) Statistical, (2) Case history method and (3) Psychoanalytic method. They have also been used to discover crimes. Now these methods will be described in some detail as follows :

1. Statistical method. The statistical method finds its best exposition in the words of Cyril Burt. He complied a list of some specific situations or circumstances. And with the help of this inventory he attempted the discovery of circumstances that are peculiar to the healthy ones. Some of these situations are described as follows :[1]

(1) Circumstances of heredity — (a) physical, (b) mental, (c) temperament (also signs of mental diseases).

(2) Circumstances of environment :

(a) Situation in the home — (i) poverty, (ii) defective

1. Burt, C., The Causal Factors of Juvenile Crime, *British Journal of Psychology* (1923), pp. 1, 12-27.

family relations, (iii) defective discipline, (iv) bad characters in family.

(b) Situations outside the home — (i) neighbourers, (ii) conditions outside the home, (iii) friends' circle.

(3) Physical conditions.

(4) Mental conditions — (a) intellectual, (b) emotional, (c) interest, (d) emotional aberrations, (e) mental complexes.

On the basis of the above list of circumstances and conditions Cyril Burt tried to discover the causes of juvenile delinquency. Some circumstances were noted through observation while others were measured through testing. The most important cause of juvenile delinquency turned out to be emotional. And crime appeared to have intimate relationship with the presence of tuberculosis and other serious diseases in the physical condition of the parents. In the environment, the status of the family was found to be the most important. Physical and mental condition of the adolescent himself was found to be of secondary importance. Accordingly, Cyril Burt came to the conclusion that the main factors concerning juvenile delinquency were defective discipline, defective relations between the parents and emotional aberrations.

2. Case history method. Another important method of discovering the causes of juvenile delinquency is the case history method. The statistical method does not reveal the singular and actual causes as it does not include a study of the personal life of the juvenile delinquent under consideration. In the case history method, efforts are made to collect all information concerning every aspect of the subject's personality, as well as most of the circumstances of his life. The observer collects all relevant information concerning the school, home, family and any other important field of the life of the subject. Knowledge of the subject's ambitions, frustrations and problems is gained through mental tests, personality inventories and actual interviews. Detailed information is sought at the hands of the subject's parents, near relatives and intimate friends by interviewing all of them. And, on the basis of all such information that comes to hand, a complete case history is developed. The example of one such study is the book called *The Jack Roller* by Shaw.[2] Study of the case history revealed many factors that could have led them to find crime attractive, for example, bitter criticism of all others, unceasingly blaming others, ostentatious desire to attract the attention of others, rationalisation instead of insight, inability to understand oneself and unfounded suspicion of others, etc.

3. Psychoanalytic method. The third and the most important method of discovering the causes of juvenile delinquency is the psychoanalytic method in which the external circumstances of the subject are not the only subject of enquiry. What is attempted is the analysis of his subconscious mind. Psychoanalysts have recourse to many methods such as dream analysis, word association and other psychological tests with the help of which they can probe the unconscious element in the individual's mind and uncover the hidden and submerged causes that compel him to a life of crime and disorder. In their book *Roots of Crime,* Alexander and Healy have written that the criminal tendency cannot be understood by discovering certain incriminating things by the statistical method nor by making inferences from the results of individual method.[3] To understand the criminal mentality we should understand those psychological processes that are in the background of all human behaviour. It need not be specifically pointed out that psycho analysis cannot be said to be the one method that can discover all the causes of delinquent behaviour among juveniles. In fact, none of these three methods taken alone can help in probing the causes of juvenile delinquency, and it is best to make use of all these three methods. Such an approach is the best as it throws light on the causes of crime by highlighting the internal and external conditions and the peculiarities of his personality.

CAUSES OF JUVENILE DELINQUENCY

According to the novel approach and concepts of modern criminology, the causes of juvenile delinquency have been divided into two classes — personal and social causes. In crime, two special factors are at work — internal and external. Internal factors include physical and psychological factors while the

2. Shaw, D.R., *The Jack Roller,* Chicago University Press (1930).
3. Alexander, D. and Healy, W., *Roots of Crime,* Psychoanalytic Studies, 1935.

external factors consist of social elements. Criminals have been divided into two categories by the American criminologists — (1) social criminals, (2) personal criminals. Social criminals, in particular, are the result of social circumstances. Walter Recklace has pointed out two specific causes of crime — (1) constructive and (2) circumstantial. Some other criminologists have divided the various causes of crime into two parts — (1) sociogenic and (2) psychogenic. Here the causes of juvenile delinquency will be divided into three classes for convenient study — (1) social causes, (2) psychological causes, (3) economic causes.

Social Causes

Of the various causes of juvenile delinquency, the most comprehensive are the social causes. Among them, the main ones are — (1) family, (2) school, (3) criminal area, (4) bad company, (5) recreation, (6) war, (7) social disorganisation, (8) displacement.

1. Defects of the family. Of the causes of juvenile delinquency, Elliott and Merill accept distorted family influence to be the most potent. Of 4,000 juvenile delinquents in Boston, Healy and Bronner found that about 50 per cent of them came from divided or broken families. The major situations in the family that cause it are : (a) broken families, (b) attitude of parents, (c) character and conduct of parents, (d) effect of criminal relatives. In order to understand the importance of family as a cause of juvenile delinquency, it is necessary to comprehend these factors.

(a) ***Broken families :*** A study of juvenile delinquency has revealed that the greatest number of delinquents come from broken families. A broken family, as the term indicates, is one in which family ties have been destroyed. A family is not constituted by a number of people living together but by their mutual intimate relationships. Absence of this intimacy results in the breaking up of a family, and it is in broken families that juvenile delinquents develop. In any such family, a child is not looked after properly. In the opinion of some specialists, broken families are more apt to arouse criminal tendencies in families than in male juveniles. The child care society of Bombay had 386 boys and 16 girls under its care in 1947. Of these children, the parents of two boys and two girls were serving prison sentences, two boys and five girls were under the influence of extreme indiscipline, six boys and nine girls were the victims of moral insecurity. In a broken family, the relationships of husband and wife, parents and children, brothers and sisters lose their healthy nature. Hence, it is only natural if the children choose the wrong path that ruins their lives.

(b) ***Attitude of parents :*** In the family factor in juvenile delinquency, another important condition is the relations between the two parents. According to the preface writer of *Women of the Street,* a probing and searching analysis of the prostitutes of London, the problem of the prostitute has its origin in the relationship between the child and parents. Often when the child is deprived of love and is scolded constantly on every opportunity, he develops feelings of revolt and hatred so that he runs away from the house at the earliest opportunity and falls into a life of crime. Disregard on the part of parents induces feelings of insecurity in the children with the result that they develop mental complexes. If the parents try to conceal many facts of their own life from children, the tendency towards crime is only aggravated. One of the most common query that children are apt to put before their parents is where did they come from, or where their younger brothers and sisters have come from. When they are told all sorts of lies by their parents, while they learn the truth from their servants or other people outside the family, a sense of insecurity is induced in them, because they feel that their parents do many things which they fear to tell their children and this injures their feelings. This sense of insecurity leads many children to sex crimes.

(c) ***Character and conduct of parents :*** The child's personality is considerably influenced by the character and conduct of its parents. One rarely comes across a child who has been able to mould its behaviour according to socially accepted values and conceptions in the face of his parents' telling lies, hypocritical behaviour, sexual immorality and thieving. In a study conducted by Miss Elliot, 67 per cent parents in broken families and 44 per cent parents in united families were engaged in immoral behaviour. If the mother is already involved in prostitution, the child will have little hesitation in following suit, and with the worst conceivable consequences.

(d) ***Influence of brothers and sisters :*** A child's personality is susceptible to the influence of his brothers' and sisters' personality apart from the personality and mutual relationship of the parents. This influence is more potent in the case of girls as they are not exposed to external influences as much as boys who remain in the home for a considerably less period of time. If the senior children in the family manifest criminal tendencies, the youngsters are invariably influenced by it. If the elder sister shows criminal tendencies or is engaged in immoral behaviour, the younger sister is more apt to follow her example.

It is evident from the foregoing description that the situation within the family has an a major part to play in turning children into criminals. But this need not lead one to the conclusion that all children in a broken family will turn out to be criminals. Healy and Bronner studied 372 broken families and in only 20 per cent of them one of every two children was a delinquent.[4] In 336 families in which each had 6 children, only 12 children were engaged in criminal activity. Such a study seems to indicate that the family being broken is not the sole cause of juvenile delinquency, but no criminologist will refuse it that such a condition is undoubtedly a most potent cause.

2. Defects of the school. After, the family, a child's personality is next influenced by the school. But one major form of juvenile delinquency is absconding from school. In 1947, Williamson found in his study that playing truant from school, theft and sex crimes were the major forms of juvenile delinquency, and even among those running away from school or roaming outside the school claimed the greatest attention and interest among children. Analysing the causes of such behaviour, Williamson came to the conclusion that it was caused by criticism at the hands of parents, gaining membership of a gang of criminals, punishment by the teacher, weakness in some subject, and a level of education that is above the child's ability and capacity. Children who run away from the school

4. Healy and Bronner, *Delinquents and Criminals : Their Making and Unmaking,* The Macmillan Co., New York, pp. 121-25.

usually spend their time in the worst sort of company and commit all kinds of crimes. This is one of the major problems confronting the teachers. It is for this reason that in most big cities, students are not allowed to view matinee shows in film exhibitions, but preventions of this nature do not help solve the problems. One of the major causes of increasing indiscipline in the present time is that education is taken as stuffing the brain with information rather than building up character. It need hardly be said that it is these factors that make the child lose interest in study and try to avoid school with the result that he falls into a life of crime.

3. Crime-dominated area. According to the results of a study by Clifford, Shaw and Mckay, some areas are not appropriate for the development of children. It is a matter of common knowledge that the neighbourhood casts important influences upon the child. Using the statistical method, Mailer came to the conclusion that in New York, juvenile delinquency was greatest in those quarters where the level of life was very low, child mortality was very high, there were no means of recreation, residences were not permanent. In a community that is unstable there are no social taboos or laws. Pickpockets are found in great abundance in and around hotels and other places where travellers stay since there is always some traveller or the other there. Clifford, Shaw and Mckay studied juvenile delinquency in nearly 15 towns to discover that the rate of juvenile crime was highest in the centre of the town and lowest at its furthest reaches. From this they concluded that the social traditions of backward and low economic status areas distinguish the pattern of crime from the average groups. And these patterns are maintained in juvenile delinquent groups. In this way, big towns have certain areas where there is an abundance of criminals, and these areas are called criminal areas or crime-dominated areas. It should here be remembered that Shaw and his assistant Henry Mckay have not accepted the place of residence as a cause of crime but have tried to show instead that crimes are found to be the highest where conditions of poverty, mental aberrations, family disorganisation, diseases, infant mortality and other forms of disorganisation, are constantly maintained, or existing. Tendency to displacement is also found to prevail in crime areas. Having studied crime areas in Chicago and other cities, Shaw and Mckay came to the following conclusion :

(a) Rate of crime differs from one settlement to another. In some areas boys are not arrested, while in other areas, a fifth of the criminals were captured every year.

(b) In winter the rate of crime increases around the factory area and decreases in the suburbs. Rate of crime decreases in proportion to the distance from the town's centre.

(c) The rate of crime is also high in the areas where there is a greater tendency to abscond from school.

(d) In areas where the rate of crime was high in 1930, the rate was also high in 1900, despite the fact that the constitution and size of population underwent considerable change during these years.

4. Bad company. According to the famous criminologist Edwin H. Sutherland, criminal behaviour is acquired through interaction with others.[5] He says that an individual becomes a criminal when there is excess of conditions that promote the infringement of law over conditions that prevent such infringement. And, among children, some get good company while others don't. The child who gets bad company progresses towards crime while the child who gets into good company progresses to become an able and useful member of society. An individual's behaviour is influenced to a considerable extent by the conduct of his companions. In order to induce the children to accept and respect the values and assumptions of adult society around them, it is necessary to create such an atmosphere in which inspiration to criminal behaviour is reduced to the absolute minimum.

5. (a) ***Absence of recreation*** **:** Means of recreation have an important place in the child's development. It is only a good and healthy atmosphere that can provide the right sort of inspiration to the children for sensible and healthy behaviour in their spare time after schools. Inability to make proper use of one's spare time is an added instigation to criminal behaviour. Play and games are essential elements in the socialisation and ethical training of children. Inadequate, uncontrolled and

5. Sutherland, E.H., *Principles of Criminology*, New York, 1955.

improper recreation in a town is one of the causes of juvenile delinquency. In Thurston's study of 2,507 juvenile delinquents it was found that their spare time had hung heavy on their heads.

(b) ***Defective recreation*** **:** In modern times, the one means of recreation available to big and small is the cinema, which is responsible for juvenile delinquency and antisocial activity to quite an extent. New patterns of crime are presented to an individual through scenes of adventure and romance. Some films have such potent influence upon the adolescents that after their screening in some towns, certain kinds of crime increased many-fold. But the reactions of children to films are determined and guided by patterns within the house or around the neighbourhood. And different children react differently to it. Scientific studies have determined that the direct influence of cinema upon the behaviour of children is very little. Actually, more important than the cinema is the child's reaction to it which keeps on functioning on the basis of his previous experience and reaction to social and cultural circumstances.

6. War and post-war conditions. Increases in the rate of juvenile delinquency have been found during war and post-war periods. In countries that actually participate in the war, the children's education is considerably hindered and affected. It often happens that in wartime the father is on the front fighting the war, while the mother goes to the factory to earn. Hence, children are not properly looked after. Lack of any control leads to much promiscuous mixing between girls and boys with the result that sexual crimes increase. In wartime, wherever there was bombing, it was the adolescents in that area who took the greatest part in looking smashed houses. Hence, the situation of war definitely encourages criminal tendencies.

7. Social disorganization. Social disorganization leads to disorganization of individuals. And disorganization of society leads to increase in criminal activity; hence it, too, is one of the causes of juvenile delinquency. In modern industrial society there is lack of synthesis and equality which creates tension. This tension inspires young men and women to crime.

8. Displacement. Displacement also influences juvenile delinquency. In studying the town Berkeley, Stuart discovered that juvenile delinquents lived in an area where there was considerable displacement, but as compared with their own respective families, they themselves were much less active and dynamic.

Psychological Causes

Till now, we have been discussing the social causes of juvenile delinquency, all data for which were collected on the basis of the statistical method. The application of the other two methods of discovering causes of juvenile delinquency — case history method and psychoanalysis — has led to some light being shed on the psychological causes of the phenomenon. Psychological causes concerning criminal activity are the following :

(1) Intellectual weakness, (2) mental disease, (3) characteristics of personality, (4) emotional instability.

1. Intellectual weakness. Having rejected Lombroso's principle, Dr. Goring advanced the theory that intellectual weakness is a cause of crime. Goddard was the main exponent of the notion that mental weakness is the cause of crime. In his book *Mental Efficiency and Levels of Intelligence* he has written that the greatest single factor or cause of crime is mental weakness.[6] After examining 4,000 children for their intelligence, Healy and Bronner came to the conclusion that 13 per cent of them had an intelligence quotient below 70.[7] This conclusion is borne out by S.S. Glueck and E.T. Glueck in their book *Unraveling Juvenile Delinquency,* who studied 1,000 criminal children in 1934 and came to the conclusion that 13 per cent children have an intelligence quotient of below 70.[8]

This contention has been objected to on the ground that it is based on the study only of those juvenile delinquents who have been produced before the courts. Naturally, the intelligent and shrewd juvenile delinquents will be apprehended far less than the backward ones. In one of their studies, C.W. Mann

6. Goddard, H.H., *Mental Efficiency and Levels of Intelligence,* Princeton University Press,1936.
7. Healy, W. and A.F. Bronner, *New Light on Delinquency and Its Treatment,* Yale University Press, 1963.
8. Glueck, S.S. and E.T. Gleuck, *Unreveling Juvenile Delinquency,* Harward University Press, 1940, p. 356.

and N.P. Mann have confirmed this view and shown that children with an intelligence quotient of less than 90 stand a far greater chance of being apprehended than brilliant children. They calculated the median of the intelligence quotient of 1,061 criminals in which the boys were discovered to have an I.Q. of 94.88 and girls of 83.77.[9] In 1947, Merrill, in his book, *Problems of Child Delinquency*, calculated the average of the intelligence quotients of 500 criminal children, measured on the modified Binet scale. The average was 92.5. Examining 2,904 healthy children for their intelligence level it was found that their average intelligence quotient was 101.8. From both these enquiries Merrill concluded that a low level of intelligence cannot be accepted as a cause of crime since the level of intelligence in juvenile delinquents is not distinctly different from that of healthy children. There can be no denying the fact that it is comparatively easier to mislead backward children, but intelligent and shrewd children are also liable to get involved in crime.

2. Mental diseases. Other criminologists have tried to establish a definite relationship between mental disease and crime. In the many studies carried out upon criminals, some mentally diseased individuals were also found. According to this view, a criminal is a kind of mentally diseased individual who is in as much need of treatment as in need of punishment. Some psychiatrists and neurologists believe that the psychopathic personality is a cause of crime. Psychopathic children are born in families where there is almost complete absence of love, affection and control. Concerning psychopathic children Tappan has written that he is very unsocialised, irritable, cruel, obstinate, suspicious, self-centred, lonely, full of feeling of revenge, backward and hyper-sexual or uncontrolled in his sexual behaviour. In an extremely advanced stage, he lacks the ability to sympathise, and is completely devoid of repentance over his own cruel doings and the pain or suffering of others. A psychopathic child of this nature has the existence of an uninvited guest in his own house. He is never loved by any one, but is instead the butt of every criticism and abuse in

9. Mann, C.W. and N.P. Mann, Age and Intelligence of a Group of Juvenile Delinquents, *Journal of Abnormal and Social Psychology,* 1939, Vol. 34, pp. 351-60.

the house. It is only natural that the child should react to such behaviour with feelings of unhindered obstinacy and homicidal tendencies. In his book *Juvenile Delinquency* Tappan has described the case of a psychopathic child, Isaac. He was a very intelligent child of 14, accused of theft, truancy from school, unnatural sexual practices and general indiscipline. He was a beautiful child who almost invariably impressed all strangers. He was the only child in the family, and his mother died while he was an infant. His father deserted him at the age of 2, following which he was disgustedly and disinterestedly cared for by one relative after another for short periods. Finally, he was sent to an orphanage. All these causes led to the manifestation of many complexes and aberrations in his childhood.

Isaac never paid attention to daily routine and showed no respect for authority, always giving evidence of obstinacy and bitterness in his conduct. He put forward all kinds of impossible and unrelated demands. His behaviour towards the two individuals whom he loved very much did not differ from his general behaviour. These two individuals, a farmer and a social worker, did their best to cure the child. Generally he was made aware of the folly of his ways and the nature of his behaviour. His interest in agriculture was encouraged. As a result of sympathetic behaviour over a considerable period, these two individuals came very close to Isaac, consequently becoming his ideals that went so far as to assume the form of his self-consciousness and awakening. Feeling of disgust with his previous ways was aroused in him and he then came to seek their advice in whatever he did. When Isaac manifested this tendency towards better adjustments, ideals of better behaviour were gradually put before him. Due to the self-confidence and persistence of the two individuals, Issac succeeded in reorganising his future, to be selected in the United States Air Force in 1941 at the age of 21.

Some psychologists and criminologists have criticised the conclusions reached by the study of psychopathic criminals. Sutherland writes that a neurologist studied the prisoners in Illinois prison. And studying the symptoms he found that 98 per cent prisoners were psychopathic. When some other psychologists studied the prisoners in the same prison they found only 5 per cent of them to be psychopathic. Actually, this term has been used in so many varied senses and on the basis of so varied symptoms by different psychologists and psychiatrists that it has been left with no specific meaning that can be used to elucidate scientific facts.

3. Characteristics of personality. Tendency to crime is also found to have close relationship with characteristics of the personality. Personality is the method of an individual's adaptation to environment. Criminal children resort to illegal modes of such adaptation. Hence, juvenile delinquents have been found to possess some characteristic features of the personality that shed light on the causes of their delinquency. In his book *Unraveling Juvenile Delinquency,* Glueck pointed out that the degree of freedom, irresponsibility, revolt, homicidal tendency, suspicion, lack of control, some forms of sadism, emotional and social maladjustment, extrovert behaviour, etc., in juvenile delinquents is much higher than in normal children. Immaturity in sentiment and lack of emotional balance were found to be some eight times more than in the normal child. A normal child is comparatively well-behaved, less explosive, peaceable, obedient and social. The juvenile delinquent, on the contrary, is found to be naughty, explosive, anything but peaceful, disobedient and unsocial. Glueck also discovered considerable difference between the general interest and forms and recreation of normal and abnormal children. A delinquent child was found to take much interest in work of an adventurous and dangerous nature. They were found to take considerable interest in seeing pictures and films. Among his interests and modes of recreation were found such practices as cigarette smoking, gambling, staying away from home, breaking things, and travelling without tickets, etc. He is often the member of one or the other gang. On the contrary, normal healthy children were found engaging in games. In some study it has been proved that female juvenile delinquents exhibited considerable emotional instability and immaturity.

4. Emotional instability. In this way, emotional instability is one of the most important causes of crime. A child's personality is rendered unbalanced through lack of love and affection, emotional insecurity, very strict discipline, feeling of insufficiency and inferiority, and reaction of revolt. Such a state of mind inspires the child to criminal behaviour. In their studies, Healy and Bronner saw that 93 per cent of all juvenile delinquents manifest symptoms of emotional imbalance. A detailed analysis of these juvenile delinquents presented the following emotional patterns and influences :

(a) Forty-six prisoners or criminals showed that feelings of insecurity, lack of acceptability, extreme discrimination of an unfavourable nature, inferiority and not being properly understood existed in their minds.

(b) In twenty-eight criminals, lack of affection had led to suppression of their normal and abnormal desires.

(c) Thirty-four criminals showed that they felt inferior or inadequate in school life, family life, in the friend circle or in play.

(d) Thirty-four criminals showed signs of emotional imbalance as a result of bad behaviour of the parents, conditions of family life, mistakes of parents and lack of proportion in the family.

(e) In Thirty-one criminals, feelings of extreme hatred and jealousy towards fellow mates were very strong.

(f) In Seventeen criminals, illusions of an unhappy life, based possibly on past experience were found existing.

(g) Nine criminals clearly evinced the presence of self-condemnation and awareness of having committed crime due to some past criminal behaviour. These feelings were both conscious and unconscious.

Economic Causes

Crime and poverty are intimately related. Study conducted by Shaw, McKay and Elliott revealed that among juvenile delinquents, majority belonged to families of unskilled labourers. This discovery has the support of Bonger and Fornasiri, as they, too, advocate that poverty acts as an incentive to crime. Concerning these juvenile delinquents, Mirrill has written that a low family income compels the children also to share the burden and to neglect their education. Atmosphere in the factory and mill is such that it leads the male and female child to crime. Sometimes children are entrusted with carrying messages to the homes of seniors where they often see all kinds of sexual practices. This has the worst effect on them, and they become tendentious towards crime. Statistics show that among juvenile delinquents, employed youngsters involved in crime number ten times the unemployed ones. Girls working in hotels or presentation houses are easily lured into sex crimes since their wages are low, their residences are dirty, hours of work are long, and there is no shortage of individuals who want to lure them to a life of crime. In fact, children in poor families have many desires that remain unfulfilled, and it is to satisfy them that they turn to crime. Poverty also induces sense of dissatisfaction and inferiority, another spur to criminal tendencies.

Yet, this is no reason to conclude that crime and poverty are invariably related. In fact, poverty is not the cause of crime; rather, the cause of crime is the psychological factors that arise in poverty and guide boys and girls to crime. In the treatise *Juvenile Delinquency,* Tappen has written that poverty is related to crime, but mainly because along with the subnormal economic situation other elements of the child's training and experience are also active, and these elements are more important in determining the reaction to character, values and laws. Family quarrels and distensions, delinquent gangs and inadequate education, are factors that are more active than the preferred attraction of non-conformity to law and order. With the help of his study, Cyril Burt has exhibited that one cause of there being such a large number of poor people among all criminals that are apprehended is that being poor, they cannot escape the clutches of law and police whereas the richer elements find it comparatively easier to avoid embarrassment. In the study conducted by Cyril Burt, only about 19 per cent juvenile delinquents were found to come from extremely poor families, while another 37 per cent of them came from the average poor families. But, according to Burt, the main reason for this large proportion was not poverty but instead the ability of the children of richer families to avoid being apprehended. Whatever the cause to which the high rate of juvenile delinquency among poor families may be attributed, no criminologist can contradict the fact that poverty and juvenile delinquency are closely related. When children of poor families see individuals of very rich families using many different kinds of things, but are prevented from doing so by the lack of wealth, they develop feelings of hatred, avarice and jealousy that ultimately lead them to crime.

The foregoing exhaustive treatment of the social, psychological and economic causes of juvenile delinquency makes it clear that the principle of specific causation does not properly apply to this phenomenon. In fact, no modern criminologist and psychologist can refute the fact that the causes of crime are many and varied. A person's activities are his modes of adjusting to his environment. And in this adjustment individuals who apply socially acceptable means are called healthy while those who use unsocial and abnormal means for this adjustment are called criminals. Thus, a child becomes a criminal through the cooperation of many causes, social and individual, familial, psychological and economic. Hence, in order to rehabilitate the juvenile delinquent as a healthy member of society, it is necessary to understand all these causes and to remove them. It is a matter of no little satisfaction that this fact has been experienced in all progressive nations with the result that juvenile delinquents are everywhere cured rather than punished.

REFORM OF JUVENILE DELINQUENTS

Modern welfare states aim at reforming the juvenile delinquents so that they may become responsible citizens when they grow old. The following are the most important methods to realise this objective :

1. Probation. In this method the juvenile delinquent is kept under the supervision of a probation officer whose job is to look after the delinquent, to help him in getting established in normal life and to see that the delinquent observes the rules of bail-bond. Thus, the delinquent not only gets a chance to reform himself but also gets advice and concrete help for this purpose.

2. Reformatory institutions. Institutions such as reformatory schools, certified schools, auxiliary homes and borstal schools are devised to reform inmate delinquents. These institutions aim at all-round progress of the delinquent. In the words of Tappan, "The object of the system is the all-round development of character and capacities, moral, physical and vocational with particular emphasis on the development of responsibility and self-control, trust increasing with progress."[10]

Whereas the above measures are adopted by the state, the psychologist adopts psychological techniques for the reform of juvenile delinquents. Of these the important ones are the following :

1. Play therapy. In this technique the delinquent children are given opportunities to participate in such plays as give expression to their repressed motives and help in the development of creative energy. In play therapy individual as well as group plays are utilised.

2. Finger painting. In this method the child is given plain papers and some colours. He is allowed to paint in his own way by means of his fingers. The purpose is not painting but expression of repressed motives in the child, which leaves him serene and healthy.

3. Psychodrama. In this technique the child is allowed to participate in different roles in group drama and thereby manifest his repressed motives.

Besides the above-mentioned specific techniques, the psychologist can reform delinquents by creating healthy atmosphere in the family and by providing adequate, healthy recreation. Finally, cure of juvenile delinquency requires coordinated and concentrated efforts of teachers, guardians and the government.

QUESTIONS FOR EXERCISE

1. Who are delinquents? How do they differ from Criminals?
2. Explain psychological causes of delinquency. Suggest methods of cure.

10. Tappan, P.W., *Juvenile Delinquency,* p. 777.

3

Psychology of Drug Addiction

What is Drug Addiction?

1. W.L. Linford. "Drug addiction may be defined as a state of periodic or persistent intoxication, detrimental to the individual, to society or both and characterised by the following features :

1. A strong drive, need or conclusion to continue taking the drug.
2. The development of tolerance, with a tendency to increase the dose to produce desired effects.
3. Physical and emotional dependence."

Physical dependence results from an altered physiological state, which necessitates continued administration of the drugs in order to prevent the appearance of a characteristic series of symptoms referred to as the abstinence syndrome or withdrawal state. According to Rees, "The term drug habituation has been applied to the person who has a strong drive or need or compulsion to continue taking the drug on which he is emotionally dependent, but he does not develop the withdrawal state characteristic of addiction."

2. The World Health Organisation. "It has suggested that the term drug dependence should be applied to both drug addiction, drug habituation and all types of drug abuse.

Drug dependence is defined as a state arising from repeated administration of a drug on a periodic or continuous basis. Its characteristics will vary with age involved."

Individuals may become dependent on a wide variety of chemical substances, with a diversity of pharmacodynamic effects ranging from stimulation to depression. All such drugs have at least one effect in common, in that they are capable of creating a state of mind in certain individuals which is termed psychic dependence. This is a psychic drive which requires periodic or chronic administration of the drug either for pleasure or to avoid discomfort.

True drug addiction is associated with physical dependence, which is an adaptive state characterised by intense physical disturbance when the administration of the drug is stopped or its action is counteracted by a specific antagonist.

Many of the drugs causing physical dependence also induce tolerance, which is an adaptive state characterised by diminished response to the same quantity of drug or requiring a larger dose to produce the same pharmacodynamic effect.

Drug dependence and drug abuse can occur without the development of tolerance.

Harmful Effect of Drug Addiction

All addictive drugs have powerful actions on the central nervous system and their harmful, adverse and detrimental effects are related to neurological and behavioural changes.

The nature of the effects varies according to the class of drug; dependence may be emotional or physical or both. All addictive and dependence-producing drugs create emotional dependence, that is to say the drug has to be taken as a means of coping with life's stresses and to produce various effects desired by the person on his emotions, drives, perpetual powers, conflicts and problems.

Physical dependence varies in type and severity according to the class of drugs. It is marked with opiate drugs and less marked with drugs such as marijuana and amphetamines.

CHARACTERISTICS OF DRUG ADDICTION

The features of drug dependence are characteristic for each generic group of drugs as follows : morphine and allied drugs, barbiturates, alcohol, cocaine, amphetamines, hallucinogens and cannabis.

1. Opiates and their synthetic equivalents. If morphine and other opium derivatives and their synthetic equivalents are given over a period of months, striking changes occur in the central nervous system. Reflexes are originally depressed but later become hyperactive and an increase in the dose of the drug is required to depress the reflexes as tolerance to the drug is established and, also, because of the greater degree of over-activity produced by the usual dose if the administration of the drug is delayed.

This hyper-irritability which occurs during drug dependence affects multi-neuronal arcs at all levels of the central nervous system, from the spinal cord to the cerebral cortex.

Physical dependence is a real physiological disturbance, largely independent of psychological influence.

The characteristics of dependence on this group of drug include a strong psychic dependence, manifesting itself as an overwhelming drive or compulsion to continue taking the drug and to obtain it by any means for pleasure or to avoid discomfort.

The development of tolerance which requires an increase in dose to maintain the initial pharmacodynamic effect.

The early development of physical dependence which increases in intensity, parallelling the increase in dosage. This necessitates a continuation of drug administration in order to prevent the appearance of the symptoms and signs of withdrawal. Withdrawal of the drug or the administration of a specific antagonist precipitates a definite characteristic and self-limiting abstinence syndrome.

The abstinence syndrome with morphine appears within a few hours of the last dose, reaching its peak in 24 to 48 hours and subsides spontaneously most often within 10 days.

The first signs are development of anxiety, restlessness and feelings of tension, followed by frequent yawning, profuse sweating, running of the nose and eyes, dilation of the pupils, trembling, goosefleshes, diarrhoea and cramps. These symptoms increase in intensity for the first 24 hours and twitching of muscles occurs, together with vomiting, loss of appetite, inability to sleep and increase in respiratory rate.

The effects are predominantly parasympathetic but sympathetic over activity also occurs, such as rise in body temperature, respiratory rate and systolic blood pressure.

All substances in this category possess, in varying degree, a capacity to induce physical dependence. They are mutually interchangeable, in that substitution of one for the other will maintain tolerance and physical dependence and prevent the appearance of abstinence phenomena.

Withdrawal effects appear more rapidly with heroin and, although present with methadone, are very much less severe.

Pethidine addiction is particularly associated with doctors and nurses. Tolerance is not as marked as with other drugs in this class and is not as complete. Large doses of pethidine produce muscle twitching, tremors, confusion, hallucinations and even convulsions. Inability to work is greater than with morphia addiction.

2. Barbiturates and drugs like meprobamate, glutethimide, chloral, paraldehyde, chlordiazepoxide and other trunquillo-sedatives. These give rise to a pattern of subjective and objective effects which resemble that with alcohol. For example, symptoms of intoxication include ataxia, dysarthria, impairment of mental function, loss of emotional control, confusion, poor judgment and, occasionally, a delirium. Withdrawal of the drug is characterised by an abstinence syndrome, which is entirely different from that following the withdrawal of opiates and the opiate group of drugs.

The signs occurring most consistently in the usual order of appearance include anxiety, involuntary twitching of muscle, intention tremor of hands and fingers, progressive weakness, dizziness, distortions in visual perception, nausea, vomiting, insomnia, weight loss and a precipitous drop in blood pressure on standing or even on sitting.

Other effects which may be hazardous to life may occur including hyperpyrexia, grand mal-convulsions and — or delirium resembling alcoholic delirium tremens.

Abrupt withdrawal is hazardous because of the serious effects and the difficulty in controlling them.

3. Amphetamines. Chronic intoxication with amphetamines shows the following features : anorexia, nervousness, insomnia, tremor, irritability, loss of weight and, in sufficiently high doses, a schizophrenic-like psychosis with hallucinations.

Abrupt suspension of administration produces marked somnolence, apathy and inertia.

If the dose is not sufficient to cause anorexia, nervousness and insomnia, the abstinence syndrome may be minimal or absent and a return to normal behaviour occurs.

4. Cocaine. Cocaine is a powerful cortical stimulant producing euphoria and excitement, with feeling of increased muscular and mental strength. Its pleasurable effect is of short duration and the addict has to take dose at frequent intervals in order to produce sustained effect.

Following the feeling of euphoria, there usually occur marked feelings of anxiety and fear, sometimes with hallucinations and paranoid delusions. To counteract this associated fear and anxiety, cocaine is frequently taken in combination with the opiate drugs, particularly heroin.

The unpleasant effects produced by cocaine are more marked when it is taken intravenously and include mainly sympathomimetic effect such as nervousness, hyper-reactive reflexes, sweating, hoarseness, increase in pulse rate and blood pressure and, with high dose, a psychosis.

Paranoid delusions may constitute a real danger, as the intoxicated person might mistake the identity of individuals, even of friends around him and interpret their behaviour to mean that they were going to harm him.

Tolerance develops but physical dependence is not marked. Psychic dependence is sufficient in some patients to rate cocaine only second order of preference to heroin.

5. Cannabis Sative (Marijuana). Marijuana is an intoxicant and its characteristic effects occur within a few minutes when it is smoked but, after ingestion by mouth, half an hour to an hour may escape before the appearance of symptoms. The effect of an oral dose may list from five to twelve hours.

The effects are a feeling of power with distortions of time, space, kinaesthetic and body image perceptions which are usually regarded as pleasurable. Mild inebriation takes place immediately following smoking, a voracious appetite for food occurs which is just the reverse of the effects induced by opiate drugs.

Marijuana diminishes inhibitions, increases suggestibility and increases auditory sensitivity.

The drug is misleading and particularly dangerous because it does not appear on the surface to be addictive, as its withdrawal produces no clear abstinence syndrome in the majority of people.

Psychic dependence can be marked and addicts, when deprived of the drug, have a strong desire to consume it whenever it is available but those who are mildly addicted can take it or reject it at will; but in many parts of the world it is often the first step to heroin addiction, particularly among teenagers and young people, who first of all become habituated to marijuana and then pass to heroin or cocaine mixed with heroin.

6. Glue Sniffing. During recent years there has been a marked increase in the inhalation of industrial solvents to produce feeling of intoxication. The following solvents are involved : toluene, benzene, acetone, ethyl acetate, diethyl ether and hexane. Probably, the most commonly used in aeroplane glue, which contains toluene. The acute effects are similar to alcoholic intoxication, and ataxia and dysarthria are common. Hallucintions occasionally occur, and some solvents produce long-lasting neurological damage.

CAUSATIVE FACTORS OF ADDICTION

There are three main factors operating in the occurrence of addition :

1. The pharmacological and physiological properties of the drug;
2. The personality, degree of stability and attitudes of the individuals and
3. Environmental, social and cultural influence.

1. Pharmacological and Physiological Factors. Addictive drugs are usually those which produce some noticeable subjective effect within a short time of their administration. The effects are desired by the individual either to escape from problems or to be relieved of anxiety or to gain pleasurable or new experiences.

With regard to the drugs which produce physical dependence, it has been shown that there are minimum requirements regarding daily dosage, interval of administration and total duration for the establishment of physical dependence. For example, with barbiturates the daily intake needs to be 0.5 g. at six to eight hourly intervals for four to six months.

2. Personality. Addicts show the whole range of personality characteristics from the normal to the neurotic, psychotic, psychopathic and sexually deviant.

Although many addicts show marked personality disorders with emotional instability, immaturity and impulsiveness and, although these undoubtedly increase vulnerability to addiction, these traits are also quite common in non-addicts. It is also clear that a number of addicts were previously normal, stable, well-adjusted persons.

It is also important to bear in mind the harmful effects of drug dependence and addiction on the person's behaviour and interpersonal relationship. The behaviour changes, the falling off of reliability and efficiency, the need for deception and the measures needed to obtain drugs to counteract abstinence syndromes can all exert adverse effects on the person's disposition and personality, but these are not necessarily permanent, as follows-up studies of addicts have shown.

The drug addict is a person with certain personality characteristics, who happens to have selected this way of coping with his problems for a variety of reasons of which he is usually unaware. Not the least of these reasons is his access to a social group in which drug use is both practised and valued.

3. Social-cultural aspects. Addicts can come from all social classes and from all races and countries but there tends to be a difference in prevalence which is related to cost, availability, degree of social acceptability, religion, economics, class consciousness, ethics, group mores and many other factors which influence the acceptance of certain drugs.

Moslems, in general, reject alcohol but accept the consumption of hashish, although both are officially banned by the Moslem religion.

Oriental opium-producing countries show a much higher rate of addiction than do others, such as Scandinavia. Many observers have noted that Orientals keep their opium habits under much closer control than do non-Orientals. In the United States three of the States, New York, California and Illinois account for approximately 77 per cent of the known addicts, most coming from the large cities. Of these, 25 per cent of known addicts are native-born whites. Negroes, Puerto Ricans, Cubans and Mexicans make up the rest.

In the post-war period, in New York in particular, there has been a marked increase in the use of narcotics by teenagers and young adults and one of the few intensive epidemiological studies on narcotics addiction has been carried out by Chein (1956) in New York. His group consisted of boys aged 16 to 21 years who, during a four-year period, had come to the attention of some official agency connected with narcotics. It was found that the districts in which teenage drug usage flourished were usually the most overcrowded, underprivileged areas, with the lowest income, lowest level of education and highest incidence of breakdown of family life. Round about the age of 16 was found to be a particularly susceptible time and it was thought that at this age there was no major institution playing a controlling role or strongly involved with their lives. The control group which had opportunities but had not become drug addicts differed from the addicted and effects of drug usage and also that the attitudes of significant adults were such as to disapprove and lessen the tendency to drug addiction.

It may also be said that the use of drug creates a fraternal spirit which may lead to social organisation which, in turn, is reinforced by the rejection of the addict by society. Further strengthening occurs by economic and psychological factors. The prohibitions placed on the use of drugs may, to some extent, make the consumption more attractive to youngsters.

PREVENTIVE MEASURES

Measures which could help in the prevention of drug addiction are the following :

(a) ***Research :*** It is urgently needed into the personality attributes and environmental factors conducive to addiction.

(b) ***Legal measures :*** These measures are such as making the unauthorised possession of drugs illegal which would help to control traffic in drugs. In the United Kingdom new regulations in 1968 confined the right to prescribe heroin and cocaine to addicts for their addiction to licensed doctors working mainly in hospital clinics. The Misuse of Drugs Acts (1971) provides, among other things, methods for the rapid and effective control of over prescribing of controlled drugs.

(c) ***Medical measures :*** These would include care in prescribing dependency producing drugs.

(d) ***Early diagnosis :*** Early diagnosis, treatment and rehabilitation of the addict are needed.

(e) ***Educative measures :*** These should provide relevant information about the dangers and effects of various drugs with a view to influencing the attitudes of teenagers, young adults and society generally to drug usage.

QUESTIONS FOR EXERCISE

1. Define drug addiction and discuss its harmful affects.
2. Explain features of drug addiction in important groups of drugs.
3. What are the factors concerned in drug addiction? What measures have been suggested for prevention?

Part II

Psychology of Social Behaviour

4

Communication and Interpersonal Relationships

The process of communication is a critical factor in the establishment of sound human relations in an organisation. The social structure of an organisation has superior-subordinate relationships at different levels. These are linked together by processes of communication.

What is Communication?

Communication is a process of transmitting and receiving a message in social interaction. It includes all the processes through which information, attitudes, ideas or opinions are transmitted and received. Thus, communication is the kind of information that is generated, transmitted, received, processed and responded. While a person is communicating he is trying to share an information. The basic component of a general communication system is an information source which has a message to be sent or conveyed through some channel to a certain destination. The message is coded by the encoder in a form that can be transmitted. The coded message, then, is transmitted in the form of a signal through a transmitter. The signal moves through a channel to a receiver which recovers the message from the channel. The receiver then decodes the signal and reconstructs the message and transfers it to the final destination.

In most communication systems, the signal passing through the channel normally gets mingled or mixed up with other signals coming from what is referred to as 'noise' sources. Anything which interferes with or disturbs the transmission process in communication is referred to as noise. Noise has a great disruptive effect in the communication system and it creates a discrepancy between the signal transmitted and the signal received. The different elements or components and the processes which are common to all forms of communication can be schematically represented. Communications theory is the branch of psychology that deals with communication in all its phases — human, mechanical, institutional. The related disciplines of psychology, neurology and electronics are included as they apply to communications. Particular emphasis is lent to developing models and parallels between human communication and machines. In communications theory, an ensemble consists of a *sender,* which encodes messages that are then transmitted in signal from through a *channel to a receiver,* where they are then decoded. Analogies are drawn between electronic communications units and the human organism. The sense organs are receivers that transform stimuli (encoding) into signals (nervous impulses) that are sent through the channels of the nerves to the brain, where they are interpreted (decoded).

Example of Communication

An example of a communication system as schematically represented is a communication between two persons. Suppose that two persons are walking on the bank of a river. One of them suddenly notices a snake in front at a certain distance away from them and he wants to make the other person aware of the presence of the snake. He (information source) generates a message and codes it into a form that can be transmitted. The message may be "Be careful, there is a snake. Don't step on it." In this case, the information source itself is the encoder. He (encoder) activates his vocal organs (transmitter) which convert the message into a series of vibrations (signals). These vibrations are then carried through the air (channel) to pressure sensitive ear drum (receiver) of the other person. The vibrations received are then converted by his cochlea (decoder) into appropriate impulses and stimulations which are then carried to the brain making the person (destination) aware of the presence of the snake. Thus, the information source gets his message through to the destination. In this process, it is possible that the vibrations in the air produced by the vocal organs may be mingled or mixed with other vibrations or sound waves present in the air. These constitute the noise. If there is too much noise in the system, then instead of hearing the message, "Be careful, there is a snake. Don't step on it," the receiver may interpret it as "Be careful, there is a snail. Don't step on it". In this example, the source, encoder and transmitter are one person and the receiver, decoder and destination are the other person.

Direction of Communication

Effective communication promotes a better understanding between persons and groups in an organisation. Information moves from one level to another in an organisation along different channels. In large organisations such as a government department or an industrial or business organisation, communications normally flow in three directions — downwards, upwards and laterally.

1. Downward communication. A lot of information in large organisations moves downwards from the top level to the lower levels of the organisation. Downward communication generally includes orders, instructions, etc.

2. Upward communication. Upward communication moves from members at the lowest level to intermediate level personnel up to highest level. Upward communications generally include reports, suggestions and grievances.

3. Lateral communication. In addition to these, there are channels and mechanisms by means of which communications are maintained laterally from people on one organisational level to others on the same level.

Elements of Communications

There are three major elements in communication. They are the source, the message and the destination :

1. The source. The source may be an individual who is speaking, writing, drawing or gesturing. It could also be a communication organisation such as a newspaper organisation, a publishing house, a radio station, a television studio or a cinema house.

2. The message. The message may be in the form of ink on paper, sound waves, light, movement of the hand, a flag, or any other signal which could be interpreted meaningfully.

3. The destination. The destination may be an individual listening, watching or reading, or engaged in some other activity.

Encoding of the Message

The encoding of the message is an important process in communication by the source or the sender. The individual who wants to transmit some information or convey his feelings to the receiver puts it into a form that may be transmitted. The message or information in one's mind cannot be transmitted until they are coded into spoken or written words or symbols. After encoding the message, it is transmitted in the form of a signal, spoken words, written words or symbols. When it reaches the receiver or the destination, the message gets decoded to derive a meaning from the received message and interpret it in the same way as thought of by the sender. In human communication one person is the source of encoder, another person is the decoder and destination and the signal is the language and symbols.

FORMS OF COMMUNICATION

There are mainly two forms of communication — verbal and non-verbal.

Verbal Communication

A verbal communication is always equated with speaking and writing which require the use of language. It may be either written communication or oral communication.

(i) **Written Communication.** In written communication printed materials, pamphlets, magazines, newspapers, notices, posters and so on serve the purpose of conveying the message or information from one person to another. Usually written communication is used in organisations with a large number of members. Written communication plays an important part in the total functioning of such organisations in the form of letters, reports, records, instructions and so on. In large organisations any communication from the top level personnel which becomes part of the formal instructions, rules or policies is mostly in a written form.

Following are the advantages of written communication :

(1) *Permanence* : A written communication has a permanence which is found lacking in the oral communication.

(2) *Adequate length* : In the case of a written communication, the coverage of the message or information to be communicated may be of adequate length and may be duplicated and distributed to all individuals who should receive it.

(3) *Authoritative* : Writing provides authority to the communication.

(4) *Accuracy* : Another advantage of written communication is the accuracy in the receipt of the information by individuals.

Written communication, however, suffers from the following disadvantages :

1. *Slow* : It is slow and time consuming as compared to oral communication.

2. *Formal* : It also lacks the personal or informal face to face contact with the persons from whom the communication is generated.

3. *One way process* : It is a one-way process and there is no chance for the individuals to have immediate exchange of ideas or to seek clarification from the source.

(ii) **Oral Communication.** There is always face to face and personal contact between the sender and the receiver of the communication in oral communication. Oral communication has following advantages :

1. *Enough opportunities* : In it the individuals have enough opportunities to exchange ideas, ask questions and seek clarifications.

2. *Flexibility* : An oral communication can be made flexible and it can be adapted to suit the levels of understanding of the receivers.

3. *Easy* : It can be made more easy, simple and can be transmitted faster.

4. *Faster* : In the case of oral communications, the sender gets to know the feelings of the receivers much faster as compared to written communication. However, it cannot travel very far unless certain devices like loudspeakers and radio are used.

Non-Verbal Communication

Communication can also be non-verbal or without the use

of language. The green and red colour codes used at a traffic junction denoting 'go' and 'stop' respectively is an example of non-verbal communication. Similarly, all traffic signs are means of non-verbal communication. The attitudes and emotions of a person can also be communicated through non-verbal forms of communication. Facial expressions, gestures, changes in body position and head movements, express a person's positive and negative attitudes towards an object, situation or an idea. Non-verbal communication is generally used to communicate the feelings, emotions, likings and preferences of a person.

Effective Ways of Communications

In order to make the communication effective, it is necessary that the source has the following characteristics :

1. Clarity. Adequate and clear information.

2. Accuracy. Message is encoded fully, accurately and effectively in transmittable form.

3. Speed. The message is transmitted fast and accurately enough to the intended destination or the receiver.

4. Efficiency. The message is decoded in a pattern that corresponds to the encoding and that the destination or the receiver is able to handle the decoded message so as to produce the desired response. When all these are accomplished with relatively high efficiency, the communication becomes successful.

5. Tuning. Communication becomes successful when it meets a number of requirements. If the communication is to be effective, it is necessary for the sender and receiver to be in tune with each other.

6. Experience. The source or the sender can encode a message only in terms of the experience he has had. Similarly, the destination or the receiver can also decode the message only in terms of the experience he has had. If a person has never learnt a particular language, he can neither encode nor decode in that language.

7. Commonness. If there is commonness in the experience of the sender and the receiver, communication becomes easy. If there has been no experience common to both the sender and the receiver, communication becomes difficult and it would be very difficult to get the intended meaning across from one to the other. This difficulty is normally seen when a person having no background in science tries to read a chapter on the theory of relativity or when a person tries to communicate with another person who cannot follow the language of the speaker.

8. Easy encoding. Therefore, in order to make the communication effective it is necessary that the source or the sender should encode in such a way as to make it easy for the receiver to relate it to parts of his experience which are similar to those of the source. When an information source gets his message through to the destination with an acceptable minimum of distortion or error, communication is effective. If the sender feels that the receiver may need more exposure to the message, he may repeat the message over and over again to make sure it is heard and decoded properly. Alternatively, he may give more examples and analogies to make the receiver follow the message properly.

9. Requirements of communication in organisation. The success of communication in an organisation depends upon a number of requirements :

(i) ***Commonness :*** In order to make communication effective, it is necessary to ensure that all the members of the organisation know the channels of communication. There are certain organisations which require their members to communicate only with the personnel immediately above or below them. In certain organisations, members at different levels in the line of authority are permitted to transmit communications to any one else regardless of position and status of the members.

(ii) ***Familiarity :*** Whatever may be the system in the organisation, every member of the organisation should be familiar with the channels of communication for a smooth flow of communication.

(iii) ***Reaching all the members :*** The effectiveness of communication is maximum when the communication is made to reach all the members of the organisation almost at the same time. If a communication involving a number of members is not received by all of them at approximately the same time, rumours tend to spread among the members, thereby creating a feeling of insecurity among the members.

(iv) ***Short lines of communication :*** To avoid delay and spreading of misinformation, it is necessary to have short lines of communication. Short lines of communication also help correct and accurate transmission of messages and avoid misunderstandings and misinterpretations of the communications.

10. Authoritativeness. A communication is generally considered to be effective when it is authoritative, and when the members of the organisation understand it properly.

11. Consistency. The communication should be seen as consistent with the purposes of the organisation and should be compatible with the interests of the individuals and groups.

12. Two-way process. Communication should be a two-way process in which all members receive an equal opportunity to convey their ideas, feelings and reactions to each other. Better understanding among the members of an organisation exists when there is a free flow of information both upwards and downwards in the organisation.

13. Through mass media. In the case of a large group of people, one of the effective ways of communication is through mass media. These are used for communicating with people who may be physically away from each other. But they all receive the message or the information approximately at the same time. The different mass media used for communication are : newspaper, radio, television, films, various kinds of posters and bulletins used for different purposes.

BARRIERS TO COMMUNICATION

Often misunderstandings and breakdowns in communications occur due to certain barriers to communication. Barriers to communication can be both physical or psychological.

1. Physical barriers. These involve absence of some required physical instrument such as loudspeaker, etc. For example, if the boss of a large organisation with a large number of members wants to communicate with his subordinates, he may not be able to make all of them hear clearly what he says unless he has a loudspeaker. Lack of public address system in the organisation may prove to be a physical barrier to communications in such situations.

2. Psychological barriers. The great strides made, in recent years, in electronics and satellite communication systems have helped to overcome the physical problems of communication to a large extent. But there still exist many psychological barriers to communication which stand in the way of accurate and adequate communication. These psychological barriers to accurate and adequate communication between individuals and groups of individual are the following :

(i) Due to the inadequacy of the language in communicating the reality and experience.

(ii) Due to the tendency of the individual to assimilate the incoming information according to his own experiences. Misinterpretations and breakdowns in communication are in part due to the differences in the experiences of the persons attempting to communicate and the persons to whom the communication is addressed. Even though two individuals speak the same language, they often fail to communicate adequately and appropriately because of the differences in their personal experiences.

(iii) The psychological barriers to communication are also in part due to the emotional character and mental limitations of human beings.

(iv) The major barrier to mutual interpersonal communication is the individual's tendency to judge and evaluate or to approve or disapprove the communication received without giving proper thought to it.

(v) Communication is blocked when a person tries to evaluate the message or information received from his own point of view rather than trying to understand and look at it from the point of view of the sender of the communication. Communication is facilitated when a person tries to see the received information, idea or attitude from the point of view of the sender and when he tries to achieve the sender's frame of reference in regard to the message received.

From the above discussion of the effective ways and barriers of communication it is clear that in order to make a communication effective and successful, it is necessary to ensure that the communication is expressed in such a way that it is easily understood by those to whom it is addressed. The messages should be coded in such a manner that they can be interpreted without distortion.

Every organisation requires a system of communication in which orders and information can move from higher to lower levels, from lower to higher levels and laterally at different levels. The proper functioning of the organisation depends upon the system of communication which channels the information correctly throughout the organisation. The smooth flow of work depends to a large extent upon the accurate and rapid transmission of information to different levels. Thus, the system of communication is an integral link in the chain of human relations.

ATTITUDES

What is Attitude?

Attitude is a specific mental state of the individual towards something according to which his behaviour towards it is moulded. For example, due to differences in respective attitudes of the Muslims and the Hindus towards cow slaughter, their behaviour towards the cow differs. The nature of attitude will be further clarified by the following definitions :

1. Allport. "An attitude is a mental and neural set of readiness, exerting a directive dynamic influence upon the individual's response to all objects and situations with which it is related." This definition reveals the following facts concerning attitude :

(a) Attitude is the mental or neural state of readiness.

(b) Attitude influences the reactions of the individual.

(c) Attitude changes the reactions of the individual.

2. K. Young. "An attitude may be defined as a learned and more or less generalised and affective tendency or predisposition to respond in a rather persistent and characteristic manner, usually positively or negatively (for or against) in reference to some situation, idea, value, material object or class of such objects or person or group of persons." This definition of attitude improves upon the definition by Allport in this respect that it introduces the following two elements omitted by Allport :

(a) Attitude is generally negative or positive.

(b) Attitude is a learned or acquired affective tendency.

3. Krech and Crutchfield. "An attitude can be defined, as an enduring organisation, of motivational, emotional, perceptual and cognitive processes with respect to some aspect of the individual's world." This definition is a specific attempt at the analysis of attitude and an exposure of the various elements present in it. In this way, Newcomb has written, "An expression of preference is not an attitude but a motive pattern." Hence, in an attitude the process of motivation, emotion, perception, and thought are present. Newcomb writes, "...Attitudes are defined in terms of susceptibility to the arousal of motives and not to the carrying out of a particular motive pattern.... An individual's attitude towards something is his predisposition to perform, perceive, think and feel in relation to it."

From its foregoing definitions, it is evident that attitude is a mental or neural set of readiness, system or disposition in which the motivational, affective, perceptual and thought processes are included and due to which the individual's positive or negative activity is directed to the objects, individuals and groups surrounding him.

Characteristics of Attitude

An account of the characteristics of attitude will help in understanding its nature. The major characteristics of attitude are the following :

(1) Related with images, thoughts, and external objects. Attitudes are related with images, thoughts and external objects. For example, upon hearing of the Chinese attack on Indian territory, every Indian national developed a negative attitude towards the Chinese aggressors. In this attitude is involved the thought that in attacking India the Chinese have made a most unjustified and immoral move. In this attitude, some imaginary concepts concerning the Chinese aggressors are present in the mind of the individual, and these are based upon his knowledge of the Chinese attack. This mental attitude is further influenced by some external objects. Because of this attitude, the individual is persuaded to contribute his entire wealth to the national defence fund in order to help to expel the aggressor from the country. The relation of the attitude to thoughts, images and external objects is evident from this example.

(2) Directive for specific direction. Attitudes guide the behaviour of the individual in one particular direction. In the foregoing example which illustrated the nature of attitude, it was seen that due to there being a negative attitude towards the Chinese aggressors the individual was prepared to do his best to help the Indian soldiers who were fighting them. In this way, the behaviour of an individual can be predicted if there is knowledge of his attitude towards the Chinese attack. Since attitudes direct the activities of the individual, his reaction can be predicted, by knowing his attitudes.

(3) Affective experience. Various kinds of affective experiences are also attached to attitudes. In the foregoing example may be seen attached emotions of anger, displeasure and sometimes hatred to the attitude of the Indian individual towards the Chinese attack.

(4) Importance of the unconscious in the creation of attitude. The unconscious motive is an important factor in the creation of attitudes. Sometimes even the individual himself is unaware of the motives for his attitude towards a particular person or object because in fact the motive is in unconscious.

(5) Relation between the individual's needs and problems. Attitudes are related to the person's needs and problems. When China attacked India, every Indian was faced with economic, political and other problems which thereby became all the more glaring. This led to a very direct interference in the fulfilment of his day-to-day needs since it is only natural for the populace to suffer many hardships. In this way, being related to needs and problems a negative attitude towards the Chinese is developed in the minds of the Indian people.

Functions of Attitude

Social attitudes play an important part in directing man's social behaviour. Man's behaviour is influenced by his beliefs, assumptions and decisions. And these are affected by the individual's attitude towards different persons and objects. They are the motivated forces. Hence, it is only natural for the individual's social behaviour to be influenced by these attitudes.

Beliefs and Attitudes

Attitude and belief are fairly intimately related. To put it in the words of Krech and Crutch field, "A belief is an enduring organisation of percepts and cognitions about some aspect of individual's world." A person's beliefs are not always scientific because beliefs are formulated on opinions even without knowledge although knowledge is helpful in the formulation of beliefs. Beliefs can be real as well as imagined or unreal. Sometimes even faith is the basis of belief, in cases where the individual believes even when any favourable evidence is not forthcoming. When any attitude is based on belief, belief may be called the cognitive aspect of attitude. But sometimes belief may also run counter to attitudes. The fact of the matter is that there is no invariable relation between belief and attitude, and attitude is not based upon belief. It is not necessary for it to concur with belief. In the individual's social behaviour the greater influence is caused by attitudes because they are the actual motives of behaviour. There is no question of a belief being in favour of or against an individual or object. Only attitudes are in favour or against. For example, in India one comes across many people who harbour a favourable opinion for communist philosophy while many others are antagonistic to it. On the other hand, knowing and accepting that the earth is round is a matter of belief and there may be no question of a favourable or unfavourable opinion.

Attitudes are the motivating forces behind man's social behaviour. It is because of attitudes that the individual's behaviour exhibits consistency and system. In the absence of a permanent organisation the individual would be a new person in every situation. His behaviour will be organised only by the immediate pattern of stimuli and his economic needs. But because the individual possesses some or the other attitude towards every person and object his behaviour is marked by a continuity. For example, if an individual has a negative attitude towards communism he will always be seen opposing the communist party. But while having beliefs opposed to the communist thought the individual may not indulge in any antagonistic activity. In the same way, when it is felt that the people have a positive attitude towards the government's plan it may be expected that they will do their best in the way of cooperating with the government. Having formed an attitude the individual may come to an instantaneous decision in any matter and he need not contemplate every time.

The child develops in a social environment. In this social environment he gains the experience of different objects, individuals, institutions, associations, etc. With differing experiences he formulates different types of attitudes towards them. In this development of attitudes there is some contribution of beliefs, decisions and assumptions. In this manner, by the time he attains adulthood, his attitudes become quite firm and these also direct his social behaviour. In this way, it is evident that social attitudes play an important role in social behaviour. Hence, the social behaviour of the individual is better understood if prefaced by an understanding of these social attitudes. But there is also a limit to the accurate prediction of the social behaviour of the individual on the basis of the knowledge of his social attitudes because, for one, it is difficult to know an attitude in its entirety and secondly, attitudes also keep on changing.

Attitudes also influence the individual's abnormal behaviour. For example, some people believe in the existence of ghost, witches, etc., and consequently they develop specific and peculiar attitudes towards certain objects and animals such as the temple or the snake. And because of these attitudes they indulge in many kinds of religious rituals. It is difficult to change these attitudes because it is difficult to adduce evidence to the contrary. An individual not only formulates attitudes towards external objects but possesses attitudes even about himself. These attitudes have much importance for his social adjustment. His behaviour may become abnormal if he forms a wrong attitude towards himself. For the individual's behaviour to be desirable his attitude towards himself and external objects should be favourable.

Development of Attitude

Although attitudes are described as permanent one should not be misled thereby into thinking that they are not susceptible to change and development. The stability of attitudes is relative, meaning that once an attitude has been formed changes in it can become steadily more and more frequent. But attitudes do change and develop. While many factors concur to make the attitude permanent there are some factors which are continually causing change in it. And even otherwise the permanent attitude towards an object does not come into being all of a sudden but it is the result of steady development. An attitude changes and develops at a slow rate and at different rates in different individuals.

Determinants of Change in Attitude

The important factors which are responsible for this change and development in an attitude are the following :

(1) Cultural determinants,

(2) Psychological determinants and

(3) Functional determinants.

(1) Cultural determinants. Researches of the anthropologists have affected the development of different attitudes of people belonging to different cultures. Eskimos appear to be individualists, the Arapesh peace loving while the Mundugumor are apparently ferocious, aggressive and non-co-operative. The Nagas are head-hunters. The Bhils are fighters while the Santhals are plain and innocent. The Swazi tribe of South Africa is peace loving and innocent, while the Zulu tribe which inhabits an area very near it is murderous and aggressive. The reason behind all this difference is culture. And MacIver and Page have correctly written that culture is the manifestation of our nature in our modes of living and thinking, in our daily routine, literature, in religion and pleasure. In this way, culture is the sphere of values, modes, affective attachments and intellectual achievements. Modes of living and thinking, art and literature, religion, etc., of the Indian and English, cultured and primitive people are due to their different culture. Fundamentally, everywhere, man possesses the same biological motives but culture varies the mode of satisfying these motives and needs. Culture also changes form. For example, the turmoil evident in the adolescents of most cultured and civilised societies is not to be seen in the same age group in the societies where there are fewer restrictions upon relationships between the people of different sexes. It is hence apparent that culture is an important factor in determining our attitudes towards various objects and individuals.

Many psychologists have made important researches upon the effect of cultural factors upon attitudes. In 1934, Carlson's research revealed the fact that the beliefs and mental attitudes of University students are influenced by their religious impressions. In this study, Carlson noticed that the upper middle class Jewish students possessed generous attitudes towards God, war and birth control. On the other hand, Catholic Christian students exhibited extremely conservative attitudes. Protestant students exhibited neither extremely conservative nor very liberal attitudes. Before Carlson, scholars named Harris, Remmers and Ellison used the statistical method in studying conservative students and showed that students related to the Church or any other religious institution are more dogmatic than students who have no relation with any religious institution. In 1936, Stagner studied students studying in the costlier and moderately costly or middle class institutions. This study showed that students of the former institutions were, in comparison with students of the latter institutions, more tendencious towards Fascism. Stagner also found out that the beliefs or thoughts of children and their parents concerning internationalism and related matters do not differ.

(2) Psychological determinants. Along the cultural determinants of attitude the psychological determinants are also important These include different types of tensions, needs, expectations, affective experiences, perceptions, etc. All these tend to influence the attitudes of the individual. For example, the people who have witnessed the cruelty and misanthropy of the Muslims can be excused if they possess antagonistic attitudes towards them. On the other hand those who have come into contact with Muslims who have given evidence of their patriotism and sacrifice will not be found possessing any antagonistic tendencies towards them. This difference in attitudes is the outcome of experience and observation. All parents have high expectations of their children and for this reason they have love and affection for them. But sometimes these expectations and hopes are dashed. In this case some parents are seen developing hostile tendencies towards their children. Our attitude will be a positive one towards all those who can and do help in the fulfilment and satisfaction of our needs. Many of the child's needs are fulfilled by his mother. Hence, it is only the rare individual who is seen possessing a hostile attitude towards his mother. On the other hand, most people have affection for their mother. We tend to create in ourselves hostile attitudes towards all objects and individuals who give us painful experience or which cause an increase in the tension in our lives. On the contrary, positive attitudes are formed for all objects and individuals who give us pleasant experiences and serve to reduce the tension in our existence.

(3) **Functional determinants.** The next class of determinants which cause changes in attitudes is that of the functional determinants. These include the type of personality, belief, propaganda, etc. Attitudes differ because of the type of personality. If an individual is an introvert, then it is natural that his attitudes towards many objects and individuals will differ from the attitudes of an extrovert towards the same objects. Commonly, introvert individuals are seen possessing an unfavourable attitude towards social contact whereas the extrovert is very social. Beliefs also exert very important influence upon attitudes. It is only the belief of the Hindus due to which they possess an attitude of such deep devotion towards an idol that they are prepared to sacrifice their blood if it is in any way slighted. On the other hand, the Muslims possess an attitude of hostility towards the idols because they have no faith in them. Propaganda is the most important artificial means of causing changes in attitudes. One objective of propaganda is the control or conversion of the attitudes and beliefs of the public. As has been said before primary propaganda gets hold of one of the existing attitudes while in secondary propaganda attitudes are changed or created. In much the same way, in propaganda old beliefs are ousted and new beliefs are instituted in their place. For example, every political party tries to convince the public that it is the only party which can really introduce welfare in society. Everyone speaks of himself as the real representative of the public and wants to diminish or even finish the belief and confidence enjoyed by the other parties. But in changing beliefs it is necessary to be aware of attitudes because beliefs cannot be changed by force. If the public does not have an attitude in any particular direction it is useless to

introduce any propaganda favourable to it. For this an attitude should first be created in the minds of the people.

PREJUDICES

What is Prejudice?

Prejudice, as is evident from its name, is the preconceived attitude towards some subject or some individual. It is not unusual for people to make assumptions about some individual or object without being possessed of all the relevant information. In India, the Hindus possess prejudice towards the Muslims while the Muslims are prejudiced against the Hindus. And even within the Hindu community itself, members of the higher castes are prejudiced against those belonging to the lower castes. Prejudices of this kind are based not on experience and knowledge but on various fears, emotions, ignorance, etc. And even within the higher strata, individuals are seen harbouring prejudices for each other. Taking only India, one finds prejudices of all kinds among the people living in different parts of the country. These prejudices differ from one region to another. It is also true of the different social classes. In America, people are seen harbouring extremist and vicious prejudices against the black-skinned. The darker skinned people also reciprocate this feeling.

From the foregoing description it should not be deduced that prejudice is always against someone or something. A prejudice can both be against as well as in favour of. But in both cases it is based on superstition, ignorance and prejudgement and not on knowledge or experience. Almost every mother harbours some favourable illusions about her children and because this prejudice is colouring her vision she fails to see their defects. In society one sees the processes of co-operation as well as conflict. The people with whom one co-operates one forms favourable prejudices for them whereas the prejudices are against those with whom one comes into conflict.

Definition of Prejudice

The word prejudice denotes the activity of formulating an opinion concerning something without any attempt at investigation to find out its true nature. Evidently, prejudices are improper and unintelligent. The following are some definitions of prejudice, and it would be as well to consider them :

(1) According to James Drever, "Prejudice is an attitude, usually with an emotional colouring, hostile to, or in favour of, action or objects of a certain kind, certain persons and certain doctrines." In this definition, prejudice has been shown to be some attitude conjoined to which is some emotion. Hindus harbouring communal prejudices use derogatory names in referring to the Muslims and avoid them. People belonging to the higher castes hate those that belong to the lower castes. In America, the white people are wont to register disgust upon seeing the Negroes and they are shy of sitting with them. In all these examples, there is in evidence an attitude of a special kind towards some people or some groups and to this attitude is also attached the emotion of disgust and fear.

(2) According to Ogburn, "Prejudice is a hasty judgement or opinion formed without due examination." As has been pointed out at an earlier juncture, in a prejudice, the individual forms an opinion without examining the subject. For example, many Hindus are prone to assume that all Muslims are by nature unpatriotic, and do not take the trouble to find out whether they are actually so or not. In much the same manner, the Muslims look upon every individual belonging to a different sect as a non-believer, a sinner and a liar. This is an opinion formed without adequate examination.

(3) Kimball Young has defined prejudice in a more comprehensive manner. According to him, "A prejudice is a composite of stereotypes, myths and legends in which a group label or symbol is used to classify, characterise and define an individual or a group considered as a totality.... It means 'prejudgement', the making of a decision or the adoption of an attitude or a belief in advance. It is a perversion of a rational judgement by self interest or group interest. It is usually accompanied by strong emotional likes and dislikes." In this definition, prejudice has been said to be a stereotype, a prejudgement, an irrational judgement to which are conjoined strong emotions of likes and dislikes. This definition of prejudice comprehends practically every aspect of it.

(4) According to Krech and Crutchfield, "Prejudice refers to attitudes and beliefs that serve to place the objects of the

attitudes and beliefs at an advantage or disadvantage, racial prejudice refers to attitudes or beliefs concerning any minority, racial, ethnic or national group that are disadvantageous to the members of that group." In this definition, prejudice has been described as the attitudes and beliefs of an individual or group of individuals towards an object, either favourable or hostile. Racial prejudice is an excellent example of it.

It is evident from the foregoing definitions of it that prejudice is one such conglomeration of stereotypes, beliefs, attitudes, prejudgements, legends, etc., to which the emotions of like and dislike are customarily attached and which precipitates an object or an individual or a group of individuals into a favourable or unfavourable condition. In India, examples of prejudice may be seen in casteism, linguism, regionalism, communalism, etc.

Prejudice in Social Relationships

Prejudices are important elements in the determining of social relations. In the mutual social relationships of individuals belonging to different Indian tribes, races, communities, regions, languages, etc., prejudices are readily apparent. At almost every place, one sees emotions of hatred and disgust for each other in the people. The high caste people exhibit a distaste, for communicating with those belonging to the lower castes. The Brahmins are prejudiced against non-Brahmins. The trading class Baniya has no inclination to communicate with or even to tolerate the Kayasth. And, despite the fact that they have been living together for quite a few hundreds of years, the relations between the Hindus and Muslims continue to be dominated by their mutual prejudices. Some people are exploiting this psychological fact to serve their own interest by trying to prejudice people of one part of the country against those occupying other parts. People of this kind have demanded the recognition of south India as a separate state. The mutual relationship between the white-skinned and the dark-skinned people of America is entirely coloured with white racial prejudice. In this way, due to prejudice and mutual hatred, competition and conflict are evinced by different communities, groups and individuals. On the other hand, people are found supporting individuals and groups blindly and unreasoningly because of prejudice.

Nature of Prejudice

The main facts concerning the nature of prejudice, as expressed in the foregoing account, are the following :

1. Prejudice is based upon ignorance. The prejudice that exists between two different groups, parties and individuals is the outcome of ignorance on the part of both. This ignorance leads to creation and adoption of different kind of false beliefs and assumptions about other people.

2. Prejudice can both be in favour of and hostile to. The existence of prejudice leads to the acceptance of one object while it also causes the rejection of some other object. So, in this way, prejudice may be in favour of some group of individual and it may also be against the same. The prejudice that exists at the root of casteism leads to bias in favour of one's own caste and hatred and disgust for the other castes.

3. Attitudes and emotions are attached to prejudice. If the prejudice is favourable the attitude attached to it is one of approval and acceptance while an unfavourable or hostile prejudice is accompanied by the attitude of disapproval or rejection. At the root of regionalism is a prejudice and because of it, the individuals who give credence to this creed harbour affection for the people of their own region in addition to supporting them. On the other hand, they not only oppose the people belonging to the other regions but also exhibit hatred and disgust for them. The prejudiced individual is not very balanced and logical in his conversation. The fair-skinned people not only deem it necessary to maintain social distance with the dark individuals, they even manifest open disgust when they are confronted by the latter.

4. Legends and stories are conjoined to prejudices. At the root of some of the communal prejudices existing in India are some legends as well as historical facts. The Hindus give currency to various legends concerning the unpatriotic, cruel and unjust behaviour of the Muslims. Similarly, the Muslims reciprocate this tendency by circulating different legends among themselves concerning the Hindus and their behaviour and nature.

5. Prejudice is motivated. A motive is a mental or neural set which affects the reactions of an individual towards some object, individual, group, etc. A prejudice is motivated and at the base of it are superstition and irrational judgement.

6. Wrong beliefs are included in prejudice. Each and every individual has his own world and his own circle in which he formulates certain beliefs and convictions on the basis of what he has seen and heard. These beliefs may be good as well as bad. But in either condition his behaviour is influenced by these beliefs. Prejudice, whether in favour of or against, is usually founded on false and wrong beliefs.

7. Prejudice is hasty, prejudged and an irrational decision. Because of a prejudice a person reaches a decision. In other words, a prejudice finds expression in the form of a decision. These decisions are reached very hastily without any reference to experience or to reason. For this reason, prejudices almost always prove to be harmful.

Factors Producing Prejudice

The factors that result in the creation of prejudice can roughly be divided into two classes — psychological and social. Of these the social factors render assistance in the creation and production of the prejudice whereas the psychological factors are the individual bases of prejudice.

A. Psychological Factors

The psychological factors of prejudice are many and varied. In India, one finds all sorts of psychological factors such as the emotions of hatred and jealousy, mutually contradictory beliefs and the tendencies of conflict, etc., at the root of the prejudices maintained by people belonging to different castes, religions, regions, etc. When the sense of self-respect of an individual is hurt, he fosters hatred and disgust for other groups and individuals and forms prejudice against them. If the prejudice is to be eliminated, as a preliminary to it, its psychological causes must also be removed or destroyed. The main psychological factors are the following :

1. Abnormal personality. Many of the abnormalities of the individual are the causes of his prejudices because by rationalizing his abnormal tendencies and behavioural patterns he forms different kinds of preconceptions. For example, in communal riots, the abnormal tendencies of the individual are expressed in the form of aggression or pugnacity, whatever the argument that he puts forward to justify his behaviour. Many kinds of mental diseases are also the causes of prejudice. For example, an individual affected by paranoia which is a mental disease, tends to look upon all those surrounding him as his enemies and he doubts the bona fides of everyone. And for this reason he formulates prejudices of all kinds about the other.

2. Frustrated needs. Every individual has many kinds of physical and psychological needs and if they are not satisfied, they become frustrated. They are then manifested in the form of hatred, disgust, pugnacity, etc. And because of his frustrations, the individual forms unconsciously, different kinds of prejudices concerning different individuals and groups.

3. Maladjustment. It is not given to an individual to acquire perfect adjustment between himself and his circumstances and the other individuals in society. As a result of many causes, mental complexes of different kinds are formed in them. Their life becomes marked by discontent and hopelessness. They also fail to sublimate their anti-social tendencies. Hence, they become possessed with tendencies of hate, fear, disgust, etc., for other individuals and groups, and as a further consequence of this, they form all kinds of prejudices.

4. Self-defence. Every individual wants to protect his self and ego and if it is injured he reacts violently. In this reaction he develops emotions of hatred, disgust, etc., for the individual or group that is responsible for this injury and consequently forms all kinds of prejudices concerning them.

5. Motive of self-regard. Every individual wants to maintain his self-respect and self regard. This motive of self regard is not restricted only to his own personality. In addition to the development of his own ego, he wants to see intact the self-respect of his relatives, companions, party, group, etc. As a result of the link formed between them and the motive of self-regard, the individual forms prejudices towards them.

6. Desire of social conformity. In every society, some customs, laws, superstitions, notions, etc., are prevalent. In his desire for social conformity the individual accepts these without reflecting upon them and adopts them in the form of prejudices.

7. Learning. One very important psychological cause of prejudice is learning. The individual often learns or acquires his prejudices from the society. For example, the children of the Hindus and the Muslims have no prejudices to begin with but their parents do possess some communal prejudices. These adults inculcate into the child's mind that the Muslim is bad or that the Hindu is a non-believer. In this way, the child acquires these prejudices from his parents either by emulating them or by being taught by them.

In fact, most of the prejudices are acquired. The importance of learning and education in the removal of prejudices is shown by the part it plays in their acquisition.

B. Social Factors

In addition to the above mentioned psychological causes there are some social factors that are instrumental in the formation of prejudices. The main ones among them are :

1. *Social distance*: In every society different groups possess specific status with in the social strata. Some are higher, others are at a lower level. This is social status are separated by the proper social distance. To take an example, the Brahmins are believed to possess the highest and the Shudras the lowest status in the social stratification of the Hindu society. The social distance between these social classes is so great that the Brahmins look upon the Shudras as lowly and impure creatures. If a Brahmin child even touches the child of some Shudra, the former is given a bath to rid him of the supposed defilement caused by this touch. As a result of this strict formulation of his activities, the Brahmin child forms a prejudice in his mind that the Shudras are untouchable and impure.

2. *Cultural differences*: An important factor at the root of prejudice is the cultural differences. Every individual regards his own culture as the most superior and regards every other culture as inferior by virtue of its being different from his own. In this way, the distance between different individuals influenced by different cultures increases because there is no meeting point between the two. This distance ultimately assumes the form of hatred. Consequently, these individuals develop prejudices against each other. For example, people who profess their allegiance to ancient Indian culture hate and despise those who prefer Western culture. By virtue of this hatred, they form all kind of prejudices against the one who profess their liking for Western culture. They seem to consider the latter as the very manifestation and the figure of immoral conduct, corruption, unpatriotic feelings, prodigality and ostentation although it is not at all essential for an individual who likes Western culture and adopts it to possess all these faults and shortcomings.

3. *Social taboos and restrictions* : Many groups are characterised by social taboos and restrictions upon mutual behaviour between the individuals. To take a well-known example, among the Hindus it is not or at least was not permissible for a person of a particular caste to marry someone of a different caste. Further, the socially higher castes are not permitted even to eat with members of the lower castes. The result of such social taboos and restrictions is that the social distance between the various social classes continually increases and all kinds of prejudices are created. There is another way in which the restrictions upon the mutual conduct between individuals of different sexes exert their influence. In view of the many varied restrictions upon mutual behaviour between men and women that are imposed in the civilised societies, these individuals have to repress their sex need or have to satisfy it in some unnatural way by which disturbance and conflict are very much aggravated and all kinds of prejudices are the inevitable result.

4. *Social phenomena* : In addition to the above-mentioned social causes that cause prejudice, there are some social circumstances and social phenomena that cause the creation and formation of prejudices. To take an Indian example, communal tensions not only cause communal riots and conflicts but also prejudices in the minds of the Hindus and the Muslims. Differences in the various customs, traditions and practices prevalent in different societies also become the causes of prejudices.

C. Other Factors

The fore mentioned social and psychological causes are not all the causes of prejudices. They do not exhaust all the sources from which prejudices may stem. There are other causes also, but only the important ones are mentioned below :

1. ***Historical factors*** **:** At the root of all the prejudices that the Hindus and Muslims entertain against each other there are some historical causes also. It is a historical fact that the original followers of the Islamic religion were not the native product of the country but came from foreign strands and forced many Hindus to convert to the Islamic religion. Many of the Muslims also heaped injustices upon the luckless and helpless Hindus. On the other hand, some of the Hindu kings gave a severe answer to this unjust behaviour of the Muslims. These historical incidents are now old and are of interest perhaps only to the academician. But nevertheless, many individuals cannot bring themselves to forget the old history and times when the misanthropic activities of Aurangzeb endangered the existence of Hindu religion or when the Mohammadan mothers coaxed their children to sleep by frightening them in talking of Harisingh Nalva. Because of this even today there are many Hindus and Muslims who entertain feelings of hatred, disgust, etc. for each other, and this leads to the fostering of all kinds of prejudices.

2. ***Geographical factors*** **:** Some causes of prejudices are also geographical. In India people living in different regions are found fostering all kinds of prejudices concerning their brothers who live in other parts of the country. To take an example, many stories concerning the so-called foolishness and imprudence of the Sikhs are prevalent in U.P. People living in different geographical zones look upon those of their own regions as fellow-beings while people from different regions are apt to be looked upon as strangers. The result of this is that they form favourable prejudices for their own people while concerning the others they are unfavourably prejudiced.

3. ***Political factors*** **:** Some political causes also encourage the formation and excitement of prejudices. For example, in India, many parties, propelled by political interests, try to prejudice the public against their rivals by indulging in campaigns of bitter recrimination and even going to the length of concocting false tales of a prejudicial nature.

4. ***Economic factors*** **:** There are some economic causes of prejudice also. People influenced by the communist outlook tend to regard every rich individual and each capitalist as a cruel, corrupt, immoral and degraded person. They believe that all rich people are heartless. On the other hand, the rich people as a class tend to consider their poorer brothers as uncivilised, ill, behaved, crude and unrefined people. Evidently, the notions of both these classes of people are prejudiced because of economic difference. This fact is all the more clearly manifested when individuals of different economic status come into close con tact.

STEREOTYPES

What is Stereotype?

In modern social psychology, the word stereotype is accepted neither in its literal sense nor in the sense employed by Lipmann. It is consequently necessary to begin an account of it by giving some definitions of the term as presently used :

1. According to Kimball Young, "...It is best defined as a false classificatory concept at which, as a rule, some strong emotional feeling tone of like or dislike, approval or disapproval is attached." This particular definition of the term points out the following two characteristics of stereotype :

(a) It is a concept that causes false classifications.

(b) To it are attached the feelings of like and dislike, approval or disapproval.

In this way, stereotypes help in the classification of individuals just as Shikarpuri, Sardarji, etc., are some words that are used only for some specific kinds of individuals and to them are attached the feelings of like or dislike, approval or disapproval. At this stage, it should be remembered that classification of individuals in this way is completely unjustified. But this fact does not alter the fact that human behaviour and experience are influenced by stereotypes.

2. According to Charles Bird, "Stereotyped responses are perceptions of meaningful arrangements of ideas having their origin primarily in feelings and emotions rather than in some characteristics of the stimulating circumstances." In this definition of stereotype Bird points out that their origin depends not so much on external circumstances as on the feelings and emotions of the individual himself. This definition further points

out that in stereotype thoughts and perceptions are mutually entangled.

In this way, a brief definition of stereotype can be expressed in saying that stereotypes are those concepts in which perceptual experience and thought are mutually entwined and to which strong emotional or affective tendencies of likes and dislikes, approval and disapproval are conjoined, and which perform the function of false classification.

Function of Stereotype

Stereotypes hold much importance for the experience and behaviour of the individual. In this connection, many experiments have also been made and these have succeeded in throwing some light upon the influence of stereotypes in social behaviour. The following facts need to be pointed out in connection with the influence of stereotypes upon experiences and behaviour :

1. Direction and guidance of human behaviour. Stereotypes guide and direct the behaviour of the individual. As has been pointed out at an earlier juncture, we divide any objects or individuals into various classes on the basis of stereotypes. This has the advantage, however redoubtable, that it saves the labour and trouble involved in thinking about each object and individual separately. In actual fact, in the present life struggle man does not get the time or leisure to go into all the details concerning every object or person unassisted. In these circumstances his behaviour is directed by stereotypes. In the political field particularly, much of the conduct is based upon stereotypes. For example, on the Indian political scene, the victory in elections of the Congress party is taken almost for granted and it also usually happens that way. For this reason, many of the people vote for the Congress although such a state of affair cannot be said to be particularly happy. This tendency is present everywhere. Hartmann experimented upon 160 individuals of the central country of Pennsylvania and showed that they possessed political stereotypes and were influenced thereby. Hartmann composed a questionnaire containing 20 questions of which 10 were such that if the subject answered them in the affirmative, he could be pronounced a radical. If the answers to the remaining 10 were in the affirmative, the individual would be a conservative. It was deduced from the study conducted by Hartmann that the subjects possessed political stereotypes because of which the Republicans, Democrats, and labour groups were believed to compose the best classes while the international Radical reform, technocratic and the communist groups were believed to be the lowest classes.

2. Assistance in forecasting. It is often possible to base predictions concerning the behaviour of the individuals on stereotypes. For example, in the Indian Army the Sikhs and the Gorkhas are believed, by convention, to be the best soldiers and on the basis of this stereotype predictions are made in war concerning the behaviour of the efforts of these two classes of soldiers. Similarly, some people entertain stereotypes concerning the educated women and often make the mistake of predicting their conduct on the basis of this stereotype. If, for example, you have formed the opinion that the Bengalis are irritative and pugnacious then you can conclude of any Bengali that he will fight.

3. Control of social behaviour. In every society there prevail some stereotypes which perform the function of controlling the social behaviour of the members of society. For example, in India the Kshatriya believes that the most unpardonable sin that he can commit is to run away from the battlefield, and because of this many Kshatriyas cannot even entertain the idea of running away from the battlefield. Even in the progressive and lax age of modern era, the sexual behaviour of the Indian women is controlled by the stereotype of fidelity. It is said that the Indian woman establishes sexual relationship with only one man in her life and he is her husband. In the same way, the behaviour of the various castes is controlled and directed by the stereotypes prevailing about them. It is said that it makes no difference whether a Kayastha is uneducated or dead. The Kayasthas are believed to be rich of pen. Wealth is believed to reside in the stomach of the Baniya while the Brahmins are believed to be religious and sacrificing. The Kshatriyas are said to be experts in the art of warfare. These stereotypes do undoubtedly have some influence upon the behaviour of the individuals belonging to different castes.

4. Utility in commercial propaganda. The influence in controlling and directing the behaviour and conduct of the individual, that a stereotype has, is fully exploited in the commercial field. There is no tonic in the world three or four bottles of which can turn a skinny individual into a fat bulk of muscles and energy. Yet any number of producers create a stereotype of this kind concerning the tonic that they are producing. Once the stereotype is circulated, propaganda becomes an easy process. In the same way, there is probably no soap that can whiten the skin but to various soaps this kind of stereotype is attached.

5. Employment in educational institutions. This importance of the stereotype is made use of by educational institutions. People infer the nature of the educational institution from its name. For this reason, educational institutions are named on the basis of stereotypes, *e.g.*, Dayanand Anglo-Vedic College, Modern Art School, Sanatan Dharma College, etc. It should be remembered that it is not at all necessary that the Modern Art College should be actually modern although the people may deduce that it is so, and are encouraged to patronise it.

6. Importance of stereotype in experience. The existence of stereotype is felt not only in conduct but also in experience. In one of his articles Sherif has written that liking some prose depends upon the author who has composed it because the readers generally form some stereotypes concerning the different authors. These stereotypes are generally connected to those authors who influence the experience of the readers. Sherif selected some 26 essays and writings of Stevenson and to them he attached the names of 16 different authors following which he handed them over to students and enquired of their response to these articles. Although all the articles had been composed by Stevenson, the different students chose only those articles which bore the name of the author for which they already had appreciation and praise in their hearts. It is a matter of general knowledge that to begin with the works of an author are appreciated because of their worth but as the stereotypes are attached to his name his work wins praise merely because of his name.

In one of his experiments Rice proved that because of stereotypes figures or symbols concerning different persons are formed in the minds of the people. Rice selected the photographs of the Prime Minister of a European country, a labour leader, a Russian diplomat, a money lender, a member of the American Senate and a mill-owner. Now a list of these various occupations was prepared and handed over to the subject along with the photographs, he was then instructed to coincide the photograph with the occupation. From the results of the experiment it was deduced that the subjects had formed stereotypes and mental images concerning the occupations and the individuals who are occupied therein on the basis of the photographs appearing in the newspapers and the descriptions and account given. On that basis they had selected the occupations and the corresponding photographs of the individuals. It is a matter of common experience that a mental image is conjoined or attached to the common features seen existing in individuals or objects that are known by the same name. For example, in India if someone is referred to as Baba, the mental image that comes to the forefront is one of an old man and if the name employed is 'Dadi' one visualises an old woman although it is not at all necessary that the persons addressed by these two names should be old and bent. Similarly, the vision that one is apt to see when the word 'Bahu' is uttered, the word is the equivalent of daughter-in-law, is of a young woman with a long veil drawn down on her face although few of the modern married girls are at all of this kind.

7. Effect upon perceptions. Stereotypes influence perceptions in addition to affecting behaviour and experience. When we have formed the opinion in our mind that the Muslims are a dirty people then we are apt to notice only their dirty actions oblivious to their all other actions. Similarly, if a person has formed the stereotype that women love children or that they are of a sacrificing and delicate nature then he will see them in this light. A similar kind of stereotype is seen existing that concerns the Sikhs and you will come across a number of people who will describe incidents that they have perceived that concur with this prejudice. In this way, the stereotype influences the behaviour, experience and perception, in fact every aspect, of the individual.

INTERPERSONAL RELATIONSHIPS

An Individual is a member of a number of groups in his daily life. Groups differ from one another in a variety of ways. They differ in their purposes as well as in their structure. The structure of the group refers to the nature and characteristics of the interrelationships among the members and the distribution of functions among them. Two groups may have the same goal but their structure may be different.

Organisation

In the case of some groups, the members are differentiated with respect to their functions in connection with the task of achieving a common goal. Such a group is called an organisation. In an organisation, the members have a mutual responsibility to the achievement of their goal. But their functions may vary from one another and different members may contribute in different ways towards achieving the goal.

Formal Structure of the Organisation

Most of the organisations have a formal structure. This helps in prescribing the responsibilities and duties to different members. The formal structuring also helps in conducting the functions of the organisation in an orderly manner. In the case of a highly structured organisation such as an industrial or business organisation, the functions of the various members are generally clearly specified.

Organisational Chart

The formal structure of an organisation is generally presented in the form of an organisational chart which indicates the interrelationship among the various jobs and the functions of the various personnel in the organisation. The organisational chart provides the flow of work in the organisation, its jobs, its systems of communication, supervisory controls and the like. The members of the organisation are differentiated in terms of their functions in the organisation.

Differentiation of Functions

There are, generally, two types of differentiation of functions in an organisation — horizontal and vertical.

1. Horizontal differentiation. In the case of horizontal differentiation, different individuals in the organisation perform different functions on the same level. The functions of the members are coordinate in nature. There is a more pronounced relationship and interaction among the individuals, who hold jobs of the same rank in the organisation. The work in the organisation is of such a nature that the productive activities of one person influence those of others.

2. Vertical differentiation. In an organisation having a vertical differentiation of functions among its members, some individuals guide or direct the activities of others. The functions of the organisation involve a superior-subordinate relationship. In organisations having vertical differentiation of functions, some members always occupy positions superior to others. The formal superior-subordinate relationships in organisation help in the proper allocation of authority and responsibility among the individuals occupying different positions or ranks.

Common Basic Structure

Though there are differences in organisations, there is a certain basic structure common to most organisations. Among the common characteristics very often found in most of the organisations are those related to human relations, involving the patterns of activities and relationship existing between individuals.

Advantages of Good Human Relations

Following are the advantages of good human relation in an organisation :

1. Good human relations in an organisation help to make the members of the organisation organised and motivated to work together in accomplishing a task.

2. They lead to the development of a productive and satisfying group effort in achieving the common goal of the organisation.

3. Since interaction between people is an essential feature in most of the organisations and their work situations, good human relations are an important factor in the operation of almost all organisations, whether they be governmental or private, industrial or business.

4. Every organisation consists of a group of people having varying interests, needs and aspirations. All of them continually

make adjustment to the formal tasks which they are required to perform. In the process of performing the allotted tasks, each member tries to adapt his own interests to the demands of the people with whom he comes into contact.

Conditions of Good Human Relations

Good human relations in an organisation are possible in the following conditions :

1. Social adjustments. The operation of an organisation involves a set of social adjustments between the individual members or groups of people and the formal demands of the work activity. Each member has to perform his job and duties. Each one needs to be in contact with certain other persons and objects. Each one has his own activities.

2. Social system. In an organisation, the individual's role is considered mainly in terms of his activities and the way he fits into the activities of others. Thus, an organisation can be considered to be a system of relationships in which each individual occupies one position and functions according to the demands of that position. The system includes not only the processes and equipment or machines needed for accomplishing a task but also the set of activities and relationships by means of which people work together for achieving the goal.

3. Patterns of behaviour. The social adjustments between the individual members or groups of people and the formal demands of the work activity gradually lead to the development of certain patterns of behaviour and attitudes with reference to the work activity. These patterns of behaviour constitute the social system of the organisation.

4. Social status and role. Each individual fits into a definite place within the total system. Each individual joining the organisation gets informally trained in his duties and jobs in the organisation. He gradually comes to know his place and his role in the social system, the behaviour and attitudes he can expect from members of the organisation and the behaviour and attitudes expected of him. He soon learns whether his interests and attitudes are acceptable to the group members and whether he is liked by them or not. He learns all that he is required to learn in order to be able to meet the demands of all the members at different levels in the organisation with whom he needs to have contact in his work situations. He, thus, soon becomes part of the social system of the organisation. The patterns of behaviour and the positive attitudes which develop among the members of the organisation ultimately result in a productive and satisfying effort aimed at accomplishing the goal of the organisation.

5. Type of internal relationship. The role of a person in an organisation and the place he occupies in it is determined not only by his values, interests, motives and attitudes but also by the way he relates to his group. Regardless of his position in the organisation a person trying to perform a task is part of the social structure of the organisation. Relationships with other members of the organisation may often influence motivation to work hard or not, remain at work or keep away from it. It is clear then, that in order to keep the members of the organisation organised and motivated to perform their tasks, it is necessary to devise strategies for effecting sound human relations in the organisation.

Factors Promoting Better Human Relations

1. Understanding social system. To develop sound human relations in an organisation it is necessary to understand the social system and the recurring pattern of behaviour of its members.

2. Creation of suitable conditions and opportunities. The development of good human relations in an organisation depends mainly on the creation of conditions and opportunities which would lead to the development of positive attitudes and motivations among the members of the organisation at various levels.

3. Interaction and leadership. Some of the factors that affect human relations in an organisation are the kind and process of interactions among the members of the organisation, the kind of leadership or supervision in the organisation and the process of communication.

4. Common needs, interests and expectations. The needs, interests and expectations which the majority of the members of the organisation share in common and the formal demands which the organisations make upon their members also have some bearing on human relations in the organisation.

ORGANISATIONAL BEHAVIOUR

Process of Interaction in Organisations

Every organisation can be seen as a coordinated system of activities directed to the achievement of the goals of the organisation. In an organisation different members are grouped to form different groups, each of them having characteristic functions and activities. Each of them operates in a very definite and predetermined way but all aim at accomplishing the goals of the organisation. The relationships among the members in an organisation may be formally imposed or may arise out of informally-developed interactions among the members.

Kinds of Interactions

There are mainly two kinds of interactions among the members of an organisation. One is the interaction arising out of the work and the other is the personal interaction that occurs as a result of being put together as members of a group in an organisation.

1. Interactions arising out of the work. The interactions arising out of the work can be classified into two major categories — those arising out of the superior-subordinate relationships and those arising out of coordinate relationships.

(i) ***Interactions among superior-subordinate relationships :*** Most of the industrial, governmental or business organisations have a system of authority ranging from the top level boss to the lowest level supervisor. In such organisations, practically everyone has a person superior to him in the organisational set-up. In a government organisation, the Section Officer is superior to the clerks in the section and the Section Officer in turn is subordinate to the Under Secretary and so on. Similarly, in a bank the officer occupies a superior position to the clerks or cashiers but is subordinate to the bank manager. In bigger organisations the structure is normally linked from top to bottom by a series of superior-subordinate relations. These linkages, running from top to bottom, form the lines of authority by which the person at the top normally controls and directs the entire organisation. The superior–subordinate relationships in an organisation constitute the problem of leadership of supervision which has a crucial bearing on human relations.

(ii) ***Interactions arising out of coordinate relationships :*** In between the top and bottom levels of authority in an organisation, there are generally a number of positions which constitute the supervisory hierarchy system with those at each particular level having the same rank in the structure. For example, between the General and the soldier in the Army, there are a number of positions such as the Junior Commissioned Officers, Second Lieutenants, Lieutenants, Captains, Majors, Lieutenant-Colonels, Colonels, Brigadiers, Major-Generals, and Lieutenant-Generals. All persons at each of these levels have the same rank in the structure. Coordinate relationships occur among individuals holding the same rank since they all function at the same level though each one of them may perform different functions. A person's position in the structure of the organisation determines, to a great extent, his behaviour and his relationships with others. It also determines the way he thinks about his job and the organisation. Thus, the principal of a school acts and thinks differently from the office superintendent; the teacher thinks differently from the office clerk and so on. In an industrial organisation, the manager thinks and acts differently from the engineer. The engineer is different from the accounts officer and the skilled workers are different from the office clerks. But every one must adjust his behaviour to his position in the structure. Each one must adapt himself to the needs of the job and the responsibility entrusted to him. This would help in maintaining the coordination of activities required for the proper functioning of the organisation.

2. Personal interactions. In addition to the interactions that arise out of the work situations and within the existing organisational framework, there also occur patterns of relationships and activities which develop as a result of social contacts among individuals. These are of two types — friendly and unfriendly :

(i) ***Friendly relations :*** For each individual there are patterns of individual friendships and dislikes and from these individual friendships emerge the cliques, the informal leaders and their followers. From these personal relationships arise the formation of groups that stand together on issues of mutual interest and the groups that oppose each other.

(ii) ***Unfriendly relations :*** The unfriendly relations sometimes emerge as a result of conflicts arising out of the work in the organisation. They may also arise out of the personal differences that occur due to one reason or the other. Sometimes, these unfriendly relations among the members of an organisation result in aggressive behaviour which leads to unproductive efforts.

The friendly and unfriendly relations or the indifferent and antagonistic behaviour are in most cases influenced by the formal structure or by the intentions of the superior personnel or the top boss. However, they are not directed by the formal structure of the organisation. The different patterns of relationships and behaviour constitute the human element in the organisation and they have a direct bearing on the development of human relations in the organisation.

Individual Roles in Organisations

The development of good human relations which can foster affirmative attitudes and motivations in groups of people in an organisation also depend upon the kinds of roles assumed by different members of the organisation. Though every member of the organisation functions in a different way, the part played by some members is more dominant and important while that of others is less important in terms of achieving the goal of the organisation. Every individual in the organisation is assigned certain functions and he does them in the way and at the time prescribed in order that the goal of the organisation may be achieved. Each member has a certain position or status. The duties, functions and position of the individuals constitute the role of the individual in the organisation.

Kind of Roles

As a member of an organisation, an individual may be required to play different kinds of roles :

1. Roles adopted on particular occasions and for specific purposes.

2. Roles that are permanent in nature and may be assumed for longer durations.

3. Roles related to the achievement of the purposes of the group with which a person performs a task. Such roles facilitate the coordination of the effort of the group. They may be concerned with the solution of the problems facing the group in connection with the achievement of the group goal.

4. Roles concerned with the functioning of the group as a group. These are concerned with maintaining or changing the ways of working of the members of the group so as to keep harmony in the group.

5. Individual roles which are directed towards satisfaction of the needs of the individual. These are concerned with the achievement of certain individual goals which may have no significance either for the accomplishment of the group task or for the functioning of the group.

6. Formally assigned roles. The role of an individual in an organisation is determined by many factors. In most cases, the functions and roles are formally assigned to the members by the organisation. In such cases, the individual performs certain functions because of the position he occupies in the organisation. However, in carrying out these formally assigned roles there are individual differences among the members in performing a task and, therefore, each individual needs to be treated differently. While carrying out a job, two individuals may perform equally well though both of them may function in different ways. Therefore, for the development of good human relations, it is necessary to assign appropriate roles to each individual and also to adjust the characteristics of the job according to the personal attributes of the individuals.

7. Assumed roles. In many organisations, the functions of the members and the specifications of jobs are not clearly laid down. In such cases, the roles are sometimes assumed by an individual due to his unique and individual personality. There are roles which the individual believes he ought to adopt in order to satisfy the expectations of others. An individual also assumes roles which others believe he should adopt while functioning in an organisation. Sometimes an individual, due to various reasons, may not adopt the roles which he thinks he should adopt and others may not feel that he is adopting the role expected of him. In other words, the role the individual

seeks to assume may not correspond with the role he believes he ought to adopt. Two individuals performing the same task but possessing different abilities and personality traits may assume entirely different roles in an organisation. An officer in a bank or an executive in a commercial organisation who believes more in authority and responsibility may adopt the role of a strict boss. Another person who is more sociable may seek to establish himself as a friend of his subordinates.

8. Informally imposed roles. In certain cases, the roles may be imposed informally upon an individual by other members of his group. A person more educated than others in the group may be considered as an adviser by his group members. An older member of the organisation having more experience than others in the group may sometimes be considered as a counsellor by others because of the knowledge of the organisational matters acquired by him during his long years of service in the organisation. Roles are also sometimes thrust upon certain persons because of the positions they occupy in the organisation.

Behaviour According to Roles

The roles that an individual occupies in an organisation also prescribe the behaviour expected of him. Certain kinds of behaviour are considered as an essential part of the individual's role. The appropriate behaviour for a role may be prescribed by the individual himself or by the members of the organisation.

When the members of an organisation act in ways that are neither desired by them nor expected by others, difficulties in interpersonal relations occur. This often leads to the development of negative attitudes and lack of motivation among groups of people, hindering the development of good human relations in the organisation.

FORMS OF INTERACTIONS

The members of an organisation try to develop different forms of interactions between them. Some of them result in cooperative efforts in the organisation.

1. Cooperation. Cooperation requires the people to contribute their maximum efforts towards the common goal of the group or the organisation. Cooperative effort involves division of labour and sharing of efforts among the members of an organisation. It helps the members to share the fruits of their achievement. It helps them to surmount their difficulties. It is not possible for a single individual in an organisation to identify the difficulties and find solutions to all the problems. When an individual works in cooperation with others in a group, he gets the benefit of the experience and knowledge of the whole group and the difficulties which otherwise are not surmountable can be easily overcome by the group.

2. Competition. Another form of human interaction is competition. Competition calls for one individual to do better than other individuals. Individuals cooperate in groups to compete with other groups. In such cases, members of the particular successful group share the recognition and reward secured by the group. In the case of competition between two individuals, only one person enjoys the recognition and reward.

Incentives

Both cooperation and competition may themselves be regarded as incentives. The term incentive refers to a spurring force that is introduced as a means of achieving a goal. When cooperation and competition result in satisfaction for the members of the organisation, one finds positive attitudes and motivations among them fostering better human relations in the organisation.

Persuasion

In certain work situations in an organisation, cooperation or competition among its members may not occur spontaneously. The members may need to be persuaded to cooperate or compete in order to achieve a certain goal. Persuasion is done in a variety of ways. In persuading, one may need to appeal to the emotions and feelings of the members in order to direct them to make efforts for the accomplishment of a satisfying task. Sometimes one may persuade a group to act in a specific way by providing appropriate and adequate incentives. However, persuasion may fail to work in the case of certain individuals. The stronger the opinion of the person, the less he becomes susceptible to persuasion and change of views and activities.

Supervision and Leadership

A major factor in the development of sound human relations in an organisation is the kind of supervision and leadership provided in the organisation. The personality and behaviour of the leaders or those at the higher levels in the organisation influence the attitudes and behaviour of those at the lower levels. The reactions of the members to the organisation are generally reflected by their reactions to their leaders or those who are superior to them in position and status.

QUESTIONS FOR EXERCISE

1. Why are human relations important in organisations? Describe the factors promoting human relations in an organisation.
2. Describe the kinds of interactions that take place among the members of an organisation.
3. What is the place of cooperation and competition in a group situation?
4. Describe the importance of communication for the development of human relations in an organisation.
5. Describe the major elements and processes that are common to all forms of communication.
6. What are the different forms of communication? List the major factors that determine the effectiveness of communication.
7. List the common barriers to communication. Give examples of situations where communication is blocked by physical and psychological barriers.

5

Psychology of Group Behaviour

A child's social development takes place gradually as he advances in age. The newborn baby performs very few social functions, being both consciously and unconsciously concerned with the fulfilment of his physical needs. But before long, he exhibits signs of reacting to individuals who help him fulfil these needs. The only thing that his early activities show is that he has started understanding the objects and individuals in his environment. By the time he completes his first year he forms specific patterns of behaviour regarding the adults with whom he comes into contact. He is also influenced by their interests and other things.

Similarly, as the child grows older, the patterns of his play also evince many significant changes. When he is two months 'old, the only thing he is capable of is holding the wooden block proffered to him. But when he is two years' old, he plays with his toys without the need of any external intervention, besides which he tries to dispossess other children of their toys and to take all toys for himself. Gradually, the feelings of 'I' and 'mine' develop and strengthen, but at the same time he also learns what 'you' and 'yours' mean. In the third year, he also recognises the right of other individuals over his toys, thereby learning to share his possessions with others. It is only after this period that the child shows any desire to co-operate in group games.

Moving from the egocentric behaviour of the first three years to the pre-school period, the child's conduct begins to appear socialized. In infancy, the child is almost completely egocentric and selfish, not being inclined to give any of his possessions to any one else. As his social development progresses towards ultimate maturity, he learns to divide and share his own with others and to co-operate with them. Even then, the intelligent children maintain some independence and individuality. Most of the child's games in the pre-school period are egocentric. On entering school, he enters the first stage of his socialization and immediately becomes a member of the group of his own sex. Boys group with boys, and girls with girls. In school, the child is particularly sensitive and susceptible to other's behaviour towards him, particularly the conduct of his seniors. Till four or five years of age boys and girls play together. As the child gets greater opportunity to meet boys of his own age, his socialization accelerates. In the words of L.B. Murphy, "He becomes a member of a small world of children, all near his own age, although differences in age may vary with the arrangement in different groups." This world of children furnishes, from this time on, a major part of his social diet. He is constantly assimilating this, by direct imitation of patterns of other children, by spontaneous reaction to things which they do or to situations which they create, by resistance to this pressure, by repeated experience of tensions aroused by their mere presence. In the kindergarten and montessori education systems, the child's social development is further facilitated by the opportunity that children get to play together. It has been pointed out before, too, that in this age group one can find groups of children formed on the basis of sex differences. But it is equally usual for two children of opposite sexes to become quite friendly and intimate due to reasons of proximity or convenience or the absence of other children. The truth of the matter is that the presence of sex distinction among children's play is the result of criticism or interference from seniors. In this age, friendship normally lasts for no more than a couple of days. Some children of course find it easier than others to make friends.

Living in the group, the child gradually evolves the communal sentiment. As he grows, he also acquires notions of propriety and impropriety, although children are seen differing in their individual opinions on this point. These concepts are primarily influenced by the attitudes of parents and teachers. The child himself, in his play, shows little or no consciousness of sex difference, as state of mind that is normally found to exist in the childhood that immediately precedes the period of adolescence.

GROUP FORMATION

Between the age of 6 and 12, the child begins adjusting rapidly to his changing and varying social world. Now he is usually a member of one or the other group, which exhibits a code language, places of meeting a leader, special purpose of various activities, etc. The members of the group evince a definite loyalty to the group, do not hesitate to obey the orders of the leader and to emulate him and experience considerable freedom and independence. These same groups later on, in adult life, manifest themselves in the form of committees and societies. In this age, boys and girls form their groups among members of their own sexes, because of a definite and clear differentiation between their habits, interests, desires, etc.

He is particularly anxious to win esteem in the group. Sometimes, in the group he indulges in activities that are considered specifically anti-social. In the case of children who indulge in such activities, fundamentally a great responsibility lies in the environment within the home and family. In families where the parents have no hesitation in giving praise and affection to their children, it will be seen that the young individuals indulge in proper and desirable activity. On the other hand, neglected and consequently rebellious children are apt to indulge in detestable actions, and later on turn into juvenile delinquents. It is necessary that the teachers keep an eye on the development and active manifestation of such tendencies within the child groups within his domain. Groups provide opportunities for the development of the qualities of leadership, so that in their adult and more responsible years, the boys and girls can turn to leading the nation. It should be kept in mind that all children do not evince the same liking for the group. Some children tend to avoid groups and prefer to stay with one or two children of their choice. There may be occasions of conflict between these individualistic boys and the bigger groups. And, there is no essential rule that members of the group are intelligent while these boys and girls who tend to shun the group are slow-witted. It is perfectly possible for the opposite to be true. Secondly, there may be some personal reasons which may actuate the individual to stay away from the group, but generally it is best to live in the group, as it benefits the individual's social development. The child's social development is influenced in an important manner, by the mutual interaction between childhood groups, competition, conflict and co-operation.

In adolescence the groups are not as well organised and systematic as the groups of childhood, and their purpose is mostly social. Important social activities of young men and women are dances, singing sessions, picnics, mountain climbing, etc. In Western countries, in all such outings the number of individuals from either sex is almost equal, so that every one has his companion. Some boys and girls do not participate in such a big group, but choose to develop relations with an individual of the other sex. But people who choose to live in big groups do not entertain a good opinion of such solitude lovers. One finds considerable loyalty in conflict and even physical violence. Members of a particular group have the same conversational style, dress, modes of conduct, etc., and they mostly prefer to be together. Adolescents talk incessantly of their school and college, but they also show considerable interest in philosophical issues, national and international matters, professions, games and other subjects of universal significance. But their greatest pleasure is derived from their conversation on the other sex. Leaders of adolescent groups are chosen on the basis of health and energy, loyalty, enthusiasm, sportsman spirit, organisational skill, originality, sympathy and many other qualities of personality.

Definitions of Group

The group has been defined in a variety of ways by sociologists and social psychologists. Each of these definitions emphasises some one or the other features of the group, according to the viewpoint of the scholar who has advanced the particular definition. An analytical description and discussion of the definitions of the group will bring out its nature. Some main definitions of the group are the following :

1. R.M. Williams. "A social group is a given aggregate of people playing inter-related roles and recognised by themselves or other as a unit of interaction." In this way, the group is an aggregate of some people. The roles of these people are related to each other. The group is considered a unit, by every member of it, in which the conduct of the people is inter-related. It is recognised in the same light even by individuals external to it.

2. Ogburn and Nimkoff. "Whenever two or more individuals come together and influence one another, they may be said to constitute a social group", write Ogburn and Nimkoff in their treatise *A Handbook of Sociology*. This definition of the group is oversimplified but the least it does is to convey the information that a collection of individuals can be considered a group only when they influence each other. In other words, they should have an awareness of each other.

3. R.M. MacIver. "By group we mean any collection of social beings who enter into distinctive social relationships with one another." This definition makes it abundantly clear that there must be social relationships between the individual members of a group.

4. J.P. Gillin and J.L. Gillin. "A social group thus grows out of and requires a situation which permits meaningful inter-stimulation and meaningful response between the individuals involved in common focusing of attention on common drives, motivations or emotions." This definition of the group treats as essential the mutual actions and reactions as well as mutual stimulations between the members. Some motives, drive, interests, emotions and stimuli are common within the group.

5. Edward Sapir. "Any group is constituted by the fact that there is some interest which holds its members together." The members should also be persuaded to co-operate with each other through some common interest.

6. Elredge and Merrill. "A social group may be defined as two or more persons who are in communication over an appreciable period of time and who act in accordance with a common function or purpose." According to this definition, besides a common purpose, communication for an adequate and proper period is also essential in a group.

The foregoing account of the definitions of group will have made it clear that group is that aggregate of persons which is like a unit and whose members have some common aims, interests, stimulations and emotions together with the mutual social relations and social interactions. Through the medium of all these, members of a group influence each other and are tied to each other. According to Bogardus, "A social group may be thought of as a number of persons, two or more, who have some common objects of attention, who are stimulating to each other, who have common loyalty and participate in similar activities."

CHARACTERISTICS OF GROUP

It is a difficult task to point out the characteristics of group. Even then some characteristics of group can be described. These are as follows :

1. The members of a group are related to each other. Simply a gathering of persons cannot be called a group. The members of the group should be inter-related. In fact, this social relation is called a group. Cuber has written, "A group is any number of human beings in reciprocal communication." MacIver and some other sociologists have also admitted the social relations to be the fundamentals of the group life.

2. Group implies a feeling of unity. A feeling of unity is essential for every group. By virtue of such feeling members of a group treat each other as their own and a sense of sympathy develops between them.

3. Members of a group have a sense of we-feeling. By a sense of we-feeling, the members of a group help each other in performing their duties; and they defend collectively against the harmful powers. They treat others as the outsiders and try to make their groups prosperous and self-sufficient.

4. The interests of the group members are common. A group includes those persons who are related to each other in such a way that they should be treated as one. For it, the interests of the persons of a group should lend to be common because this similarity promotes unity.

5. There is similarity of behaviour in a group. As the interests, ideals and values of the persons of a group are common, similarly the behaviour of the persons also tends to be similar. A group is not merely an aggregate of persons, but it is a continuation of their behaviour.

6. Control of group over the actions of the members. The main reason behind the similarity of behaviour in group life is that the actions of the members are controlled by the group. In each group there are some customs, norms and procedures which are acceptable to everyone and the dissenting members of the group are given punishment. Even if the group fails to punish a person disobeying these, he shall be severely criticised by public. In this way, every one has to obey the social norms. In fact, without some norms, the existence of group life is practically impossible.

7. The members of a group are affected by group characteristics. Each group possesses some social characteristics which separate it from the similar and dissimilar groups. These characteristics affect the members constituting the group. The affect may be of different nature for different persons, but still all the members are affected by the group.

8. Common values. Each caste has its own specific common values that help to distinguish it from other castes and also tie its members in the thread of unity. In this way, the social values of the Brahmins and the Shudras, the Kshatriyas and the Vaishyas, can be seen differing considerably. The caste panchayats are very vigilant in enforcing the obedience to these social values and people who deviate from them or transgress their bounds are exterminated from the caste. They are subjected to social isolation and ostracism. They cannot marry within the group. In a similar vein, the example of family can also be considered. The social values of the members of a family are common and are traditionally respected and communicated to the succeeding generation. They are clearly expressed in the mutual behaviour of the members. Thus members of the social group are bound together in the tie of common values.

9. Mutual obligation. The relationships between the members of a group are further strengthened through their mutual obligation, beside their common social values. The family is a fine example of this. In the family, all the members have complementary obligations to each other. Children obey the orders of parents and try to conform to their desires. Husband and wife love each other. The husband fulfils the needs of the wife, while the wife obeys the orders of the husband besides cooperating with him in all activities. In this way, the members of the family are bound to each other by the ties of mutual obligation.

10. Mutual expectations. In a group, the members are entitled to expect love, sympathy and co-operation from others. In the family, the husband expects his wife to love him while his wife expects reciprocation of this affection. When this desire is turned into despair, the family relationship is destroyed and divorce is imminent. In the same way, the parents expect their offspring to accede to their wishes while the children expect from their parents love and sympathy coupled with help to rise in future. The disintegration of the family sets in when these desires are not fulfilled. While the family is a much close knit social unit, even the neighbourhood is related to each member through mutual expectation. In all social groups that human beings form members have expectations of each other. If the people of one's own clan were not to share in one another's joys and sorrows, then what is the use of any clan. All individuals hope that in times of joy and sorrow the people belonging to their clan will participate and render the occasion befitting of a social being. And so long as this mutual expectation is being fulfilled, the organisation of the group is maintained intact. If in any school, the student were to refuse to show obedience to his teacher and the latter were to abstain from helping the student in his pursuit of knowledge, how long can such a school last? Thus, a group retains its existence only as long as its constituent members fulfil their responsibility by satisfying the mutual desires among them.

The example of the family as a group can serve to illustrate the aforementioned characteristics of group. Among the members of the family there are relationships such as husband-wife, father-son, brother-sister etc., and all of them work for the interests of the family in a mood of mutual co-operation. Each member treats every other member as his own, and despite all the differences that there may be between their attitudes and tendencies, they share some common ideals and values. It is because of the common interests that the family works as a well-knit unit. Family control is exercised on each member. Disobedience of the laws of the family leads to serious altercation between the head of the family and the children while even the senior members do not escape censor. Each member bears the indelible stamp of his family characteristics. This characteristic is so prominent that the study of an individual's behaviour, affords some clue as to the type of family in which he must have been bred. These characteristics of the group are to be found in other groups in greater or lesser degree.

Social organisation is the organisation of groups. And social groups are the units of social organisation. Hence the integration and the disintegration of social organisation are dependent upon the integration or disintegration of the groups. The group, as is evident from the term applied to it, is a conglomeration the basis of which is social relationships. The family, for example, is a social group.

TYPES OF GROUPS

Some important classifications of groups are as stated below :

1. Cooley's classification. (i) ***Primary Groups*** — In which there are face to face, strong and co-operative relations between the persons such as a family.

(ii) ***Secondary Groups*** — Where strong, personal and warm relations are not found as in political parties.

2. Sumner's classification. (i) ***In-Group*** — In these groups the members have common object and common interest and a sense of well-feeling. The members of the in-groups treat others as outsiders. These groups can be formed on the basis of relation, country, political interests, economic interests, etc.

(ii) ***Out-groups*** — Groups other than in-groups are out-groups.

3. Miller's classification. (i) Vertical, (ii) Horizontal.

4. Gidding's classification. (i) Public, (ii) Private.

5. Elwood's classification. (i) Sanctioned, (ii) Unsanctioned.

6. Gillin and Gillin's classification. (i) Based on blood-relationship, (ii) Based on physical traits, (iii) Based on situation proximity, (iv) Based on cultural interests.

7. Ward's classification : (i) Voluntary, (ii) Involuntary.

In fact, to classify groups is a difficult task. In this connection, Cuber has rightly written, "Sociologists have devoted a great deal of effort to the difficult problem of classifying groups into types. At first, though this would seem easy to do but perhaps after further reflection, it will be found to present numerous difficulties which are so great, in fact, that at present we have no overall systematic classification of groups which is entirely acceptable to all sociologic scholars."

WHAT IS LEADERSHIP?

Before entering upon a detailed study and discussion of it, it is necessary to determine what leadership is. As usual, different scholars have defined it differently, each according to his own propensity. An investigation into these definitions will make the nature of leadership clear. Some important definitions are the following :

1. Sprott. Any one who acts as a model to others is often called a "leader". According to this definition, leadership is attribute of that person who is an ideal for the other members of the group. Evidently, only a wrestler can be the leader of a group of wrestlers, while only a person acquainted with political techniques and means can lead a group of politicians. In both circumstances, the term leader is used only for that individual who guides the others, or who is the ideal of others. It is only because he is the ideal that the other members of the group follow him naturally and it is due to this that he wields so much influence upon the other members. The followers of the leader acquiesce to the wishes of the leader. They want to apply his teachings in their lives. They are even prepared to lay down their lives at his wish. According to Freud, the leader becomes the ego-ideal of the followers.

2. Lapiere and Fransworth. "Leadership is a behaviour that affects the behaviour of other people, more than their behaviour affects that of the leader". In every group every member bears some relation to the others and all of them influence and affect each other. In these mutual relationships and the mutual influences, the individual who exerts the greater influence but is, in his turn, not influenced quite so much becomes the leader. In this way, then, this definition sheds light upon the interaction between the leader and his followers. The leader leads, suggests, orders and guides. Other people follow him.

Difference between Leadership and Domination

It is clearly evident from this mutual interaction that

leadership and domination are not synonymous terms. The leader does not remain unaffected by the followers. He is also affected by them just as they are influenced by him, though not in the same degree. From the psychological viewpoint, the behaviour of the leader towards the followers as addressed to their leader shows the predominance of elements of dedication and surrender. But one rarely comes across cases in which the behaviour of the leader is exclusively dominating while the follower completely surrenders himself. In this way, what is most and invariably noticeable in the interaction between the leader and the follower is that the behaviour of the leader influences the conduct of the follower more than does the latter's influence that of the leader. Leadership can be seen anywhere where there is such conjunction between domination and self-surrender. It is not necessary for this that the leader always direct the follower along the right path. A leader is always a leader whether he directs the follower along the right path or along the wrong one, and so long as he remains a leader, the followers have no choice but to follow him.

In their masterly treatise, *Society,* MacIver and Page write, "By leadership we mean the capacity to persuade or to direct man that comes from personal qualities apart from office". This definition indicates the difference between leadership and office. An individual does not become a leader merely by occupying an office which carries responsibility. It is a matter of secondary importance that his important office is of assistance to him in his endeavour to become a leader. Actually, leadership depends upon the individual qualities of the person and not the office that he holds. For this reason it is seen that sometimes nobody is inclined to pay attention to the utterings of the constitutionally elected leader while they are all ears for some other person. In the political sphere, the politician cannot hope to hold his post if he is lacking in the personal qualities of leadership. And as to what these personal qualities of leadership are will be investigated further on.

Putting it briefly, leader is that individual in the group who performs special tasks, makes suggestions, orders and shows the way, who appears before the others as the ideal, who is respected by all the others and whose suggestions and orders are implemented. Leadership is the term which denotes the behaviour or functions of this leader. In this way, the leader affects other individuals in such a way that they surrender themselves and follow his dictates. The process of domination or dictatorship differs from that of leadership. In his book, *Leadership or Domination,* Pigors writes, "Leadership is a process of control in which by the assumption of superiority a person or group regulates the activities of others for purposes of his own choosing."

CHARACTERISTICS OF LEADERSHIP

The following are the characteristics of leadership :

1. Leader is the ideal of the followers. As has been stated earlier, only that person assumes the station of leader in any group who is the ideal of the other constituents and he retains his leadership only as long as the people continue to look upon him as the ideal.

2. Leader is a respected and revered person. In order that he may be the ideal of the people of the group, it is essential that the leader is as respected and revered as he is great.

3. Leader is shown regard. In the mutual behaviour and interaction between the leader and the followers, the latter manifest much regard for him and are even prepared to lay down their lives in preventing the leader from suffering any injury. He does not have to coax or to persuade the followers to act on his decisions. His word is law to them. This show of regard also has the effect of encouraging the leader and is constant reminder to him of his duty towards those who have placed so much trust in him.

4. The leader's order is a command. Just as the child cannot disregard the order of the parent, the followers in a group cannot disregard the orders of the leader.

5. Leader and the followers influence each other. In studying the mutual behaviour between the leader and his followers, it must be kept in mind that the influence is not entirely one-sided. Both mutually influence each other, through of course this mutual effect, the influence exerted by the leader is by far the greater. From this another fact that emerges is that a successful leader should make a constant note of the psychology of his followers. He should respect them and do nothing that can injure their feelings. It should be his constant endeavour to win their hearts rather than trying to display his power and influence. Only then can he hope to be their beloved leader.

6. Leader determines the group's conduct. All the members of the group obey and carry out the order of the leader. In this way, the position of the leader in the group is central and the most superior. His followers are always turning to him and constantly attending to him. Whenever any difficulty is posed they turn to him expectantly for the solution and do whatever he sees fit. It is in elucidating this very point that Seeman and Morris write, "One tentatively adoptable definition of leadership emphasizes its influence aspect, leadership acts are acts by persons which influence other persons in shared direction."

7. Leader controls the other members of the group. Every group is composed of many members. The process of leadership is determined by their specific kinds of relationship. In the words of Pigors, "Leadership is a concept applied to the personality-environment relation to describe the situation when a personality is so placed in the environment that his will, feeling and insight direct and control others in pursuit of a common cause".

Leadership and Office

The foregoing treatment of the station and the functions of a leader in his group is enough to make it clear that leadership is dependent upon some personal and individual qualities and that it is distinct from office. It cannot be denied that an individual can become a leader with facility if he is occupying a high and important post. As Shartle and Stogdill have written, "Persons who occupy positions which are commonly presumed to demand leadership ability are proper and likely subject for the study of leadership". But merely by his occupying an office that demands the qualities of leadership it cannot be concluded that the individual possesses the qualities usually found in a leader. It is, of course, necessary that if he is to continue in that post for long he must possess the requisite qualities. For example, if a person lacks the qualities of an army general he cannot successfully lead the army for long. On the other hand, the individual who possesses these qualities can become the general. It is only due to this difference in leadership and office that many so-called leaders are divested of their status; generals are murdered by their own armies while new persons come to the forefront in the leadership.

Authority and Leadership

From the foregoing delineation it is only too apparent that there is appreciable difference between authority and leadership. Authority possesses the element of domination. The authoritative individual also resorts to power in order to have his notions accepted. To authority is further conjoined self-exhibition. People are afraid of dominance and authority. Leadership, on the other hand, does not exhibit any of these qualities. Although the leader is a dominant figure, he does not assert his authority. The successful leader does not employ force and has no need too. The public is not afraid of him but shows respect for him. The leader also behaves lovingly and benevolently towards his subordinates. He looks more to his duties than to his rights. He presents an ideal to the public. Thus, it is clear that leaders should not run after authority. In doing it their qualities of leadership suffer and sometimes in the greed for authority they even lose their leadership. In the political field, incidents are not at all uncommon in which a leader is seen forsaking authority in order to maintain his leadership.

TYPES OF LEADERSHIP

Different types of leadership have been described by different scholars, and this classification of leadership is made on bases which differ. The following are some of the main bases :

(1) Origin of leadership.

(2) Purpose of leadership.

(3) Nature of leadership.

(4) Nature of the relation of the leader with the followers.

The different types of leader in these various classes will now be described.

1. Classification on the basis of origin. The following types of leadership have been accepted in the classification based on origin. It need not be pointed out that a perusal of them will throw light on the origin of leadership :

(i) ***Executive appointed leadership :*** As is evident from the name given to this particular type of leader, he is appointed by the executive and his leadership stems from the office or post to which he is appointed by the executive. The class of government officers is of this type.

(ii) ***Leader appointed by group :*** These leaders are elected by the group. In India, the public leaders of panchayats, local groups, the Lok Sabha and the Rajya Sabha are elected by the group.

(iii) ***Self-appointed leader :*** But there are some leaders whose authority derives neither from the executive nor the group because it is not vested in them by these groups. They advance because of their individual qualities and having attained the central position, lead the people. They are also recognised as such because of their qualities. Leaders like Mahatma Gandhi, who were liked by the public, belong to this class. Here one may be assailed by the doubt that the self-appointed leader may impose himself upon the public inspired by the desire for leadership. But, in actual fact, this is not inevitably so. Hence, the term self-appointed is employed merely to point to the fact that leadership or authority is not bestowed upon them by any electoral body but their leadership is accepted because of their personal qualities.

2. Classification on the basis of purpose. Leadership can also be classified on the basis of the purpose for which it is meant. Different groups make efforts for the achievement of different aims in their respective individual spheres. The individuals who appear to be the most qualified and the most resourceful in the attainment of these purposes are accepted as leaders in these respective spheres. There can undoubtedly be any number of spheres of this kind but here only the intellectual, the artistic and the executive will be described. In this way, this classification includes the following types of leadership :

(i) ***Intellectual leadership :*** Intellectual leadership is needed in the intellectual field. In the fields of philosophy, science, etc., the greatest thinkers can be said to be the intellectual leaders because they show the way and the others follow them. Freud and Shankaracharya were leaders of this category.

(ii) ***Artistic leadership :*** In the field of art, only the great artists can provide the leadership. Artists like Tansen, Premchand and Rabindranath Tagore can be said to be leaders.

(iii) ***Executive leadership :*** In the sphere of administration it is the authoritative personality who becomes the leader. For example, the district magistrate in every district is the leader of the district in the sphere of administration, and his orders are respected and carried out by every one.

3. Classification on the basis of nature of leadership. Leadership, as found in different individuals is also classified on the basis of its nature. For example, some leaders are exclusively authoritarian while some others are more faithful to the democratic ideal. The following are the classes into which leadership is divided on the basis of its nature :

(i) ***Authoritarian leader :*** The authoritarian leader is an individual who likes to assert his authority. Hence he conducts himself as his fancy takes him. He does not consult any one in taking decisions and leads by creating fear into the hearts of his followers and subordinates. He does not solicit cooperation but prefers to issue orders and punishes those who disobey him while those who fall into line with him are rewarded. He keeps all his authority in his hand and appoints reliable subordinates at crucial positions. Evidently, the leader of this kind is an officer and an authoritarian. And to be accurate, he should not be called a leader.

(ii) ***Democratic leader*:** This type of leader is of a democratic mould in his thoughts, modes of action and conduct. He takes advice from every one and is always anxious to enlist the cooperation of any one who is willing to give it. His leadership is based upon sympathy, belief and affection. He does not call himself a leader and neither does he take all the authority into his own hands. With the authority vested in him he speaks of himself as the humble servant of the public.

4. Classification on the basis of nature of relation with followers. Leadership is classified also on the basis of the nature of the relation of the leader to his followers. The relation of the leader with his followers depends on the leader. They differ from leader to leader. Some leaders are connected with the executive, others are leaders because of their important position in the group, some are leaders because of their ability, efficiency or capability while others lead because of their ability in getting work done by their power of persuasion. The following are their classes :

(i) ***Institutional leader*** **:** In every institution, there is some individual who occupied the highest post, just as there is the Vice Chancellor in a University who is looked upon as the highest official or supreme authority. His orders are appreciated and implemented because of the authority vested in his chair. Actually, the institutional leader is not leader but the officiating head.

(ii) ***Dominant leader*** **:** The dominant leader is so called because he maintains a relation of authority and dominance with his followers or subordinates. He does not rule over them, however successful he may appear because of his power and authority.

(iii) ***Expert leader*** **:** In many spheres it is not unusual to see the most efficient and capable individuals becoming the leader in their own specialised field. The basis of their contact with their followers and subordinates is their special ability and efficiency. Leaders of this type do not put any premium on maintaining social contact with their followers, understanding them or even knowing their thoughts. Being specialists, people come to them for advice from time to time, respect their opinions and these experts show the way when difficulties crop up in other's paths. Expert leaders are experts, and should not be considered as leaders.

(iv) ***Persuasive leader*** **:** The persuasive leaders win the heart of their followers and do their best to maintain the closest social contact with them. These are the real leaders. It is only this kind of individual who really exhibits all the qualities of leadership.

QUESTIONS FOR EXERCISE

1. Describe the formation of group.
2. "The structure of the group may vary according to the function that the group plays in a given situation." Discuss.
3. Bring out clearly the structure and characteristics of groups.

4. How would you study a group? Describe interactions in a group.
5. Make a functional analysis of groups and indicate the impact of the group on the behaviour of the individual. Refer to relevant studies.
6. What is a social group? Explain its structural characteristics. State the functions of social group for the individual.
7. What is a social group? Explain with illustration the main types of groups.
8. Give a classification of social groups and explain their main characteristics.
9. How are groups formed? Explain the various ways in which groups are classified.
10. What do you understand by leadership? Point out the characteristics of leadership.
11. Define leadership. Distinguish between various types of leadership and point out the various elements which enable the leaders to influence the followers.

6

Psychology of Crowds and Audiences

An amazing occurrence and yet by no means an uncommon one is the rapidity with which a crowd gets together at the smallest provocation such as a heated discussion between two people, or even the excited peroration of an enthusiastic orator. Common parlance gives this conglomeration of protoplasmic forms the name of crowd. And here, as everywhere else, scientific treatment demands that every term be scientifically defined. Thus even a word as commonly used as crowd has been defined so that it may not be improperly used.

WHAT IS CROWD?

Some of the ways in which crowd has been defined are the following :

1. According to MacIver, "Crowd is a physically compact organisation of human beings brought into direct, temporary and unorganised contact with one another." This definition of crowd is too general. According to it, if some people were to stand together for a short time at any place, their group would constitute a crowd.

2. To quote Kimball Young, "A crowd is a gathering of a considerable number of persons around a centre or point of common attraction."[1] This definition indicates a characteristic feature of crowd which is that the attention of the people is focused at one point. This definition is more adequate from the viewpoint of social psychology. McDougall also has written, "Not every mass of human beings gathered together in one place within sight and sound of one another constitutes a crowd in the psychological sense of the word." A most interesting

1. Young, K., *Handbook of Social Psychology* (1953), p. 387.

description of this has been given by Gillin. What you can do is to stand in some well frequented street and to stare fixedly at the top of a very high building, it being immaterial whether there is or not any object of interest. In a short time you will be surrounded by curious people who, while looking skywards, will be inquiring of their neighbour as to what is up there to hold the attention of so many people. This group brought together by a common curiosity is a crowd. As soon as their curiosity is satisfied they will resume their routine activities and the crowd will dissolve. This description clearly depicts the nature of crowd.

3. In the opinion of Britt, "A crowd then involves a temporary physical gathering of people experiencing much of the same reactions from the same stimuli." According to this definition, a crowd is characterised by reactions towards a common object. Thouless also points out the necessity of a common interest in a crowd. According to him, "A crowd is a transitory contiguous group organised with the completely permeable boundaries, spontaneously formed as a result of some common interest."[2] In Cantril's view, a crowd possesses common values and common emotions. To quote him, "Crowd is a congregate group of individuals who have temporarily identified themselves with common values and who are expressing similar emotions."

In this way, briefly, crowd is a temporary, direct and unorganised group of individuals whose curiosity, values and emotions are temporarily identical and which arises because of common interest or common stimuli.

An enquiry into the process whereby an audience is transformed into a crowd must be preceded by defining audience and indicating its characteristics thereby distinguishing it from a crowd. According to Kimball Young, "The audience is a form of institutionalised crowd."[3] In this way, an audience is a crowd formed for a specific period of time, based on some specific laws. Sprott has written, "We have called the audience an institutionalised crowd because in the vast majority of

---

2. Thouless , R.H., *Central and Social Psychology*, p. 258.
3. Young, K., *Handbook of Social Psychology*, p. 399.

situations, which we should call audiences, there is an accepted pattern of conduct, a formal beginning of formal end."[4]

Characteristics of Audience

Kimball Young has mentioned the following three characteristic features of an audience :

1. Specific Purpose. Every audience has a definite purpose, such as witnessing a dramatic representation or listening to a poetry recital.

2. Predetermined time and place. An audience collects at a specific place for a predetermined period of time.

3. Standard form of polarisation and interaction between the performer and the audience. The audience attends to the performer and is affected by the speech, action, etc., of the performer. The audience can be seen laughing or crying simultaneously with the actors in a stage play.

Difference between Crowd and Audience

Crowd	*Audience*
1. No predetermined aim.	1. Predetermined aim.
2. Collects of itself.	2. Is invited.
3. There is no definite time or place.	3. Time and place are determined.
4. Behaviour is not certain.	4. Behaviour takes place by definite modes.
5. People stand shoulder to shoulder and stimulate one another.	5. Conduct is not stimulated by the presence of member.
6. Members react to the influence of an internal stimulus of the crowd.	6. The stimulating cause is external to the group.
7. Members are motivated by emotions and soon become uncontrollable.	7. People are reflective and keep in mind the propriety or otherwise of any conduct.
8. The intellect of almost all members becomes inactive.	8. Members do not lose their discrimination.
9. Uncontrolled, unorganised and disordered.	9. Controlled, organised and orderly.

4. Sprott, S.H., *Social Psychology*, Methuen and Co. Ltd. (1952).

Crowd	*Audience*
10. No definite pattern of polarisation and interaction.	10. Definite pattern of polarisation and interaction.
11. Attraction point is some incident.	11. The focal point can be any such thing as intellectual, apparent, inapparent, material, etc.
12. Power increases with number.	12. Numerical strength does not have so much influence.

In spite of so many differences, crowd and audience also have many points of similarity. In both cases many people collect near one another at one place. Both have some common focus of attention or interest. There are some emotions in both. It is not necessary that an audience would be organised or that its members should act rationally or that its polarisation should be in only one direction. In a cinema hall it takes next to no time for the audience to conduct itself like a crowd. If some violence were to break out between a few people in a hall, an audience can become as dangerous as a crowd, can throw chairs at one another, can tear up the screen and can set fire to the cinema hall. The audience continues to behave sanely and collectively in a picture house as long as the film continues to run uninterruptedly but if there is any interruption due to whatever cause, the resulting conduct leaves nothing to choose between the behaviour of a crowd and of an audience. People make all kinds of noise to register their disapproval. They whistle and generally create pandemonium. In the 1905, meeting of an organised group such as Congress held at Surat, the conduct of the members of the audience compared favourably with that of any crowd. Some difference of opinion between the Left and Right Wings led to the most unruly behaviour, abusive and pungent language, use of footwear as guided missile. Actually, an audience is composed of all kinds of individuals, some of whom visit such occasions with the express intention of creating disturbance and do so at the slightest excuse. This creates disorder even in the organised audience and it takes the form of a crowd.

ESSENTIAL CHARACTERISTICS OF CROWD

The following are the essential characteristics of crowd :

1. Transitory nature. In the opinion of Kimball Young, Britt, McDougall and other psychologists and sociologists, crowd is a temporary phenomenon. To quote Britt, "The crowd behaviour then, involves three aspects — (1) Psychological continuity, (2) Polarisation of interest and attention and (3) Transitoriness or temporary character." A crowd collects because of some particular curiosity, interest or other temporary cause and dissolves as soon as its cause vanishes. If two people start fighting on the road, a crowd will collect and when they stop their struggle it will break up.

2. Polarisation of interest and attention. The members of a crowd are similar in their interest and attention. This attention is focused on any one individual, object or incident, the dissolution of which immediately disperses a crowd. In the words of Lebon, "Not just any group of individuals is crowd, but that there must be something of central importance to the group as a whole." Ross writes, "A crowd itself will not arise unless there is an orientation of attention, expectancy, a narrowing of the field of consciousness that excludes disturbing expressions."

3. Unorganised. A crowd is unorganised because it has no definite leader, objective, laws, location, functions, etc.

4. Similarity in thoughts, emotions and actions. But nevertheless the character of thought, emotions and actions is uniform throughout a crowd.

5. Mutual influence. In a crowd individuals excite the thoughts and actions of their fellow beings and are influenced by them. The capacity of suggestibility sometimes assumes dangerous proportions.

6. Sense of mass strength. In a crowd the self-confidence of individuals increases manifold because they have a sense of mass strength.

7. Gathering of sufficient persons at one place. One essential characteristic of a crowd is the gathering of sufficient persons at one place.

8. Psychological characteristics. It is the psychological characteristics of a crowd that distinguish and differentiate its behaviour from that of an individual. It is due to them that emotions, rather than thoughts, circulate rapidly through a crowd. They are the main factors in the conduct of the crowd. Following are the main psychological characteristics among them :

(i) ***Lack of the sense of responsibility*** : In a crowd due to increased suggestibility, the experience of mass strength, etc., the people do not retain their sense of responsibility and they indulge in many actions of which they would individually be incapable such as arson, bloodshed, rape, etc. In a crowd the criminal is unidentifiable, hence an individual can do anything. Ross writes, "Masked by their anonymity, people feel free to give reign to the expression of their feeling."[5] According to McDougall, one reason why any crowd is completely lacking in the sense of responsibility is also the absence of the sense of self-respect. Lebon has written, "The sentiment of responsibility which always controls individuals disappears entirely."

(ii) ***Low degree of intelligence :*** In a crowd the degree of intelligence of the members falls very low. Describing this psychological fact Ruskin writes, "You can talk a mob into anything ... it thinks by infection for the most part, catching an opinion like cold and there is nothing so little that it will not roar wild about, when the fit is on, nothing so great but it will forget in one hour when the fit is past. The low level of intelligence in a crowd is due to the tendency to imitate suggestibility, the excited state of emotions, lack of reflection, etc."

(iii) ***Lack of volition :*** Due to the low level of intelligence and the absence of the sense of responsibility as well as that of self-respect besides the influence of emotions, the power of volition is lost.

(iv) ***Heightened suggestibility***: In a crowd the susceptibility of persons to suggestion is very much increased. People lose their capacity of reflection, their emotions grow excited and powerful, and they tend to do or say what they are told by another, without thinking about it.

5. Ross, E.A., *Social Psychology*, p. 46.

(v) ***Heightened emotionality***: In the words of Bernard, "It is usually some strong emotions or curiosity impulse which integrates the crowd." Accordingly, an increase in emotionality is an essential characteristic of crowd.

(vi) ***Credulity :*** With an increase in the capacity of suggestibility and emotionality, the credulity of a crowd also increases. According to Ross, "Rational analysis and test are out of question. The faculties we doubt with, are asleep."[6] A crowd tends to believe any rumour easily.

(vii) ***Unconscious impulses***: According to Freud and other psychoanalysts, the conduct of the crowd is governed by the unconscious impulses of persons. In a crowd, due to the absence of inhibitions the repressed tendencies are excited and persons behave like insane beings.

(viii) ***Instability of emotions and ideas***: The emotions and ideas of a crowd change rapidly. There can be no predicting what it is liable to do at any moment. Ross writes, "Its hero one moment may be its victim the next."[7]

(ix) ***Inter-stimulation***: In a crowd, people excite each other. Every thought and excitement moves through the crowd like a contagious disease. Fear, anger, sorrow, delight, etc., circulate very rapidly in a crowd because of the increased suggestibility of its members.

(x) ***Influence of the leader***: The crowd is largely influenced by its leader. He can make the crowd laugh, cry, excited and can even induce it to commit arson and murder. A skilful leader can make a crowd whatever he desires. An oration by Tipu Sultan was sufficient to turn the guns of the army which was pursuing him on the enemy. In the drama *Julius Caeser,* a speech by Antony made a crowd thirst for the blood of Brutus who had been its object of worship a minute before.

(xi) ***Social facilitation*** : According to Ogburn and Kimball Young, "Social facilitation may be defined as the enhancement of one's response by the presence or activity of other person." The same process is called 'Crowd Stimuli' by N.E. Miller and John Dollard.

6. *Ibid.*, p. 55.
7. Ross, E.A., *Social Psychology*, p. 54.

(xii) ***Immorality of the crowd*** : A crowd loses its capacity to discriminate between moral and immoral or good and bad and it stoops to the most degenerate actions when in the grip of powerful emotions or when spurred on by the leader. In 1947, in India during communal riots crowds did things that cannot easily be credited. Blinded by the sense of power the crowd loses sight of all social taboos. Bernard writes correctly, "They approximate most closely to the packs and herds of the lower animals."[8] The immorality of a crowd depends on its leader. As Ginsberg has remarked correctly, "Crowds are in themselves neither good nor evil but they may be either the one or the other on occasions according to the stimulus."[9]

It is evident from the foregoing psychological analysis of the behaviour of crowd that man's behaviour in a crowd is driven or governed by instincts, sentiments and emotions. In it, the person's suggestibility, sentimentality and emotionality are heightened and intensified, and his unconscious impulses are given free reign. In a crowd under the influence of various factors such as social facilitation, influence of leader, low level of intelligence and lack of volition, an individual indulges in activities of which he is otherwise incapable. Quoting McDougall, to be brief, "A crowd is excessively emotional, impulsive, fickle, inconsistent, irresolute and extreme in action, displaying the coarse emotions and the less refined sentiments, extremely suggestible, careless in deliberation, hasty in judgment, incapable of any but the simpler and imperfect forms of reasoning, easily swayed and led, lacking in self-consciousness, devoid of self-respect and a sense of responsibility, and apt to be carried away by the consciousness of its force, so that it tends to reproduce all the manifestations ... of any irresponsible and absolute power. Hence, its behaviour is like that of any unruly child or untutored passionate savage in a strange situation ... and in the worst cases it is like that of a wild beast."[10]

---

8. Bernard, L.L., *An Introduction to Social Psychology,* Henry Holt and Co., New York (1928), p. 458.
9. Ginsberg. M., *The Psychology of Society,* p. 133.
10. Wm. McDougall, *The Group Mind,* Cambridge (1920).

KINDS OF CROWD

As a general rule, crowds can be divided into two classes — (a) Active and (b) Inactive.

(a) **Active crowd.** The active crowd, evident from the name given to it, is active. According to Burgess, the active crowd is accidental and momentary. When the wayside vendors hold their congregation, people start and then keep on collecting around them. These people are almost unwillingly attracted by the magnetic tongue of the vender or pseudo-magician who is holding the show. In much the same manner, if two bulls decide to put an end to their differences in the middle of the road or if some one fires a gun, people converge on the area with a surprising rapidity. A very detailed description of the crowd has come from Lebon. In his opinion, the individual loses his individuality and he thinks and acts in the manner of all the other members of the crowd. The entire active crowd is converted into a unit motivated by a common motive and manifesting the same kind of conduct directed towards the same end. According to Lebon, the behaviour of this kind of crowd is directed and controlled by a group mind. In his book, *Group Mind,* McDougall accepts Lebon's theory. According to this theory, the active crowd has its own personality and its own mind. This theory came in for criticism at the hands of Allport in 1924 and modern social psychology does not accept the group mind theory as an explanation of crowd behaviour. According to Allport, the individual behaves in a crowd in practically the same manner in which he is prone to conduct himself when alone. The only difference is a small degree of peculiarity. Kimball Young has written, "An active crowd is a mass of individuals who, with the common focus of attention, unleash certain deep lying attitudes, emotions and actions."[11] The active crowd has been classified into four classes by psychologists :

1. Aggressive crowd,
2. Panicky crowd,
3. Acquisitive crowd,
4. Expressive crowd.

11. Young, K., *Handbook of Social Psychology* (1951), p. 287.

AGGRESSIVE CROWD

An aggressive crowd is a crowd of people in an aggressive and destructive frame of mind, capable of any and every act of destruction and irrationality, brutality and inhumanity. They can commit arson and murder, rape and manhandling. A crowd of this kind exhibits a tremendous excitement. The air is full of much noise and all kinds of exclamations fly about. Rousing words are usually spoken. In a crowd of this kind there is and probably there cannot be any limit to inhumanity and destruction. The members of such a crowd seem either to be devoid of or to have been completely deprived of their sense of propriety and humanity. In the communal riots of 1947, the Hindus and the Muslims set fire to the residence and property of the people belonging to the other sect. Living children were thrust into burning houses and the women treated with an almost unseeable bestiality and inhumanity. People migrating from one country to another were murdered in their hundreds as they sat in trains. Entire train-loads were wiped out. Telegraphic communication was prevented by the wires being cut down while the rail tracks were removed. Villages in their entirety were burned off the face of the land and millions rendered homeless. The Independence fighters who gathered to demonstrate against the British government were also sometimes constituted into aggressive crowds. Simultaneous with the passing of the 'Quit-India' resolution was the arrest of all the top leaders of India by the British government, thus incensing the people to acts of violence all over the country because they could not accept the idea of all their leaders being imprisoned. The police outposts were frequently set fire to and government shops looted, government buildings were demolished. The Union Jack of the British Government was taken down time and again and consigned to the flames. It was replaced by the tricolour of India.

Experience and Behaviour in Aggressive Crowd

The foregoing examples of an aggressive crowd exhibit some particular features. The following are these special features. These special features are also expressive of the experiences and conduct of the members of such a crowd :

1. Intense emotionality. The most characteristic feature that immediately attracts attention is the intense emotionality of an aggressive crowd. In such a congregation, all individuals are highly excited. Even the most casual glance at any crowd of this sort will reveal this. One person will be shouting at the top of his voice, another will be waving his fists about, another will be so excited that he cannot stand still, some will be running around while many will be clenching their teeth in expression of their impotent range. The most prominent emotion that characterises people in such a crowd is that of anger.

2. Suggestibility. In an aggressive crowd, the suggestibility of every member increases. Everyone imitates everyone else. A not uncommon incident is that a child is crushed on the road by a car travelling somewhat fast. The moment this is seen all people who are near run towards the crowd, thus unnerving the driver who tries to make a getaway. But in his nervous condition he does not see where he is going and so collides with a pole, thus being foiled of his escape. The moment three or four people have arrived on the scene, the most terrible things start happening. Usually their first reaction is to pull the defenceless driver out of the car and to beat him thoroughly. Gradually, the crowd of righteously indignant people grows larger in which everyone is very agitated, angry, busy in beating. There are very few people who have seen the child being injured by the car, while most of the others have only seen the rest of the people beating someone and have gone to it with a will. They have not exercised in their minds as to why all this beating is going on. Anger seems to be contagious and it catches them and enlarges their spleen, too, and they become angry. The element of this suggestibility makes it very easy for anyone to guide the crowd and to turn its attention and behaviour in any direction that he desires.

3. Effect of precipitating causes. In the above example, the explosion of tempers and restraint came immediately the speaker was struck with the first shoe, such a blow being impossible to disregard without offence to dignity. On the other hand, the rioters were bent on offending the speaker and breaking up the meeting. In this way the actual and direct presence of two groups with contradicting interests was the perfect background for an aggressive crowd. The shoe did no more than set fire to the dry grass piled all round in the form of high tempers and low restraint. It naturally caught fire.

4. Social facilitation. Creating a disturbance in any meeting is no fun. The least bit of precipitate behaviour leads to a good and sound thrashing. In the above example, a young man gathered up his courage and threw the shoe at the leader. It was enough to encourage all the present members of the opposite group and they jumped on the stage. In this manner, the courage of the aggressive crowd improved when it sees the activities of some of the more daring elements in the crowd. They take their inspiration from such guides. The reason behind this is social facilitation in which every gesture, every loud shout and every activity counts.

5. Influence of rumour. Another common happening is people collecting in a crowd upon hearing some or the other rumour. A not unknown example is the rumour that a Hindu has been murdered by some Muslim and probably the shortest possible time one can see many Hindu youth gathered together, each of them having equipped himself with haste rather than discrimination, angrily deciding on the best form of reprisals. A motley crowd has mean while collected and the entire collection, aroused by mutual simulation to a high pitch of anger, proceeds towards the lane in which Muslims live. In such any angry mood, they are likely to make short work of anyone who defies them. No one is likely to stop and question the rationality of thrashing the poor rickshaw-puller who has probably nothing to do with the whole affair. Someone instigates the others by exclaiming that he is Muslim, kill him! and behold, he is beheaded. In this incident not even a simple person took the trouble of checking upon the veracity of the original rumour and finding out for certain whether some Hindu had been murdered in the first place. A long and impressive list of all the accidents and unfortunate occurrences that have taken place because of rumours could be easily drawn up.

6. Tendency of imitation. The above example makes it abundantly clear that in a crowd the various members imitate each other and do not employ their own reasoning power. If only one or two decide to run, most of the others will probably follow suit. If one shouts a slogan, all the others start shouting at the top of their lungs.

7. Influence of pre-existing conditions. But it is not possible for an aggressive crowd to come into existence just anyhow. If in 1947, aggressive groups of Hindus and Muslims were seen indulging in the foulest crime and causing blood to flow down streets, it was possible only because this had been succeeded by a period of intense propaganda of a communal nature indulging political parties on either side. The effect of this propaganda was continually increasing. Hence, an aggressive crowd cannot accidentally and immediately come into existence if there is no suitable background for it. It is the culmination of certain events.

8. Single line of behaviour. As is more or less obvious from the example treated of in the previous paragraphs, the behaviour of members of a crowd takes a single line. They are not inclined to pay attention to the arguments of the other side, and neither are they interested in finding out anything of the other aspect. If they take it into their heads to support a particular contention, they will find that it goes against the grain to listen to anything proceeding from the side opposing them. If they choose to contradict some position, they will equally tenaciously refuse to consider any arguments for the position. Whether they support or oppose some contention, the members of an aggressive crowd do it with a wonderful tenacity of purpose and unbending devotion to the cause they have taken up to promote.

9. Influence of low economic level. If we take a more than cursory glance at the members of an aggressive crowd, we will find that most of them belong to a low income level group. People who belong to the upper or middle classes are more resistant to excitation and are not easily to be encouraged into such rashness. Individuals of the low income group such as labourers, menials, rickshaw-pullers, etc., can easily be goaded into an aggressive frame of mind, while people who can be excited even more easily are those who are unemployed.

10. Effect of low educational level. The aggressive crowd is usually composed of people who are not highly educated and even of the uneducated. And even in an aggressive crowd composed almost solely of students, one finds that those most interested are the ones who are more interested in things other than educational and academic qualifications. One rarely comes across serious and intelligent students among the ones who usually break discipline and create nuisance. Uneducated and slightly educated people are easily excited and instigated because they are lacking in the reasoning faculty as a result of which they are prone to their emotions which overpower them and lead them to much injudicious action.

11. Importance of Leader. Of the members of the aggressive crowd, the most important is the leader. It is not necessary that there be only one leader since for expediency it is possible and occasionally necessary to have three or four leader in a group. He sets the example which the crowd vividly follows. It is the leader who lends organisation and co-ordination to the behaviour of the group. He focuses the attention of the crowd instead of allowing it to dissipate its energies in many directions fruitlessly. He excites them with his words and his gestures and inflames their emotions and passions. It is he who points out that which is to be achieved by the crowd and even becomes the first to do it. It not essential that the leader must invariably belong to a richer class or be a very intelligent person. The person who becomes the leader is the one who succeeds in influencing and impressing the crowd at any particular time and under specific circumstances, manages to excite it, directs and motivates its emotions and goads it to do what he desires. Not every one possesses these qualities while some people are endowed with a more than sufficient quantity of these capabilities. In India, during the Independence movement Tantia Tope (1857) succeeded again and again in routing the armies that followed him and also in turning the cannons against their own officers.

PANICKY CROWD

Another kind of active crowd is the panicky or fear-stricken crowd whose constituent members are almost crazed with fear to a point where they can no longer think and reason. Any person who hears of any firing that has taken place lose his composure and very soon one can witness a horde of frightened people running for their lives. A panicky crowd is a common phenomenon during wartime when people are on tenterhooks most of the time. Conditions of panic and fear reigned in people's minds during the days of Hindu-Muslim riots just after the partition of the country. Crowds of thousands strong escaped into India from West Punjab in fear of the Muslims, in their flight crossing many villages. Similar crowds of panicky

Muslims also fled for their lives from India to Pakistan. Another tragic drama was enacted in Prayag on the occasion of Kumbha, a very important religious fair held once in twelve years, an occasion on which millions of people gather for the eternal salvation of their respective souls. In the fair, there was a steep gradient on one side and on this gradient there was a bog on one side which had been cordoned off by nothing more than bamboo poles. A crowd of people was moving towards this gradient. Six feet high parapets had been built on the road leading to the gradient, on both its sides a parapet, it would be difficult to cross. It so happened that while the people were walking on the gradient a wave motion within the crowd itself disturbed the people and some of them fell. Before they could recover, others behind them were precipitated upon them by the shock wave so that a condition of confusion prevailed. An uproar ensued with the result that some of the persons on the gradient were thrown into the bog on the left side into a living grave. People who witnessed this heart-rending scene stood enthralled with their hearts in their mouths out of fear. This tended to add to the confusion with the result that many helpless women and children were crushed underfoot in the rush for safety while many others were thrown into the bog; thus death took a heavy toll of the fair.

Characteristics of a Panicky Crowd

A panicky crowd exhibits clearly some of its most characteristic features. The first is that all the members of it are almost frightened out of their wits, so that thinking is for the time being a thing beyond their power. They are concerned with the prime quest of saving their lives. Under such conditions some people exhibit extraordinary courage and never escape while some others lose their precious lives only because of their blinded running. In such a crowd every member is aware of the presence of trouble and the feeling of fear that completely encompasses all and spreads like contagion from one to another. If one dies, it is immediately rumoured that no less than ten have passed away. Organisation is a thing of the past as well as the future but not of the present. No one stops to consider the rationality of his or her decision but runs in the first direction that he sees in front of him.

Kinds of Panicky Crowd

But it is not essential for the fear-stricken crowd to be disorganised. In the example of the mammoth fair it was seen that the crowd is disorganised but if an army is routed and it is decided to retreat, they do it in an orderly and well-planned and reasoned manner so as to minimize loss of manpower as well as equipment and also with a view to speedy reorganization. They are orderly and systematic even in their downfall. They fall, but are not deprived of their dignity. In this way, psychologists accept two distinctions of panicky crowds — (i) The organised and (ii) The disorganised.

Experience and Behaviour of Members in a Panicky Crowd

The above description of a panicky crowd is sufficient to bring out some of the general characteristics that also throw light on the experience and behaviour of the people who form a part of such a crowd. Roughly speaking, these characteristics are the following :

1. Emotion of fear. The members of a panicky crowd exhibit fear and all its signs. They are excited and their hearts beat much faster than normal. Their facial expression is contorted and their minds lose all considerations of propriety.

2. Sense of crisis. The cause of the fear is the sense of crisis. All people who live in adjoining areas where there has occurred some case of arson, bomb explosion, firing, or some mass killing are conscious of a sense of crisis or catastrophe.

3. Tendency to escape. The sense of fear and crisis causes the tendency of escape to come uppermost in the minds of all the members of a panicky crowd so that everyone runs in any direction that he happens to be facing when the fact of danger hits him and benumbs his brain. They are so much full of care, for their own precious skins, that they dare not stand and stare, or even to spare a thought for their erstwhile companions.

4. Disorder. As a general rule, members of a panicky crowd do not maintain any system or order and even if it does display some signs of order, it can only be relatively organised or systematic. Probably, the only signs of organisation that one can find in any panicky crowd is in a routed army that is retreating and this, too, can be attributed to their previous training. And yet, this order is of a very scanty nature.

5. Irrationality. It has been pointed out before, too, that members of a panicky crowd lose their faculty of reasoning and their mind stops functioning.

6. Emotionality. One main cause of the irrationality of a panicky crowd is the excitement that reigns among its members. As Ross has written in his *Social Psychology*, "To the degree that feeling is intensified, reason is paralysed."[12] In another context, Ross further writes, "Masked by their anonymity, people feel free to give reign to the expression of their feelings. To be heard, one does not speak, one shouts. To be seen, one does not simply show one's self, one gesticulates."[13]

7. Lack of responsibility. In this manner, then, there is no sense of responsibility in any panic-stricken crowd. No one has the time or energy to bother about another; everyone is too much occupied with saving his own skin. Men have been seen running to safety even when they had to step over living but prostrate women and children.

8. Effect of rumour. Rumour plays an important part in creating and further augmenting fear. The moment that it is heard that some firing has taken place, people show the cleanest pair of heels. The least rumour that riots between Hindus and Muslims have broken out is enough to empty the streets of all people.

ACQUISITIVE CROWD

The third main distinction of an active crowd is the acquisitive crowd. The aim and object of each of its members is to obtain or acquire something. Why is there such a big crowd in front of the Delhi branch of the Palai Bank? The crowd consists almost entirely of people who have some deposit in the bank and immediately they heard of its going bankrupt, they have gathered to salvage whatever they can from this collapse. And for a change just look at this third-class window outside this cinema house. What a crowd! Man is fighting with

12. Ross, E.A., *Social Psychology*, Chap. III.

13. *Ibid.*

his neighbour. One enterprising person has taken to the air and is making his away towards the ticket window via the heads of the others who have queued up. The next moment fighting breaks out. That man has had his shirt torn. You will ask, what is all this hullabaloo about? Why are the people so anxious and excited? Probably you are not aware that a very famous film is to be displayed here for the first time and people are fighting to secure the tickets for the initial show. If you have any experiences of the time in which rationing of food was introduced, this scene will probably recall that time to your mind. And you will have no difficulty in understanding the psychology of the acquisitive crowd. In those days large crowds of expectant and hopeful people could be seen outside every shop dealing in food grains and other related necessities of life. In this way, it is evident that the acquisitive crowd is composed almost entirely of individuals whose object it is to gain or obtain something, be it a cinema ticket, wheat, kerosene oil, money or whatever else.

EXPRESSIVE CROWD

The fourth kind of active crowd is the expressive crowd. The very term suggests that in this kind of crowd some people have gathered to give expression or to manifest their demands or sentiments. In the democratic states that we have at present, crowds of this kind are by no means rare and hard to come by. It happened not very long ago that in an Indian University examination papers for some particular examination were rather on the strict side, allowing for no convenient and ready-made formula for success to operate. The reaction to this on the part of the student community was that they followed each other out of the examination hall and collected in the ground outside, the group soon being sizeable enough to be reckoned a crowd. The crowd formed itself into a procession and immediately proceeded to the Vice Chancellor's residence. Some people invented appropriate slogans for the occasion and these were shouted with gusto and vigour. On reaching the Vice Chancellor's residence the leaders of this crowd put forward their demand that the examination papers be reformed and the examination be arranged at some future date. In the last general elections, expressive crowds of this kind could be seen in fair abundance in towns and villages. Procession of uncouth labourers or educated students, the procession behind the hearse carrying a dead body or be it a procession in which a leader is being taken in grand style, on display for the public to see, are other instances. The desire of violence is relatively less pronounced and dominant in the members of an expressive crowd. But it can turn aggressive if forceful means are employed to disperse the crowd and prevent its members from voicing their troubles and sentiments. Generally what happens is that if this crowd is permitted to go its own merry way and the people allowed to put their viewpoint in front of the public so that they can go away with the satisfaction that their side of the case has been adequately represented then the crowd of this nature disperses once its object has been achieved. Some degree of excitement is only to be expected even from a crowd of this nature but it is never of the kind to deprive the people of their reasoning faculty. The crowd manifestly lacks all desire for violence and aggressive behaviour for escape and for any acquisition. The members of this crowd are usually more interested in voicing their ills, their opposition, anger, happiness or pain, etc. If expression of this nature is its object, then the crowd can turn aggressive and if efforts are made to break it by resorting to violent means, then it can become fearful also and take to its numerous heels.

(b) **Inactive crowd.** No crowd is completely inactive. Even the people who have collected to hear a recitation of the old religious texts are somewhat active. Just take a look at some such inactive crowd. And more particularly, the women are restive. They will be seen fidgeting or whispering. Some will be carrying on their knitting while others will be busying their fingers with the remnant of some or the other domestic chores. Yet another, while hearing the recitation will also be reciting her daily woes to her neighbour. The children too provide a very diverting occupation when they ask their mothers to put them to sleep. And, to be very fair, the male members of the crowd will also be busy in many things other than just listening. But if this fairly peaceable crowd is compared with some exhibitionist or representation crowd, a fear-crazed crowd or an aggressive crowd, the difference between an active and an inactive crowd will become clear. The actions of the crowd will not show much variation even after an hour or two of recitation from the religious texts but very easily discernible changes can be seen in any aggressive crowd even after a very few minutes. One moment the rioting crowd is seen running and next minute they are beating some unfortunate person who has obstructed them. And, then they will be running for their very lives. Evidently, the difference between an active and inactive crowd is only relative. The active crowd is somewhat more active while the inactive crowd is relatively inactive. The inactive crowd even resembles an audience. The audience can be divided into two classes : (1) Casual and (2) Intentional.

1. Casual audience. The crowd that usually collects beside the roadside to listen to the soap box orator is a good example of an audience of a casual nature.

2. Intentional audience. The audience that gets together to see a cinema is an intentional audience. In this audience, the people collect due to predetermined intention rather than a casual decision.

The intentional crowd or audience can further be divided into two classes :

1. Recreational.
2. Information-seeking.

1. Recreational audience. As is evident, the recreational audience collects together with the aim of being entertained. The audience mentioned in the last example, that collects to visit a cinematographic presentation is a recreational audience.

2. Information-seeking audience. The group that gets together for the purpose of gaining knowledge or collecting information is called an information-seeking audience. The students in the class comprise the audience which comes in this classification. Evidently, it will not be characterised by the same independence and freedom that marks a recreational audience. It is improper to leave the class while a lecture is being delivered. On the other hand, people are at liberty to leave the cinema hall whenever they like, and neither is the question of dignity quite involved in sitting there or leaving.

The following chart gives a diagrammatic representation of the above-mentioned kinds of crowd :

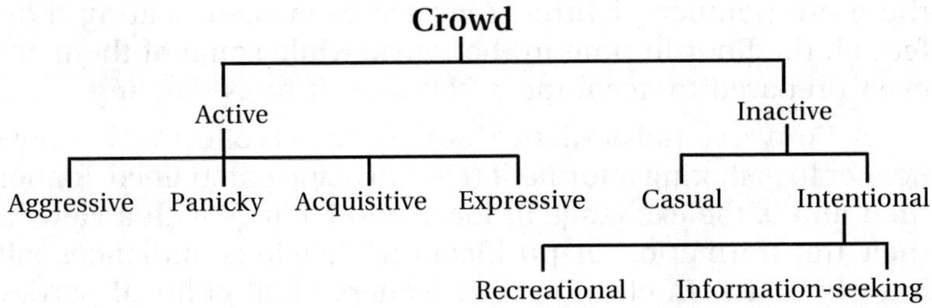

KINDS OF AUDIENCES

Audiences have been classified by different psychologists. The classification differs from one psychologist to another. Among the more important classifications are the ones made by Kimball Young, Lapiere and Britt. The views elucidated here will be those expressed by these psychologists.

Kimball Young's Opinion[14]

Kimball Young has mentioned three kinds of audiences :

1. Information seeking audience. This particular kind of audience consists of people who have collected together to seek some information or knowledge. Nowadays, one comes across many people collected outside a beetle shop listening to the news blared out by the seller's radio. And if some leader comes to town then many people gather to hear him speak and they do so in large herds. In educational institutions people gather from time to time to hear learned specialists delivering their discourses on their subjects. All these are good examples of information seeking audiences.

2. Recreation seeking audience. The members of this kind of crowd gather to be entertained rather than be loaded down with knowledge or information. Crowds gathered to witness a cinematic presentation, circus, dramatic performance, opera, etc., are collected with the idea of recreation. Their aim or object is recreation and not information. Since the aim of recreation is less serious than that of gathering information, the conduct of members exhibits a proportionate and natural

14. Young, K., *Handbook of Social Psychology,* (1951), pp. 399-400.

laxity in both organisation and control. And often one can see people not only yelling and shouting while witnessing one of the more popular pictures, they are even seen beating their feet on the floor in tune to the music while some of them are even prepared to accompany the hero if he is dancing.

3. Conversional audience. Some crowds collect with a view neither to gathering information nor to being entertained. Rather their aim is the exchange of ideas and feelings with a view to their transformation or purification. Religious audiences fall into this class. In election time leaders of all political parties can be seen vociferating to the eager crowd and trying to convert the views of their audience to their own way of thinking, if they have one. This is an example of a conversional audience.

EXPERIENCE AND BEHAVIOUR IN A RELIGIOUS AUDIENCE

Besides the description of various kinds of audience, the behaviour and experience of their members have also been hinted at. It would be advisable to include a description of the experiences and behaviour of an audience that is listening to religious recitations or a lecture, since this will throw useful light on what has been said earlier. The entire attention of such an audience is focused on the speaker. They are open to influence emanating from his words as well as his gestures and physical motions. And in some religious meetings people have been seen to go to such an extent that they have laughed and cried with the speaker. The audience that listens to a lecture and the one that listens to a religious lecture differ from each other in certain respects. In the common lecture, the greatest attention and importance are given to the person delivering the lecture with the result that the intelligence and personality of the speaker become important elements in the total influence that he is able to wield. If both are of a high order, the members of the audience are considerably influenced. These members make more use of their intelligence and reason than of their faith. They are more prone to weigh and consider what the speaker had said instead of accepting it at its face value, although the speaker can sway their emotions and change their mode of thinking. On the other hand, the speaker cannot assume an equal importance if his subject is of a religious nature. It cannot, of course, be denied that if the speaker is possessed of an interesting and attractive personality along with the ability to make even the mundane facts of life interesting and of a sweet tongue that will make the people readily swallow even the bitterest of pills, then he will be in a position to exert a much greater influence on his audience and will even hold them spellbound for hours together. But even if the lecturer cannot soar to tremendous heights in his oratory and is a pronounced bore of the mediocre type, many people will still bear the inflictions of boredom that he is reciting and not in himself. In a religious lecture, the speaker or orator does possess some individual importance, yet it is equalled if not overshadowed by the specific subject of which he is speaking. In most cases, the opinion that the speaker is expressing is ascribed either to some great and famous personality in the field or to God Himself. The person who discourses on the home-truths expressed by Christ, Buddha or Krishna expands upon their sayings rather than putting forward any original thesis. The audience is impressed by the thoughts expressed by the representatives of the Almighty God, in utter disregard of the views of the orator himself. The religious preacher cannot hope to achieve the same success if he were to lecture on other topics on which people ordinarily lecture. The local priest usually dilates upon the religious subjects of considerable lengths of time and most of the women and old men of the neighbourhood are to be found listening to him for hours together. But if he decides to take a hand in the elections and to speak in favour of one or the other political party, he is usually booed off the platform by all the youngsters of the locality, at which even the senile folk cannot repress a smile of amused tolerance and sheer pleasure in the discomfiture of the ordinarily influential priest. Some one delicately points out to him that this is no occasion for a lecture on the religious tests and that one man's meat is another man's poison, to which the priest would probably respond with a sickly smile and a forehead beaded with perspiration, thus showing his nervousness. And it certainly cannot be denied that the young folk are right in saying that lecturing in a political gathering is a far cry from the oration from the religious and sacrosanct pulpit. Finding no other dignified way out of his dilemma, the poor priest decides to abandon the unequal battle and gracefully retires to his chair off the stage. But when he returns to his congregation to continue with his more normal duties of pointing out the ways of God to man, he finds not the least reduction in numbers. He is also not harassed by any booing or any form of behaviour expressive of disgust with his oration, because the people have gathered to join him in their obeisance to their eternal creator. They had not come to have their thoughts converted to some new political ideology and the priest, too, was busy in talking of the thoughts and ideas expressed by God rather than the ideas that he may have at the previous meeting. In this way the members of an audience collected to hear a religious preaching can only boast of a low level of intelligence. Logic is replaced by faith. A consistent blind eye is turned to all glaring inconsistencies. The orator is accorded complete respect and honour. In a group of this kind, the emotions are also of a pure, clean and high order. Such meetings and audiences encourage the higher emotions such as pity, love, cooperation, sympathy, etc. The name given to such meetings in Hindi (satsang) is the equivalent of a good meeting and it gets its name from this purgation of human emotions that it achieves. The members in such a group usually maintain a high dignity and complete restrain. They do not fling criticisms of the speaker at him as they are prone to do in ordinary meetings. They passively accept all that he choose to put before them. A persian even accepts things from the orator's lips that no one could induce him to accept in his day-to-day life. In his usual mode of thinking they strike him as manifestly unpsychological but when the preacher pronounces them, he does not seem to find any necessity of contradicting him.

QUESTIONS FOR EXERCISE

1. Distinguish between Crowd and Audience.
2. Clarify the psychological characteristics of a crowd. Describe the mental conditions of a panicky crowd.
3. Distinguish between a crowd and a group and bring out the main characteristics of a crowd.
4. Mention different types of crowd. Describe psychological characteristics of any one of them.

7

Psychology of Social Tensions

Tensions may exist in individuals as well as in groups. Just as people, who hold mutually contradictory views, opinions and beliefs, tend to come into conflict, so do groups which have mutually contradictory morals, ideas, behaviour, ideals, modes, etc. Hence, social tension is the psychological tension between two or more groups. In India, for example, one finds feelings of hatred, fear, superiority or inferiority entertained by one communal group for the other in society. One comes across mutual distrust and hatred between Brahmins and non-Brahmins, Brahmins and Kayastha, Baniyas and Brahmins and even between the higher and lower sub-groups within the same caste. The casteism is the outcome of caste tensions. Despite their having lived in close continuity for hundreds of years, the morals, ideals, customs, viewpoint and other things of the Hindus and Muslims show very pronounced differences. As a result of this one may see communal tensions existing between Hindus and Muslims. And this sort of difference in respect of opinions or modes of life is to be found even among the members of the same nation hailing from different parts of the country. It is seen that the Punjabi will favour the Punjabi while the Bengali would like to benefit the Bengali before he does a good turn for someone else. The Assamese seem to be under the impression that Assam is their property and the Bengalis should be allowed no share in it. This tension has grown to such proportions that some people have utilised the natural differences between the populations of the north and south to advance the demand for a separate nation in the south. The very existence of a group that makes such fantastic demands proves the extent to which regional tensions have grown in India. The southerners seem to think that the Central government is mainly in the grip of the northerners and that these people are working to the detriment of the south. They also seem to have before their eyes constantly the history of the past in which the northern population consistently attacked the kingdoms of the south. The clash of northern swords is probably still audible to them. The result of this unfortunate situation is that they maintain a hostile attitude towards the people of the north, and this hampers healthy co-operation. At present, the situation is worsening because in addition to the casteism, communal and regional tensions we are also witnessing a linguistic tension. The language question was the origin of the recent riots in Assam, and the question of a choice between Hindi and Punjabi led to continued unrest in Punjab for a long time. The question of Hindi and Urdu was another source of heated attractions and debates in the country for a long time. Language is the medium of mutual behaviour between individuals. It is natural for a person speaking one of the Aryan languages and being unacquainted with one of our languages to appear a foreigner. Hence, it is not altogether unreasonable for people with linguistic differences to come into conflict.

Difference does not Necessarily Cause Conflict

But it does not follow from the above description the difference of caste, religion, residence, language or one of other elements will inevitably lead to conflict. Unity in diversity has been the most marked characteristic of Indian culture from the earliest days. Consequently, national organisation and unity are not considered impossible even in the existence of so many tensions. It is only recently that political parties with the most radically opposed opinions put their heads together to thrash out the question of national integration, and in this question they successfully drafted a rough outline for a programme of concerned action in this direction. It is of course a different question as to the extent to which this plan may succeed in creating national integration, but what is most important is that even political groups with opposite and often contradictory notions managed to sit down together to consider the question of national integration, and even achieved a unity of opinion regarding the methods by which it can be achieved. There may be differences of opinion regarding the fact that now India is one nation, and that despite all the variety and differences of castes, religions, languages, customs, it is possible to attain to a state of national unity and integration.

Causes of the Growth of Group Tensions

There are numerous causes that bring about group tensions. Group tension may arise if there is any contradiction between two groups on questions of language, community, residence, culture, social or economic status, etc. In this way, one may trace group tensions to a variety of causes such as physical, religious, social, cultural, economic, political, etc. Tensions increase when groups differ from each other in these or other respects. Gardner Murphy gives it the name of the sin of being different. It must, of course, be kept in mind that group tension cannot be attributed to the mere fact of dissimilarity. It is not inevitable that groups that differ from each other must also have tense relations. The fact of difference is further supplemented by some psychological factors, so that it leads to tension. It has been pointed out earlier that many prejudices, beliefs and attitudes are the root causes of tensions. Krech and Crutchfield have recognised physical, psychological and social causes of tensions. On the other hand, Kimbal Young has laid greater stress on the cultural causes and factors that lead to tension. Roughly speaking, the following causes may be said to contribute to the growth and development of tension :

1. Physical causes,
2. Social causes,
3. Cultural causes,
4. Religious causes,
5. Economic causes,
6. Political causes and
7. Psychological causes.

These various causes of tension will now be discussed in some detail :

1. Physical causes. In this particular cause physical is almost synonymous with geographical. People who live in different geographical regions are naturally apt to differ from each other in respect of their habit, diet, mode of life, anatomical features, according to the differing geographical conditions to which they have to adapt themselves. The result is that this difference leads them to look upon all people brought up in different geographical regions as foreigners. It is only natural that one should have a person of one's own nationality and avoid a foreigner whom he does not know and cannot understand so well. If this mutual distrust is further co-mingled with some other factors, then this distrust becomes more serious and leads to tensions between people of different regions.

2. Social causes. In social relationships the factor of social distance is very important. In every society, there is stratification as a result of which each particular kind of group has a special status and certain roles in society that devolve upon it and its members by virtue of their status. The relationships between two groups are determined by their respective social status. To take an example near at hand, in Indian society the Brahmins occupy the highest position in the social stratification while the Untouchables are at the other end of the ladder. Consequently, the social distance between the Brahmin and the Shudra is greater than the social distance that separates the Brahmin and the Kshatriya. The person who occupies higher status because of social distance regards the group belonging to the lower status as mean and contemptible. The offspring of people of different status are endowed with certain prejudices at their birth peculiar to the respective status. If a Brahmin child even touches the child of a scavenger, he is immediately bathed with the result that the child forms the belief that touching a scavenger results in defilement. It is evident, that prejudices of this kind should lead to the development of tensions between the various social groups.

3. Cultural causes. Culture is expressed in language, literature, patterns of living and thinking or ideational activity. The differences in respect of any one of these factors will lead to a cultural difference between groups. People tend to recede into themselves and away from people who differ from them culturally since communication of ideas and other cultural factors is impeded by lack of conformity. Each individual regards his own culture as the highest while he looks with disdain and contempt at another's culture which he regards very much lower than his own. Thus, people who harbour deep love and respect for ancient Indian culture naturally hate and mistrust people who have taken to Western culture. In Bengal it is this very cultural difference that led to tense relations between the Brahmins and other groups. Group tension can originate on any disputed element in culture. Now, in India we find tensions running high between people who speak Hindi and the people who do not, between people who speak the Assamese tongue and those who speak Bengali, and between the Punjabi population and those who would feign to foist Hindi on them.

4. Religious causes. People who have faith in different religions naturally differ in respect of their ideas about God, the world hereafter, heaven, hell, soul, etc., and other matters of religious interest. They have faith in different saints. Their methods and places of worship differ. This difference often leads to communalism since most of the religious people are convinced that it is only their own religion that preaches that truth while all other religions are no more and no less than a tissue of lies. As a result of this communal feeling, the Hindus and Muslims view the actions of each other with distrust, while they are fully convinced of each other's unmitigated folly. This only leads to more staunch communalism, and it sometimes reaches such a stage that actual conflict becomes inevitable.

5. Economic causes. Difference in economic status will directly and apparently cause a difference in the dress, standard of living, modes of behaviour, customs and ideational activity of social groups. In the materialistic culture of today, the increased importance of monetary wealth has led to social status being determined by financial success. Hence, it is that social distance increases when economic differences become more and more accentuated. This has the result of promoting conflicts and tensions between people belonging to different classes. Tensions of this nature can be witnessed the world over between labourers and industrialists, the rich and the poor and the exploiters and the exploited.

6. Political causes. The Communist Party has played the greatest part in encouraging and increasing the tensions that already existed between different economic classes. Similarly, the political organisation known by the name of DMK in the south had done much to promote the regional conflict between the north and south in India; in fact, it is responsible for it in the first place. The communal tensions between the Hindus and the Muslims have been much increased by the various communal and political parties such as the Muslim League, the Hindu Mahasabha, etc., that have aimed at political objectives. In the same manner different political groups augment the tensions existing between various lingual groups by constantly harping on this sensitive question. In the present political set-up in India, the various communal organisations are very important. In the last general elections many of the candidates elected claimed communal conformity and collusion of sympathies of the electorate and thereby secured votes that ensured their passage into the Parliament where they, in utter faithfulness towards the electors, further encouraged communalism since by only this method they could ensure a return to their present happy position. In this manner, political parties usually have a major hand in promoting and creating caste, political and communal tensions.

7. Psychological causes. Finally, the most important and the most prominent causes at the root of social or group tensions are psychological. In fact they are the direct causes of group tensions. Physical, social, religious, cultural, and economic differences cannot inevitably lead to group tensions unless mutual jealousy, hatred, contradictory beliefs, attitudes of conflict and prejudices are not implanted in the minds of members of the various groups. The presence of these psychological elements tends to accelerate the normal rate of growth of group tensions. Injury to one's self-respect normally leads people to harbour feelings of hatred for the group that is responsible for this injury. The tension between various groups is further increased by the sense of self-expression. Groups that fear each other are naturally always on the lookout for opportunities in which they may inflict injury upon the hated group. In this way, the psychological causes are the root causes of group tensions.

From the above description of the various causes due to which social or group conflicts and tensions are aroused, it is evident that no one cause is responsible for group tensions. There may be various causes that lead to the development of various tensions between sundry groups under all kinds of differing circumstances. In this connection, it is essential to maintain an open mind and a Christian attitude. At the same time it must be remembered that usually more than one causes are mixed up with any specimen of group tensions. Many different causes and all kinds of circumstances co-operate to create an atmosphere that is conducive to the growth and development of group tensions.

Once some definite tensions are created between different groups, it is not easy to rid them of these tensions. Group tensions are the outcome of certain definite circumstances and situations. Group tensions then obviously cannot be eliminated so long as these conditions are allowed to remain. In this way, then, the permanence of these group tensions is maintained for a fairly long period of time. For example, the social and group tensions that were created between the Hindus and the Muslims at the time when the dictatorial Aurangzeb was on the throne have yet to be totally eliminated. Much effort has been directed in this direction by the Congress under the guidance of great leaders as Mahatma Gandhi, but it has always reappeared in all sorts of guises. Even the division of the Indian Union can be attributed to the permanent nature of this tension, besides the communal riots that then happened and continue to occur at intervals to mar the peace and happiness of the community.

ROBBERS CAVE STUDY

Many psychologists have conducted studies to analyse the causes that contribute to the permanence of group tensions, the most prominent in this connection being the Robbers Cave Study by Sherif. This study clarifies the causes that lead to the formation of group tensions and of the causes that ensure their performance. The study, conducted in 1954 in the Robbers Cave State Park of U.S.A., 150 miles from Oklahoma, was conducted in the joint sponsorship and guidance of Sherif, his wife, Harvey, White and Hood, besides other psychologists. In this study 22 children were placed at one place, the age of all being eleven years. They were divided into two groups, both being taken to the State Park in separate conveyances. It was so arranged that the two groups should not come into any contact whatsoever. They were even put up in two separate places. So much secrecy was maintained that for a considerable length of time they were not even aware of any other group being in the State Park. This had been contrived so as to assure that the two groups may develop individual communal lives, that the member children may be able to have relationships with each other, and that they may be able to discover their relative status in the group with the result that the natural leaders may also emerge. All that was anticipated happened. The two groups were engaged in different activities that necessitated collective and communal effort. This helped to accelerate the growth of a communal life. Some of them naturally assumed the roles of leadership. The social status of each member within the group and his social prestige was determined in accordance with the role that he played in the group. The two groups were also given names. One was called the Eagles and the other the Rattlers. Both inscribed their names on their flags.

Now both the groups were introduced to each other, and some competitions were announced. To begin with, a rope-pulling contest was held in which the Rattlers defeated the Eagles, which immediately led to tense relations between the two groups. At the game the Eagles set fire to the victoriously flying flag of the Rattlers who, upon finding out next day the preparators of this indignity, promptly burnt up the flag of the Eagles. This led to some vociferous and lusty abusing on both sides. It did not take much time for this situation to worsen and lead to physical conflict. Group tension had reached enormous and almost alarming proportions. The Eagles were so much moved by this development that they immediately changed their leaders whose efficiency they had reason to doubt. The various members of the group were also upbraided for their conduct in the conflict that had led to the ignominious defeat. But where the question of facing and defeating the other group was concerned, they displayed the utmost unity and determination. At this time psychologists obtained from each of the groups their evaluations of the other group. Some stereotypes that are usually found in conditions of conflict and tension were employed. Stereotypes of both the praising and the abusive kinds were selected. In both cases there were three types of stereotypes. Among the praising kind the stereotypes were brave, tough and friendly. Both the groups chose to use these stereotypes for the edification of their own group. Each of them unequivocally described the members of his own group as brave, tough and friendly. The stereotypes of hatred or disgust were sneaky, lazy and stinking. These, with equal alacrity, were used for the other group by both the Eagles and the Rattlers. Each one of them described the members of the other group as sneaky, lazy, and stinking. From this it transpired that in every situation of tension each group uses praising and respectful stereotypes to describe the members of its own group while to the conflicting group it refers with the utmost contempt and ridicule. In India, people who have a communal bent of mind use such stereotypes to refer to people of the other group. The Hindus use the derogatory word *malechha* for the Muslims while they reciprocate the sentiment by calling Hindus *kafirs* or disbelivers in God. Both are unequivocal in their respect for their own ways and means of life, character, ideas, morals, and in the disrespect and positive hatred for the same elements in the religion of the other group. In India, tensions of this type are not characteristic of the various religions alone, but rather also of the various castes. Brahmins look upon the Shudras as untouchable but one finds that in some areas, particularly in southern India, the tables are reversed and the Shudras look upon the Brahmins as untouchable. In some villages in this area, scavengers have to stay away from the town because they are looked upon as impure and defiled. Rarely, yet truly, it happens that if a Brahmin enters into an area occupied exclusively by scavengers, he is beaten with brooms and the place upon which he treads is purified by being scrubbed with cow-dung.

Now we are concerned with the permanence of group tensions. The tensions had been easily and precipitately created between the above-mentioned two groups of children, but their removal was by no means equally easy or expeditious. All kinds of things were tried to this end. Members of both the groups were made to sit at the same table and partake of food, they were collectively taken to the picture house, and were also encouraged to do a number of other things together. But all this had no effect what so over on the permanence of group tensions. On the contrary, they began to grow. Whenever the members of two conflicting groups met, they exchanged some remarks that only worsened the situation. This made it evident that once group tensions were communicated they are apt to grow to permanence.

But the experiment did not stop here because it is not true that there is no remedy of group tensions. Efforts were made to put an end to these group tensions by creating situations in which it became necessary for both the groups to co-operate. To begin with, the water supply to the children was shut off by tying a piece of cloth to the tap, and the children were informed that the water had stopped flowing because of a probable hole in the pipe connecting the tap with the tank. Members of both groups were thirsty so that elimination of thirst became a common objective. Both were faced with the problem of obtaining water to quench their thirst. As a result of this common problem, both the groups co-operated in devising a method to restore the water supply. The psychologists had removed the ladder leading to the water tank. Both groups managed to locate it and members of both groups climbed on to it to take a look. The tank was observed to be full of water whence it was concluded that the fault laid in the tap. It did not now take long for members of both groups to get busy with their knives and clear the blockade in the tap. The result was a common jubilation at this success that led to lessening of the tension existing between them. But at the time for lunch, the hostilities were resumed. Evidently, then, a little bit of co-operation does not help much in reducing the permanence of group tensions.

Another method was then devised to bring the two militant and conflicting groups together. It was planned to rent a film from the market for the evening and to arrange a film show. The psychologists took it upon themselves to bear half of the cost, leaving the rest to be got together by the viewers themselves, neither of the two groups individually being possessed of the resources to provide the necessary amount. Consequently, the two groups pooled their resources and the plan went through, but much to their chagrin the psychologists discovered that when the film was being displayed, the two groups occupied distinct positions and did not mix up as they had anticipated. This made it clear that the tension was still continuing while the need for physical conflict had vanished.

The psychologists, evidently an industrious lot of people, did not give up at this tenacity. Eight miles from Robbers Cave there was a small lake in rocky region. The two groups were taken to camp out there. Separate transport was arranged for the two groups and they were even allowed to have their food separately. The utensils were placed at a common spot which were immediately removed to different spots by each of the two groups. But the problem that now faced the two groups was that of purchasing things from the market. It could only be brought up to their hilly lake by means of the truck but that would not start it despite the best efforts on the part of the driver. As the truck was facing up the incline, nothing was to be gained by pushing it either. There was only one method and that was to tie a rope to the truck and to haul it, a job that required a fair amount of manpower, no less than twenty persons sufficing. There was nothing that could be done to avoid co-operating. The two groups had to suffer this humiliation. The rope was affixed to the truck and both groups caught hold of one end and pulled with a will. The truck finally started to the delight of everyone who had helped pull it. Co-operation had won the day. The food was purchased and brought to the camp without a single note of dissent. It was prepared with both groups assisting. After this there came a further occasion when the truck had to be hauled by the combined efforts of the two groups, and this time they displayed even greater willingness to co-operate. On this occasion, the two different ends of the rope were not grasped by each group collectively but rather without much discrimination. They mixed up for the pull. This led to increased intimacy between the members of the two groups and the intimacy increased to such an extent that when all of them were asked to select their individual friends each and every one chose his friend from the other group. Now, group tension had been ended, and a situation of amity and bonhomous goodwill reigned supreme among them.

From this detailed description of the above experiment, it is evident that although group tensions tend to attain to some degree of permanence, this tension can be removed if repeated occasions occur where it becomes necessary that the contending parties co-operate in order to achieve some comprehensive common objective.

CAUSES OF THE PERMANENCE OF GROUP TENSIONS

The following conditions contribute to the permanence inherent in any group tension :

1. Competition. As is evident from the Robbers Cave experiment, competition leads to communal tension. This type of group tension is very much in evidence in matches played in various games. In election days in the political field, the competition for winning the election leads to increased tension between followers of opposing groups, and this sometimes also ends in violent action. Competition creates tension; if the competition continues, tension increases. In this way competition is one factor that lends permanence to group tensions. If competition between two groups is constantly maintained, the tension between them also does not relax.

2. Absence of common goal. From the experiment in Robbers Cave it is apparent that when the conflicting parties were faced with a common objective that had become a necessity, then gradually they lost their original hostility towards each other and tension decreased. This change of heart came about because the attainment of the common objective made co-operation essential and unavoidable. The permanence of tensions continues unabated if common objectives or goals of this nature do not make it necessary for the opposed factions to co-operate. So long as each group acts individually and aims at objectives that have no concern with the opponent, neither has the opportunity of co-operating with the other with the result that there is nothing to counteract the effect of tension, and hence its permanence is in no wise disturbed. The main reason why tensions of communal, caste, regional and other natures have achieved such a high degree of permanence in India is that in none of the cases do the various conflicting factions get any opportunity for co-operation and mutual work.

3. Absence of contact. The main cause of tension being created in the first place between the two groups of children in the Robbers Cave experiment was that they were denied mutual contact. It is a matter of common knowledge that contact between persons lessens tensions and promotes co-operation. The most commonly suggested remedy to the very serious problem of casteism in India is that the various castes should be given more and more occasions of coming together and knowing each other better.

4. Mutually contradictory assumptions and beliefs. Within every social group there are some values and assumptions that define and demarcate the behavioural patterns of the members of that specific group. These assumptions, beliefs and ideals differ somewhat from group to group, with the result that there is possibility of contradiction of ideals between the groups, and when this does happen the relations between the two attain to a tense state. For example, the main cause of high and increasing tensions between Hindus and Muslims is the difference in the values accepted by each.

5. Ignorance. One major cause of the tensions that are maintained between various groups is the astounding degree of ignorance that they harbour about each other. Group tensions are based upon prejudices. It often happens that even when people have not met each other, they form some prejudiced opinions regarding each other that govern their behaviour even when they do actually came into each other's contact. As a general rule, it is seen that communal hatred is found to exist in the greatest degree among people who have little or no knowledge of the people they are hating, and it is this complete ignorance that is at the root of their hatred and fear of others. In India the greatest majority of the people who took an important part in the communal riots were uneducated or semi-educated at most. Only those people who are unaware of the tenets of the religion they are seeking to wipe off the earth are the ones who can be excited into fighting at the call of religion. Group tensions can be and are reduced by increasing the opportunities whereby the members of these groups can come into contact and get a chance of knowing each other better.

6. Maladjustment. All the members of any society do not succeed in making a proper and desirable adjustment with their situation in society and with the other members of society. Many causes result in mental complexes being formed that tend to warp their personality and give it the air of one slightly abnormal. Disappointment and unhappiness increase. They also become restless. They cannot even successfully repress their anti-social tendencies. People of this kind naturally manifest a tense relationship with the members of the other group since in their case they can give vent to such emotions as hatred, disgust, fear, anger, etc., that they cannot express anywhere else. It gives them relief from the pressure of pent-up emotions.

MEANS OF ELIMINATING SOCIAL TENSIONS

As a general rule, it can be stated that the method of eliminating group tensions would involve all the causes that cause and inflame group tensions. Those causes that are responsible for group tensions are of the social, economic, political, psychological and a variety of other kinds. Hence, any attempt at eliminating all of them would involve social, economic, political and psychological means. What appears to be more reasonable and practicable is that efforts should be made to remove the various prejudices harboured by the members of these groups. They should be made to realise that the members of the other group are just as much human beings as they themselves, that they too have the sense to realise the importance of co-operative effort, that their life is as strewn with difficult boulders as their own and is not the bed of roses that they imagine it to be, that they too are desirous of extending their circle of acquaintances and friends. The group tensions that exist between various groups can be removed if their members are made to realize and feel the bond of unity that binds one human being to another. Here it will be advisable to mention only the major means of putting an end to group tensions.

1. Education. The most important single cause at the root of group tensions is ignorance. This ignorance takes two forms, lack of education being one of them. Group tensions grow easily among uneducated people and linger longer there. The other form of lack of education is ignorance concerning various other social groups. The result of this lack of information is that people form all kinds of misconceptions regarding the members of the other group. The Muslims are inclined to think that the Hindu is interested only in gaining ascendancy over them while the latter labours under the misconception that Muslims seem to have nothing more than goondaism to occupy their time with. The white-skinned people seem to have decided for all that the Negroes are mean, contemptible, uncultured and unintelligent. There seems to be no reason to suppose that the Negroes are any the more charitable or are too reticent to think base thoughts of the white-skinned people. This mutual ignorance only serves to augment the existing tension. Hence, the most important method of eliminating group tensions is the propagation of common ideals through the medium of education. This education should be of both kinds. On the one hand it is necessary to develop the personality of every individual in the nation by a very comprehensive programme of education, so that it will lend them a charitable attitude. They will learn benevolence. It should be seen carefully that no discrimination is exercised in educational institutions with regard to admission, scholarships or appointments on the basis of caste, religion, or any other basis. It is to be remembered that no precautions are taken to prevent this malpractice in India. Throwing light on the problem of casteism in the Maysore State Dr. M.N. Srinivas has written that the principle of casteism is the guiding principle not only in any and every appointment within the State, but it also governs the division and distribution of seats in schools and colleges. If casteism is to be rooted out from the Indian scene, then all terms relating to and smelling of caste should be removed from the vocabulary of the student. Efforts should be made to develop benevolence and toleration in the people through education. Sport and extracurricular activities should be so devised that the student should be conscious of taking part not only in a competitive sport but also in one in which he learns to co-operate. In addition to this, the student should also be acquainted with the moral ideas, customs, etc., of other social groups so that he may literally be inoculated against all attacks of prejudicial and misleading propaganda. Indian students should have some knowledge of the various people living in different parts of the country.

2. Creating of healthy literature. Education is not only confined to schools and colleges but rather is the province of all literary matter with the result that books and magazines also share the burden of educating the country's youth. One comes across many propaganda machines called by the name of magazines whose only aim is to spread false information and add to the group tensions already existing. Besides these there is also much in literature and much of the kind of literature that promotes group tensions. There are same social groups which use the medium of cheap literature as an organ of their group, whose one and only confessed aim is to deride all other groups and to praise its own proponent. It is of the essence that literature of this nature should be subjected to the strictest control. There should be very strong controls foisted on communal organs. The positive step in this direction would be the practical and continuous encouragement of good and healthy literary activity in the country. Magazines and papers that aim at correct information will always reduce group tensions and increase tolerance, co-operation and friendship in society. It is magazines and papers such as these that should receive the encouragement of the state.

3. Preparation of healthy public opinion. In fact, the total removal of group tensions calls for the growth of a healthy public opinion. To attain this end, in addition to magazines and newspapers, radio and public platforms should be used for propaganda calculated to lessen group tension. Programmes that help to reduce casteism, regionalism, linguism and communalism and to promote nationalistic feelings should be broadcast over the radio. Propaganda can also be employed to put an end to the misleading ideas embedded in the minds of the public.

4. Improving social adjustment. One important cause of group tensions is social maladjustment. People who fail to find proper adjustment with the conditions of their existence harbour, and are prey to, feelings such as hatred, fear, obstinacy, opposition, disgust, etc., and they are constantly on the lookout for an opportunity when they may be able to give vent to them against the other groups. Group tension is also a kind of adverse adjustment. Hence, one method of getting rid of it is to encourage and introduce proper social adjustment between various groups.

5. Reducing social distance. And social adjustment between various groups can be introduced only when the social distance between them is reduced so much that there can be possibility of fruitful social intercourse between them. They should be encouraged to improve their mutual contacts. Social or group tensions can be considerably reduced by increasing the mutual contact and intimacy between members of various groups. The best and the most efficacious method of removing untouchability is to increase the contacts between the higher castes and Untouchables. This contact will help in removing the feeling of disgust and hatred for the Untouchables from the members of higher castes while the Untouchables will be able to regain some of their dignity and self-respect and along with it their confidence. Much good in the direction of removing casteism permanently from the country can be achieved by establishing mutually intimate relationship between the various castes by encouraging intercaste marriages between them.

6. Balanced development of personality. Groups are conglomerations of human individuals. At the root of group imbalance there is individual imbalance. Hence, one other method that can reduce group tension is the balanced and proper development of the personality of the members of various groups. This work should start first of all with educational institutions. In educational institutions, the help of a psychologist can be enlisted for progress in this direction. Besides the educational institution, another social institution that has much importance for the developing personality is the family. The individual's character or personality is also susceptible to influences emanating from the improvement of social associations. In brief, all methods that can help in the development of balanced personalities within the society will also help reduce group tension indirectly.

7. Youth organisation. Youth has much importance both in social conflict as well as in co-operation in society. It is essential to make special efforts in the groups of youth in order to reduce group tensions. For this it is necessary to form youth organisations formed at the national level, and the formation of which does not bow to any considerations of religion, community, language, region, etc. One example of this kind of youth organisation is the annually held Youth Festival in almost all Indian universities. Youth festivals of the kind can be arranged in every town and every village. It is necessary to organise Indian rural population, particularly the younger generations, so that community life in Indian villages can prosper and progress. If it is not achieved then it will become impossible to establish co-operation after removing group tensions.

8. Propagation of national objectives. One other important cause at the root of group tensions is the lack of comprehensive aim and objectives. It usually happens that most of the time each group is busily engaged in attaining its own selfish interests. Every religion, community and caste is busy finding and devising ways and means whereby it can benefit its own members. It is only natural that under these circumstances group tensions between various religions, communities and castes should increase. But if all these various individual groups are presented with some national objectives and some programmes of national security and emancipation then these comprehensive programmes will have the desired effect of reducing group tensions.

9. Removal of economic disparity. Another cause of group tensions is economic disparity or inequality. Economic disparity leads to the formation of economic classes. Of these classes the higher classes exploit the lower. This only leads to an increase in mutual bitterness, and it can even culminate in class struggles. Besides, economic insecurity spreads unhappiness and unrest and dissatisfaction. Hence, both economic security as well as removal of economic disparity are essential to the removal of group tensions. This fact is accepted by communist and non-communist thinkers alike.

10. Social emancipation. Many group tensions are maintained in status quo by virtue of many social causes that contribute to this end. For example, the idea of untouchability and the restriction on intercaste marriages have both been instrumental in maintaining casteism at a fairly high level of permanence. If casteism is to be removed, it is necessary that both these social evils be removed as preliminary.

11. Formal or constitutional means. Finally, it is justified to resort to all constitutional provisions to get rid of group tensions since it sometimes becomes necessary to enforce any new suggestion by the force of law to get over the natural obstinacy of the people. Constitutional methods can be usefully employed to prevent all communal activity. In India much reform was achieved when untouchability was pronounced a legal offence since it made the people respect this reform measure. In much the same way casteism can also be declared an offence and even if this is not considered a very practical step, good precedents and examples can be created by taking very stern action. Wherever there appears to be any corruption this is alleged to be the outcome of cateism. Legal prohibition and restriction can be applied to all magazines and other media of mass communication that serve to increase group tensions.

12. Specific studies of group tensions. Group tension is a psychological fact. All the methods for its elimination that have been hitherto enumerated can be successful only if particular attention is paid to its psychological aspect. Psychologists can be employed to make some special studies in this connection. For example, Gardner Murphy guided some researches in connection with communal tensions in India. Similarly, specific psychological research can be ordered in connection with casteism, linguism, regionalism and other kinds of tensions. The psychological researches can serve the purpose of suggesting practicable methods of removing these tensions. But once these methods have been evolved, what is needed is some strong steps on the part of the government and willing co-operation on the part of the public.

Having made a general study of group tension, it is now proposed to turn to the description of problems at the root of which exist social or group tensions. In India, one can come across several kinds of social conflict in casteism, communalism, regionalism and, linguism. They will now be described individually.

CASTEISM

What is Casteism?

Casteism is partial or one-sided loyalty in favour of a particular caste. When any mode of thinking assumes the form of an ism, it becomes rigid and partial. The sense of caste when it implies a specific status in society does not pertain to casteism. The sense of caste is converted to casteism only when consideration of superiority between castes and the tendency to consider the interests of one's own caste as opposed to the other castes are attached to it. In this manner the members of one caste do not hesitate in dealing fatal blows to the interests of the other castes if the interests of their own caste are furthered in so doing.

Definition of Casteism

It is necessary to define casteism if its form and nature are to be clearly and precisely understood. Some main definitions are the following :

1. Loyalty to the sub-caste. In the words of K.M. Panikkar, "In this way it is only because of casteism that the Smiths want to benefit only the Smiths while the Joneses want to come to the aid of the other Joneses. It matters little if the members of the other castes are irreparably harmed. It does not cause any concern to the Smiths and the Joneses."

2. Loyalty to the caste. But casteism is apparent also in the from of loyalty to the caste. In the words of Dr. N. Prasad, "In this way, caste has been dragged into the political arena in the form of casteism such as 'Brahmanavada' and 'Kayasthavada.'"[1]

3. Blind group loyalty. In this opinion casteism is the blind and consequently irrational loyalty to the community. In this all considerations of proper or improper, justice or injustice, etc. are thrown to the winds in the face of the interests of one's own caste, and these must be achieved. In the words of Kaka Kalelkar, "Casteism, therefore, is an over-riding, blind and supreme group loyalty that ignores the healthy social standards of justice, fairplay, equity and universal brotherhood."

In this way, then, putting it briefly, casteism is a blind group loyalty towards one's own caste or sub-caste which does not care for the interest of other castes and seeks to realise the social, economic, political and other interests of its own group. This definition of casteism includes all the preceding definitions of the concept and tends to clarify further the political aspect of casteism.

Causes of the Development of Casteism

Nowadays casteism is at its height in India, the culmination of many causes. Some of the causes are given below :

1. Sense of caste prestige. The most important cause of casteism is the desire of people belonging to a particular caste to enhance the prestige of their caste and in so doing see no

1. Prasad, H., *The Myth of Caste System*, p. 124.

wrong in adopting even the most downgraded and deleterious methods. But the prestige of the caste can be maintained only on the ground that every opportunity be availed of in order to improve the social status of members. In order to achieve this objective, every caste provides its members with all possible privileges in order to raise their social status. This tends to increase casteism.

2. Marriage restrictions. The second cause that encouraged the development of casteism is the restrictions on marriage that prevail in Hindu society. Under the caste system the restrictions that apply to marriage turn every caste into a monogamous group in which each individual looks upon himself as related in some way to all others and for this reason everyone pays proper attention to the interests of others. Such action encourages casteism.

3. Urbanisation. With the advent of the tendency to urbanisation, it became possible for all castes to collect in large numbers in towns. At the same time the lives of members of various castes became beset with problems as a result of which it became necessary to provide security for them on a communal basis. Casteism is spreading because of the necessity to fulfil this need for security.

4. Increase in the means of transport and propaganda. One factor that has assisted the development of casteism is the increase in the means of both transport and propaganda because this improvement has led to the establishment of relations between members of a caste who were previously separated because of distance. And the feeling of casteism is being rapidly propagated through the medium of newspapers and communal magazines.

Consequences of Casteism

On the one hand, casteism serves to further the interests of a small number of individuals but on the other hand it is proving harmful to the nation as a whole. Some of the major consequences of casteism are the following :

1. Hindrance in the development of nationalism. Casteism hinders the growth and development of nationalism. On the one hand, casteism has divided Indian society into many parts while on the other hand much tension and conflict between these various parts have been created on the basis of casteism.

2. Hindrance to democracy. Many of the professional leaders in the political field exploit casteism and at election time ask the people to vote for them on communal considerations and they also succeed in their evil designs. This sometimes results in the election of unscrupulous individuals who do not hesitate in crushing common interests in the consideration and promotion of caste interests. In practice, the glories of casteism are sung even behind the scene where there is professedly equality. In this way, casteism is fatal to democracy. According to K.M. Panikkar, "In fact, no organisation of society on the basis of equality is possible so long as the sub-caste and the joint family exist."[2]

3. Corruption. People inspired by the sense of casteism try to provide all kinds of facilities to people who belong to their own castes and in doing so they resort to all kinds of immoral and improper activities. In this way, extreme corruption in the society is increasing.

4. Hindrance in technological efficiency. Because the appointment to government and private services is done on the basis of caste, there seems to be a continuing increase in the number of inefficient and worthless people. On the other hand, the efficient and able individuals do not get the opportunity to find employment. Thus a great obstacle is placed in the path of the nation's industrial and technological advance.

Remedies of Casteism

The following are some suggestions concerning the solution of the problems arising out of casteism :

1. Proper education. The greatest need for a solution of the problem of casteism is proper education. The educational institutions should be able to provide an atmosphere in which caste distinctions are not encouraged while at the same time the children are allowed to develop a distaste for this kind of discrimination. A healthy point of view in the public for casteism can thus be generated. Casteism can be destroyed only by the

---

2. Panikkar, K.M., *Hindu Society at Cross Road* (1956), p. 24.

development of new psychological tendencies and behaviour patterns.

2. Inter-caste marriage. Another way of combating the continuing increase in casteism is the encouragement of inter-caste marriages. Inter-caste marriage provides an opportunity for two families belonging to different castes to come together not only for two individuals, one male and the other female, to do so. In this way, the seed of casteism shall be unable to strike root and even if it does the resulting sapling will be so weak that it will subsequently be wiped out.

3. Lesser use of the word 'caste'. One way of solving the problem of casteism is to make less frequent use of the word 'caste' so that there may be no traces of it left in the mind of the impressionable children and they should not be imbued with the idea of caste distinction. In this way, at least it will become possible to destroy the notion of casteism in the coming generations.

4. Cultural and economic equality. Another way of facing the problem of casteims is to introduce cultural and economic equality in the minds and the lives of the various castes. Inequality in the sphere of cultural and economic welfare between the races promotes jealousy and competition among them which later assume the form of casteism. Hence, the restoration of cultural and economic equality of the various races is an important step towards the abolition of casteism from the society.

Suggestions for the Abolition of Casteism

Mahatma Gandhi has compared casteism to the appendix in the human body. As long as it continues to enjoy health it serves its purpose but when it becomes diseased, the only course is to eliminate it because if it is not removed it poses a threat to the existence of the entire organism. In this way, it is opined by some people that this conflict can be eliminated from democracy only when the caste system is completely removed from it. But in the present context, in which the castes have taken on the form of classes and casteism is on the increase, it seems impractical to harbour any hope for the complete removal of casteism from society. Casteism cannot be legalised and then infringed. It is the foundation of Hindu society. A strong and tremendous revolution is needed to get rid of it. But the artificial stimulation of a revolution proves harmful in the long run of time. Hence, as long as the society is not prepared to change the caste system and to adopt some other social order in its place, it is best to confine oneself to corrections and improvements. In this connection different scholars have expressed different views and have made various suggestions. Some of the important suggestions are the following :

1. Dr. Srinivas's view. In Dr. M.N. Srinivas's opinion most of the shortcomings of the caste system can be removed and the door opened to democratic equality through adult franchise, five-year plans, the provision of education, constant progress of the backward classes and the influence of the culture of higher castes on the living standards of the lower, etc.

2. Dr. Ghurye's suggestion. According to Dr. Ghurye, the conflict originating in casteism can be removed by encouraging inter-caste marriages. Co-education should be introduced at the primary level and boys and girls should be given the opportunity to come together. This will lead to the improvement of behaviour between different sexes simultaneously with which casteism will be actively refuted. Inter-caste marriage will be encouraged and the individuals marrying out of their own castes will be instrumental in creating an atmosphere that will fundamentally be opposed to casteism.

3. Dr. Rao's opinion. According to the suggestion put forward by Dr. Rao, in order to put an end to casteism and to deprive it of its very basis, the creation of some optional groups should be encouraged in which the communal tendencies of the individual can be manifested and organised. Casteism will decrease as the number of these groups increases because the individuals will have the opportunity to express their instincts and motives outside the caste.

4. Suggestion by Mrs. Karve. It is suggested by Mrs. Iravati Karve that in order to put an end to the conflict arising out of casteism, it is necessary to create economic and cultural equality between the castes.

5. Prabhu's view. According to Prabhu, the conflicts created by casteism can be ended only when the internal aspects of conduct are influenced. For this it is necessary to try and develop new attitudes in the people. The cinema can do much towards the creation of these attitudes.

The notion of caste has been existent in Indian society for almost thousands of years. To day it has become an impediment for the progress of the country. It is necessary to change its form in order to ensure the development of national sentiment and the progress and success of democracy in the country. But this cannot be achieved in a matter of few years. For this it is necessary to determine the extent to which caste system should be developed and then all governmental and non-governmental sources in the country should be employed for the achievement of that level of development. The first step would be to remove the idea of caste discrimination from the minds of the future generation. Co-education will encourage inter-caste marriages. Further, the idea of eliminating words that indicate caste from names should also be propagated and made popular. Caste committees and associations should be prevented legally and the government should prevent appointments being made to posts on the basis of caste, whether in government or non-governmental organisations. In this way it is necessary to make efforts in every direction for the improvement of this horizon.

COMMUNALISM

India's independence was announced on 15th August 1947 and it was on that day that in every corner of the country Hindus and Muslims shed each other's blood. The inhuman behaviour seen during this communal rioting has probably no equal in the entire history of the world. Entire villages were set on fire and living children were thrown into the conflagration; women were taken in procession being beaten with whips while they were naked. At many places entire train-loads of human beings were butchered. Millions were rendered homeless while millions of others lost their property and earning; but the worst part of the whole deal is that in spite of such a costly and terrible sacrifice, communal tensions have not been put to an end. It is only recently that there were communal riotings in Bengal and other states. This spark is one that is apt to catch fire at any moment. There are some particular causes at its root. Knowledge of the ways in which communalism can be removed from the country can be had after causes are known.

Causes of Communal Tension

The following are the main causes of communal tension :

1. Geographical causes. One main cause of communalism is a geographical one. There is much communal tension wherever the Hindus, Muslims, Christians and others live in separate sections because the modes of life and conduct of the different religious groups exhibit wide differences.

2. Historical causes. Another important cause of communal tension is of a historical nature. It is an established historical fact that Muslim religionists came to India as foreigners and started converting Hindus to Islam with the force of the sword. Many of the Muslim rulers inflicted much injustice and misery on the Hindus while on the other hand, some Hindu kings retaliated in an equally violent manner to these activities on the part of the Muslim kings. It is hundreds of years since all this is going on. There came occasions, however, on which the Hindus and the Muslims co-operated with each other. In the war of freedom of 1857, Hindus and Muslims made a combined effort to win the freedom of the country. In the Congress and the Indian National Army, the Muslims stood by the Hindus in opposing the Britishers but in both the communities many people have been unable to forget the past in which the dictatorship of Aurangzeb posed a threat to the very existence of Hindu religion by his injustice and cruelty. There was a time when the Muslim women of Punjab and Kashmir quietened their children by making them think of Harisingh Nalva. This had the cumulative result of maintaining communal tension. And not only this, some people went so far as to form political parties based on communal interests which indulged in all sorts of petty quarrels. They also inflamed the minds of both the communities against each other. The Muslim League demanded the formation of Pakistan. Pakistan was formed and yet communal tensions were not relieved in any manner of speaking.

3. Psychological causes. The main cause of communal tensions is of a psychological nature. Communal rioting breaks out between the Hindus and the Muslims in the country whenever the hatred and disgust that they have for each other reaches fever heat. There are some deceptive and misleading dogmatic concepts at the root of this mutual hatred. Hindus are prone to believe that the Muslim is a born traitor while the Muslims feel that they are in constant danger from the Hindus. Tension increases because of such fallacious thoughts based on ignorance.

4. Social causes. Some social causes also promote communal tension. Even today there are many restrictions that hinder any profound relationship between the Hindus and the Muslims. The Muslims slaughter cows and this injures the religious sentiment of the Hindus while the Hindus find it objectionable to form too close a relationship with the Muslims because they believe in a different religion. Many of the customs respected by the two stand in complete contradiction. Hindus grow their religious tuft of hair which the Muslims do not. Their respective dresses differ widely. In washing hands, the Hindu pours the water so that it proceeds from the direction of the elbow to that of the wrist while the Muslim pours it so that it flows from the wrist to the elbow. These things are well-nigh insignificant but because of them these two are prone to look at each other as slightly mad. At present inter-caste marriages are exceptions in the country and it is impossible for the people to think in terms of marriages between different religious groups.

REGIONALISM

Of course, regionalism has always been present in India in one or the other form but never it has attained such magnitude as it possesses today and neither was it ever as detrimental to any national interest as it is in the present context. When there were so many states in the country it was not harmful to have regionalism in them but when the entire country has become one nation, regionalism poses a serious threat to national unity and integration.

What is Regionalism?

Regionalism is the sense of affection and attachment for people belonging to one's own region and hatred for those who belong to some other region. As a result of this, people of one region in India have started looking at people from some other parts of the country in the same light in which they are prone to regard foreigners. They want that only people of their own area should run the government in their region while they do not want to make any place for people who have migrated from some other region irrespective of the period for which they may have been living there. In this way, some people have demanded the formation of a separate state of Nagaland in the Naga area. The Akali party of Punjab has demanded the formation of Khalistan. It was on the basis of region that the state of Bombay was divided into two separate states, those of Gujarat and Maharashtra. In addition to these antics of the politicians, some people are demanding that the south should be formed into an entirely separate unit. India is a union of states. The functions of government have been divided between the central government and the respective state governments. All these states are free to act on all domestic matters. Hence, the unity of the nation can be maintained only so long as the people regard the entire country as one nation and their own country. If all the people are going to lay their faith in their own respective regions and will not accord any consideration to the interests of the nation, then it will become difficult for the union government to continue functioning. In this way, regionalism has become a serious problem for the interests of the nation.

Causes of Regionalism

There are many causes at the root of religionalism in the country, the major ones being the following :

1. Geographical causes. The main cause of regionalism is geographical. There is some essential difference between the food habits, language, life, etc., of every region and the people who live there. By virtue of these differences they come to regard each other as foreigners and they acquire an attitude of fear and hatred for each other.

2. Historical causes. As has been indicated earlier, there are some historical causes also at the root of regionalism. For example, there has been some difference between the people of the north and south ever since the time of the Aryans and it has continued. Many of the kings of the north have won over the south while there have been few kingdoms in the south which have extended to the northern part of India. Because of this, many south Indians look upon northern India as separate from southern India.

3. Political causes. But if the situation is carefully and minutely observed, it will be seen that the main cause at the root of regionalism present in the country is of a political nature. In different regions some people have demanded the formation of regional government and in this they have been inspired by regional interests and by aims of gaining power. In this direction, a major part has been played by the revolutionary Naga party guided by Phizo, the Akali party of Punjab, the D.M.K. party of the south and other political parties. The truth is that the leaders of these political parties are responsible for having propagated regionalism in these respective areas. Not only this, but even some representatives of different areas who are members of political parties give prime importance to the interests of their own regions, even interests which are disregarded by them.

4. Psychological causes. Finally, the psychological causes have contributed no less to the development and stability of regionalism. It is the wish of most of the persons that it be their area that progresses the most. This idea in itself is neither bad nor detestable but when they disregard the national interests and those of other regions for the attainment of this, then this feeling takes on the form of regionalism. Besides this, there are many individuals encouraging regionalism who express the hatred, jealousy, fear, anger, and other feelings contained in them in this manner.

5. Other causes. There are some other causes besides those mentioned above that promote regionalism. For example, it is only rarely that one comes across married couples among whom one belongs to Bengal and the other to Punjab or to Rajasthan or to Madras, for that matter. As a general rule, people belonging to different regions do not marry and hence the occasion for close contact between the two does not arise. In addition to these there are some economic causes of regional tension. In the country there are some regions that are far backward in comparison with some other regions. As a result they are often seen possessed of a sense of inferiority and they become jealous of others. People belonging to some particular sphere are seen to be particularly successful in some vocation. For example, in India, the most successful businessmen are seen to belong to Marwar, Gujarat and Punjab, and in this sphere they have a practical monopoly. In this too they are hated by some people who try to turn them out from their own regions.

Means for the Abolition of Regionalism

The following means can help to end regionalism or at least to dilute it to some extent :

1. Encouragement to transport and communication. If regionalism is to be eliminated, the people should be encouraged to indulge in travel and to increase contact with people belonging to different regions of the country. Recently, a train of religious hermits toured the country and similarly many farmers belonging to Rajasthan travelled all over the country. In India, the tradition whereby people are induced to visit places of religious importance is a good one in as much as that it helps people to travel all over the country and meet different people. In going to different corners of the country, the people realise that India is a large country and regional sentiments can be removed or rendered less effectual by encouraging transport and communication in the country.

2. Propaganda of national history. The history of the nation should be propagated all over the country so that the people may clearly realise that the history of the individual regions of the country is only a part of the history of the nation to which all the regions have made an important contribution. The propagation of the national history will help to eradicate the sense of regionalism.

3. Prevention of regional political parties. It is essential for national unity and integration that the political parties propagating regionalism and regional interests should be prevented from doing so. If they indulge in unrestricted campaigns for promoting regional interests, they should be declared illegal. Although in a democracy every individual has the right to form a political organisation in order to express his views but if it tends to harm the interest of the nation, this right should be curbed.

4. Propagation of the national sentiment. Finally, in order to remove the psychological causes at the root of regionalism, an effort should be made to propagate the sentiment of nationality in the country. It is necessary to resort to all the various media of propaganda to obtain results in this direction.

Efforts should be made to remove the regionalistic tendencies from all spheres such as government service, educational institutions, etc., and the sentiment of nationality should be encouraged.

Regionalism is a complex problem. If it is to be solved it must be attacked from all sides and furthermore such a task requires co-operation from the government and the people. Only then can this problem be solved.

LINGUISM

India is a multilingual state in which many languages are spoken. Practically every state has its own language and sometimes more than one language is spoken in the same area. Some of these languages are English, Hindi, Punjabi, Marathi, Tamil, Telugu, Malayalam, Kannada, Urdu, Bengali and others besides these. Probably, the greatest number speak Hindi which is also the national language, and their number is on the increase. But the literature of the various other languages has also been appropriately developed. For example, the literature of Bengali, Punjabi, Tamil, etc., is by no means of a lower intellectual stature than that possessed by Hindi. The presence of many languages in a country is no defect in itself. An increase in the literature of the various languages is an increase in the literary wealth of the nation itself. When the people try to develop the language that they speak and do not attend to the other languages, it is not a matter that is likely to cause concern to one who has the interests of the nation at heart but when the difference of languages becomes a pretext for tension between people speaking different languages then it does become a grave matter. When one language is considered superior to the other languages which are considered both inferior and detestable, and there is a blind and unconsidering acceptance of such a view, then this tendency is christened linguism. Like all the other isms that one is apt to run across, this linguism is also harmful for the communal interest.

Problem of Linguism

During the past decade or so, linguism has been gathering momentum and force till now it has become a definite threat to the unity and integrity of the nation. In Punjab, the problem of choice between Punjabi and Hindi has created lots of conflict and tension while in Assam the language question has even resulted in bloodshed. In Bengal, Bengali is opposed to Hindi and a serious problem in linguism has thus taken shape. Besides the problems of regional languages, the proponents of Hindi, English and Urdu are creating tension in the entire country. It often happens that the language movement is only a disguised political move and on close observation it will become clear that there are not many literary persons but mostly politicians who cause lingual movements. For example, the movement for the Punjabi language in Punjab is attached to the demand for a Punjabi Suba.

Causes of Linguism

What are the causes at the root of linguism? As it is, linguism is a complex problem and it is difficult to make a complete analysis of all its various causes. Nevertheless, the following are some of the important causes briefly stated :

1. Geographical causes. Linguism is like the other tensions mentioned previously in as much as it too has a geographical cause. Different languages are spoken in the different parts of India and these individual languages also have a lot of varieties since the dialect differs from one town to another. Language is the medium through which people express their thoughts and feelings and make them known to others. And it is through language that they come to know each other. Hence, it is natural to feel a bond of intimacy with one who speaks one's own tongue while one feels lost among people who speak some other language than one's own. Every language has its own literature. This literature is everywhere influenced by the local geographical conditions, rivers, plains and mountains, local vegetation, animals and local culture. It reflects the life of the people who speak that language. Hence, literature bears a very definite relation to its geographical demarcation. The familiarity that a person finds in the literature of the language that he speaks is not available to him in any other literature. Hence, it is natural for a person to wish for the development and progress of the language of his own region and he does not appreciate it if the language of another region is forced on him. When this mental tendency grows more vicious and strong, when the individual acquires a sense of hatred for the other languages and the people who speak them, then tension is created.

2. Historical causes. Some of the causes of linguism are also historical. India has been attacked by one foreigner after another. These foreigners came equipped with their own respective languages. The Moghuls came and brought along Persian which mixed with the local languages and became Urdu. The Britishers put in their appearance with the English language up their sleeves. These languages found the Indian soil suitable and they prospered and grew, and their Indianization also occurred. Many Hindus also wrote in Urdu. If the people had recourse to reason there need have been no occasion for the problem of Urdu or Hindi to have arisen but people who turned to ancient history for their inspiration did not accept the Indianization of Urdu and kept the language as it was with an abundance of Arabic and Persian words. It was not confined to this because the literature that they created had a foreign soul.

3. Psychological causes. And yet, the most important and the primary causes at the root of linguism are of a psychological nature. At its root are the hatred for the other languages and those who speak them in addition to the respect and admiration of one's own language. At its root is the narrow-minded self-respect of the individuals. If the prejudice concerning the other languages is removed from the mind and a comprehensive and sympathetic viewpoint is adopted; it becomes possible for any number of languages to prosper.

4. Political causes. Linguism is also inspired by the political interests and aspirations of different politicians and political groups. Many communal political parties raise the language issue, instigate their people and want to win their votes during the elections. The problem of linguism has gained in complexity because of its affiliation with politics.

5. Economic causes. There are some economic causes that also inspire linguism. Some languages are financially assisted by the government which aims at their progress but people speaking other languages object to this and thus linguism increases.

6. Social causes. Linguism is encouraged by some social factors also. Some myths and legends, customs and traditions prevail in every society. That language is respected in society which provides a place for these. It also is the language that is adopted by the society. On the contrary the languages that do not respect and accept these or the languages that cater to contradicting presumptions are objected to. In this manner linguism spreads.

Suggestions for the Abolition of Linguism

Having studied the causes that cause linguism, it is now possible to turn to the means for its solution and elimination. In this context the following suggestions can be made :

1. Development of the national language. In the event of there being one national language and literature, that have been developed, people speaking the different languages will have an opportunity to communicate with each other through the medium of this national language and the tension existing between them will be sensibly lessened.

2. Encouragement to all major languages. In addition to the development of one common national language and literature, the main regional languages should also be encouraged. No language can be forced upon any region and neither can a literature be developed by putting stress upon it. The language automatically develops through the medium of usage. Once this fact is clearly understood, much of the tension caused by linguism would come to an end. In this way, the government should encourage all the important regional languages. The government should see to it that Punjabi is developed in Punjab, Bengali in Bengal and Assamese in Assam and so on in addition to which Hindi should be propagated in all parts of the country.

3. Opposition to communalism. In order to obviate the political causes of linguism it is necessary to vigorously oppose communalism in the country.

Finally, it should be remembered that in order to solve the problem of linguism, it is necessary to adopt a comprehensive viewpoint. Each language should be encouraged by the government and in every region particular attention should be paid to the regional language and its development.

QUESTIONS FOR EXERCISE

1. Explain the origin and development of group tension. Mention linguistic group tensions.
2. Describe the causes and remedies of casteism.
3. What are the psychological causes of communalism? Suggest remedies.
4. Discuss the psychological causes of regional tension. Suggest measures to eradicate it.

8

RACE AND RACISM

What is Race?

The greater the currency given to the word 'race' in scientific, political and literary texts, greater is the latitude within which its meaning is interpreted. Politicians and the common people are small fry when compared with scientists who have persisted in using the term most confusingly and unscientifically. The term 'race' has been used in a variety of differing senses, some of the following being the more important usages :

1. Particular colour. Many scientists have used the term to denote the classification of human beings on the basis of the skin's colour such as black, white, yellow races, etc.

2. Physiological characteristics. The term 'race' is also used for physiological recognition of the individual, such as Negro, European, etc. Of these all have special physiological characteristics.

3. Specific linguistic groups. The term has also been employed by some scientists to denote specific linguistic groups such as Aryans, Dravidians, etc. In such groups, each has its own particular language.

4. Human characteristics. The most comprehensive sense in which the term 'race' has been used in when it is employed to denote the entire human race. When compared with other beings in the animal kingdom, man is found to possess certain characteristic features that serve to distinguish him from the animals. It is to indicate this difference that an individual is designated the member of human race.

In addition to these more important usages of the term, race is also utilised to denote the offspring of a particular couple and their subsequent offspring in the generations to come.

But a scientific analysis would end in serious confusion if the most important term used by it is open to so many different interpretations. Hence, the need to define the word 'race' and to limit its use to only one particular concept.

The different definitions of race strike a note of discord and there is no common opinion expressed in them. Experiencing this difficulty UNESCO arranged a conference of some prominent sociologists, anthropologists and psychologists in order to determine a single concept of race. The conference gave the following judgments concerning race :

1. Fundamentally, the entire human species has one origin and all men are homo-sapients.

2. Types of group such as national, religious, geographical, cultural, linguistic, etc. are all entirely unconnected with and unrelated to race. These groups do not give indication of any race.

3. The difference found to exist between the physical characteristics of men is due both to heredity and to environment. Differences thereby arise due to the processes known as mutation and inbreeding.

4. Distinctions can be made between different races on the basis of differences in physical characteristics but not on the basis of cultural traits.

5. Some races make claims of purity but this is not true. Today pure races cannot be found anywhere in the world. The process of mixing of races originated long back.

6. Human races can be classified but these classifications are based solely on physical traits. They have no relation of any kind with mental or intellectual superiority or inferiority.

7. The inner capacity for the development of mind and culture is found equally in every race. Hence distinctions between races cannot be based on cultural differences or levels of intelligence. Intelligent people are to be found in all races.

8. It is possible that in one nation the degree of racial difference may be greater while in another nation it may be of lesser degree.

9. Evidence in support of the fact that the race has no important effect in the social and cultural differences between

various human groups has been found in historical and sociological studies. By no stretch of imagination can one conceive of any relation between changes in racial forms and social changes.

10. That from the biological viewpoint, mixing of races is undesirable, is an essentially incorrect and invalid belief.

To conclude, the race is a group of intermarrying people who are born of common ancestors, possess similar physical traits and a 'we' feelings. Inbreeding renders permanent the physical characteristics of the race and due to them one race may be distinguished from another. One major cause of inbreeding is geographical separation. Besides geographical isolation, a race originates due also to mutation, migration, selection and adaptation.

RACE AND SOCIAL CONSCIOUSNESS

Race, in addition to being a biological term, is also indicative of a sociological fact. Race may or may not be able to establish the superiority or inferiority of any human group but nevertheless it has a hand in social consciousness. In human groups of different races one finds differing cultures and psychological characteristics. And usually, they marry within their own group. And these factors lead to the creation of a 'we' feeling in them, which in truth gives rise to social consciousness. From the scientific viewpoint, theory of race has been proved weak. Hoebel has rightly written that "There is no such thing as pure race on the face of the globe today, whether there were pure races in the prehistoric past, we do not know. That there never will be a pure race in the future, is a certainty."[1] On similar lines, any definite correlation between physical characteristics and mental abilities has also been disproved by modern experiments. For example, the idea that there is a specific correlation between brains and the shape of the head has been disproved. But then, it was only on the basis of race distinction that Hitler managed to arouse a tremendous social consciousness in the people of his country in whom it took such a stronghold that it has not been completely wiped out even today.

1. Hoebel, E.A., *Man in the Primitive World,* p. 73.

In fact, the concept of race continues from generation to generation. Even today, it would not be difficult to locate some people in India who believe in the purity and superiority of the Aryan race. In Hindus intermarriage between people of different religions is forbidden only because of this race distinction. The idea of race has a direct and strong influence on the behaviour of the individual. In India, the Arya Samaj has made efforts to revive the ancient Aryan culture, inspired by the notion of Aryan superiority, be it true or a fallacious concept.

The relation between the notion of race and social consciousness can be easily understood by the example of Negroes who live in the Western countries. It is due to idea of race that the dark people are treated as different and alien to the white people in America. They are not allowed to intermarry with white people, their children are not permitted to study with the white children, they are not allowed the use of any public place, such as hotels. In certain places they have even no right to vote and to occupy any responsible position in the government institutions. In this way one finds serious and important differences in the living standards, facilities, privileges, etc., of the whites and the blacks on the basis of race. It is undeniable that distinction and discrimination do not lessen whatever truth there is in race but they do influence the personalities and social institutions of the whites and the blacks. Both of the two groups look upon themselves as belonging to different races, and the social consciousness that they develop conforms to this notion of basic differences.

In this way, then, even though the concept of race lacks any scientific basis, it plays an important role in developing social consciousness.

ARYANISM

William Jones was the first person to extract the word 'Arya' from its Sanskrit background and introduce it to the European languages where 'Aryan' came to denote all Asian languages. Later on, Max Muller used this same term for a specific group of languages. Max Muller's investigations proved that with the exception of Bask, Magyar and Finnish languages, all other European languages belong to the family of Sanskrit of India and the language of Iran. These languages were then given the name Aryan or Indo-European languages. On the basis of this similarity of languages, the existence of a common race was imagined which was called the Aryan race. This theory was given its scientific form in Count Joseph De Gobineau's essay *The Inequality of Human Races.* This essay was an attempt to prove and to establish the superiority of the Aryan race. It was elevated to its highest pinnacle by Lapouge. Indians, Greeks and Romans who spoke the Aryan languages in the past gave rise to the most highly evolved cultures and civilisations. In the following centuries, the European Aryan races made great scientific progress, on the basis of which it was believed that the rise of civilisation is particularly related to the Aryan race. No two races are identical in respect of qualities, and neither are they equal. It is the Aryan race that can develop the best civilisation. In this way, the object of Aryans was the deification of the ancestors and the establishment of the superiority of a particular race.

NORDICISM

In Europe, every country did its best to modify Aryanism and to assimilate it into its own national history. Nordicism is also one form of it. It was called Teutanicism in Germany, Anglo-Saxonism in England and Gallicism in France. Nordicism aimed at the emancipation and praise of the cultural qualities of the extinct Nordic race. According to it, only the Nordic race is capable of ruling the world. It is the most superior in civilisation. It is also the most superior in psychological and mental characteristics. It is the race that will prove to be the strongest and the best equipped to face the struggle of life. According to Nordicism, the races lose their power of generating a civilisation when they intermix and a threat to civilisation becomes imminent. The actual or real Aryan race is represented by the Dolichocephalic or white-skinned, tall and elongated headed people. They were called Nordic because they lived in North Nord. All the best artists, philosophers and politicians of ancient Greece and Rome were claimed to be Nordic. It was said that all the great historic figures, beginning with Jesus Christ, Mohammed right down to Changez Khan, had Nordic blood in their veins. The Nazis went a step further and declared the Teutonic race, among all the Nordic races, as the most superior and accomplished race in the world. After 1933, when Hitler had come into power Nordicism was at its prime with the result that it led to the complete extermination and mass eradication of millions of Jews. In 1938 when Mussolini signed a treaty with Hitler, he thought it fit to declare that the Italians were the only true Aryans. In his work, *Foundations of the Nineteenth Century,* Houstan Steward Chamberlain Staunchly supported the inseparability of the Aryan and Teutonic races. This principle had been further elaborated by Stoddard in his book *The Rising Tide of Coloured and Racial Realities in Europe.*

IS THE WHITE RACE SUPERIOR TO OTHER RACES?

Scientific investigations have finally and conclusively rejected the myth of the superiority of the white race. The following arguments are adduced to establish that the white race is not superior to other races :

1. White race is not mentally superior. Modern scientific tests have established that no race is superior to any other in respect of mental ability. In his *Scientific Aspects of the Race Problem,* Klineberg, in the essay entitled 'Mental Testing in Racial and National Groups', has proved the thesis that differences in the intelligence quotient obtained by intelligence tests are due to environmental differences rather than the result of racial differences. The intelligence quotient of a nine-year old Negro girl was found to be 200, twice the normal or average. Similarly, it was found that the intelligence quotient of North American Negroes was higher than that of the Negroes settled in the southern countries because there were better educational facilities in the North. The intelligence quotient of the American Indians and the ordinary Americans were found to differ because of their dissimilar environment.

2. Which race is not superior in culture. The proponents of Nordicism and Aryanism assume one or the other European race to be the most superior and then they believe it to be the founder of all the cultures of the world, but history provides the evidence of the fact that at a time when the European races were still in the barbaric stage, the civilisations of India and China were at their zenith, and things such as dynamite, paper and the magnetic needle had been invented. Hence, the principle of the cultural superiority of racialism is completely at variance with historical facts.

3. No race can claim purity. Modern scientific discoveries have deprived the idea of pure blood of its last vestige of respect. All races are found to possess the same blood groups. Blood has no relation with heredity, and the concept of superiority of blood is a mere figment of imagination. There is no pure race in the world today. In India one finds a mixture of the Negrito, Proto-Australoid, Mediterranean, Dravid, Mongol, Iranian, Shak, Kushaan, Pahalv, Hun, Arabic, Moghul, Afghan and East European races. Despite the tremendous disturbances on the basis of colour distinctions there is considerable mixing of the white and dark-skinned races in U.S.A.

From the above arguments it is evident that the white race is in no way superior to other races in respect of intellectual or cultural attainments.

FALLACIES OF RACISM

Hence, racism is unjustified. The principle of racism is faulty in many respects, the main ones being the following :

1. Confusing race with culture. In these theories, culture has been confused with race. It has also been assumed in these theories that the emancipation or downfall of culture is dependent exclusively upon race. This assumption has no logical ground. In fact, race does not influence culture or civilisation. The same race sometimes reaches the pinnacle of its civilisational and cultural development while at other times it falls back completely, and culture and civilisation are lost. This cycle of rise and fall in culture can be seen in the cultural history of the Indo-Aryan race and in the rise and fall of Arabian culture. Racial elements play little or no part in this rise or fall. In fact, race is neither the basis of culture, nor one of its more important factors. Culture is a social phenomenon while race is a physiological or biological factor. The elements of culture are poetry, art, philosophy, customs, institutions, languages, etc., none of which is concerned with racial elements. Culture spreads through cultural contact but race cannot spread in different areas without actual crossing.

2. Interpreting language as characteristic of race. Another defect in these principles is that language is treated as a characteristic of race. In fact, language and race have no relation. It is improper to imagine that the Aryan languages would be spoken exclusively by the Aryan race or those with Aryan blood. Despite the fact that English is an Aryan language, there are approximately twelve million Negroes in America who speak no language other than English. History records repeated incidents in which the victorious nation foisted its own language upon the vanquished people. There are also incidents in which it is the victor who had adopted the language of the vanquished nation. The truth of the matter lies in the fact that language is a part of culture and it can be learnt by an individual of any race. It cannot be associated with race.

3. Identifying race with the nationality. In these views, race has been identified with nationality. Race and nation are two different and distinct things. According to Huxley and Huddon, nationality is a specific aspect of the development of classes among men. Many different racial elements can be admixed in the organisation of a nation. In an entire nation, there can be only one racial element, and there can also be numerous racial elements resulting from their mixture. Race can be a physical or material element of the nation. Nation is a social concept while race is a genetic concept. Nation has a geographical limit while race has no specific limits. Nation is created with a view to attaining some definite purposes. The creation of the race is the outcome of natural processes. Nation is subjective; it is impossible without a national psychological oneness. Race is objective since it is based on common physiological characteristics. Briefly, nation and race are not attributes of one another.

4. Imagination of a pure race. These principles also imagine the existence of a pure race, a concept that is entirely unrealistic. In fact, there is no pure race such as the Nordic or any other race. In his book, *We Europeans,* Carr Saunders, Huxley and Huddon, have proved that there is no European nation in which there is any pure race. There is no race that can scientifically be proved pure.

Briefly, then, the principle of racism is completely lacking in any rational basis. The civilisations of ancient Egypt, Cambodia, China, Mesopotamia and Mexico were evolved neither by the Nordics nor by the Aryans. Two thousand years ago when the Nordic race had yet to cross the barbaric stage, the great civilisation of Rome was at the height of its development. And in the most advanced nations of the modern world, France, America, Germany and Italy, Britain and India, there has been almost a complete mixing of the various human groups. In the modern age no scientist worth the name accepts the validity of the concept of race, which is a harmful and baseless principle.

QUESTIONS FOR EXERCISE

1. What is Race? What are its fallacies?
2. Is white race superior to other races?

9

Psychological Effects of Social Status

What is Status?

Most people are accustomed to talking in terms of 'status' when talking of various particular people and qualifying this term by the more common words such as higher and lower. One often hears of an improvement in the status of women, of Shudras, of the Brahmins in Hindu society and of the white and black-skinned men and women in western countries, and so on. What is this social status? As indicated by the term itself, it implies the status or place of an individual in society. And, what is society? It is a web of social relationships. Hence, social status is the position of an individual within social relationships. As is evident, this can be both high as well as low. Hence, there is an order of social status in society. In Hindu society, Brahmins are much respected and considered superior to other castes besides being awarded many special privileges. Thus, their social status is high. On the other hand, the so-called untouchable castes of Hindu society are given less respect than the Brahmins and have fewer rights; hence their low social status.

It would be useful to consider the definitions of status in understanding the concept. Some definitions are as follows :

1. Definition by Ogburn and Nimkoff. "A person's status is his group standing or ranking in relation to others." This is the simplest definition of the term 'status'. In Hindu society, the status of the Brahmin is at a higher level than that of the Shudra. The leader is at the top in a group. In this way, the status of an individual is his place within the group. This status will be his ranking in relation to other positions and will be called high or low accordingly.

2. View of Martindale and Monachesi. "We define status as a position in social aggregate identified with a person of prestige symbols and actions." This definition indicates that social status is to be recognised by a pattern of prestige symbols and actions. For example, within the same college, the status of the principal and the teachers is different. How is this difference in status expressed? All the teaching staff ostensibly respect him and he is greeted wherever he may happen to go. In his presence, the teachers leave their chairs and address him in the most respectful terms. This is an example of prestige symbols. Now consider the pattern of actions. The principal keeps an eye on the work of each of the teachers, maintains order among them and directs them from time to time. There is a distinct pattern of prestige symbols related to the principal's status. This pattern differs from the pattern of prestige symbols and actions related to the teachers. Difference in the status of both is evident from this difference in these respective patterns.

3. Definition by Maclver and Page. "Status is the social position that determines for its possessor, apart from his personal attribute or social service, a degree of respect, prestige and influences." This definition of status is even more enlightening. According to it, some proportion of an individual's respect, prestige and influences are determined by his social status. In a family the social standing of the husband and wife can be gauged from the influence which one has on the other as well as from the prestige or respect that one of them receives from the other. According to this, one can know the difference in the social status of husband and wife that exists in different cultures. In the villages of India, the status of the Sarpanch is the highest. He is greeted with respect wherever he may chance to wander. In the meetings of the village he is seated upon the highest pedestal. He mediates in the mutual quarrels of the villagers, who respect his decisions and judgements. In this way, social status of an individual is that particular position in his relations with other individuals by virtue of which he is the recipient of respect and prestige, and has influence and which can be recognised by symbols of prestige accruing to him and his actions.

DETERMINATION OF STATUS AND ROLES

How is this status determind? Before going into a detailed discussion of this, it is necessary to know that there are two types of positions. Some positions are due to 'office' or title such as the post of college principal or a village sarpanch. In the case of such posts, the social status is determined by the office occupied or held, just as the person who occupies the chair of the principal is accorded the respect in accordance with his position. The rights and duties of a district magistrate do not change with every new magistrate because these duties, rights and symbols of respect are related to the magistrate's position or office and are inherent therein. Besides these, some positions derive from the family, physical capability, knowledge or skill, etc., of the individual. For example, some roles and respect symbols are related to the post of the country's prime minister. But the social status which Mr. Nehru had in India is not due entirely to his occupying the post of prime minister but rather to the qualities of his character, patriotism, knowledge and skill. The social status of Dara Singh is due to his powers in wrestling, that of Vinobaji is due to services rendered by him while the social status of Tenzing is due to his having conquered Mount Everest. In this way physical beauty or prowess, skill in music, scientific knowledge, cultural excellence, etc., or other special qualities attainable by human beings raise the status of an individual. The social status of film actresses is due mainly to their physical charms. In the same way status is lowered by defects in character. When a poor boy studies hard and qualified for the I.A.S., the status of his family is raised at the same time as his own. The daughter of a rich man loses her status when she is married into a poorer family. But factors and causes which determine status change according to the time and place to which they belong. In ancient India, it was the *varna* which determined the social status of an individual. Today, wealth is the determinant of social status. In some primitive societies, the social status of an individual bears a direct and proportionate relation to the number of wives he has. The more wives he has, the better is his social status. In some tribes, the social status of women increases with every new divorce that she gets. According to some, the determinant of the social status of an individual is his financial condition. This theory is completely one-sided. In India, the social status enjoyed by Gandhi, Dayanand, Sri Aurobindo, Rabindranath Tagore, Prem Chand and others was not due to their economic condition.

IMPORTANCE OF SOCIAL STATUS AND ROLES

This social status is of much importance for the individual. Marriages in almost every society depend upon social status. It is common knowledge and an everyday occurrence that many marriages are not contracted simply because of difference in the social status or in the financial condition of the parents of the boy and the girl. Everyone wants to marry his sons and daughters into a family on an equal or better footing in society. An individual wins respect in society by virtue of his social status. Every social status is recognisable from some symbols of respect. These symbols of respect change along with change in social status. An increase in the individual's social status entitles him to more respect than before irrespective of whether this increase or improvement is due to marriage, or the acquisition of skill in some art or knowledge or due to his having moved into some higher office. The roles of an individual also change along with his social status. Different roles are conjoined to different social positions. Actually, the very object in having differences in the statuses within society is to facilitate the division of work among people according to their ability. Kingsley Davis correctly observes, "Social inequality is thus an unconsciously evolved device by which societies insure that the most important positions are conscientiously filled by the most qualified persons. Hence, every society, no matter how simple, or complex, must differentiate persons in terms of both prestige and esteem." At some places social status grants prerogatives even in the eyes of the law. For example, in England no one can file a suit against the Royal family and in case some involvement does occur, the member of the Royal Family is always above the commoner. In ancient India, the same crimes were punished differently, depending upon the caste of the criminal. In this way, the individual gets many direct and indirect advantages from social status.

According to Ogburn and Nimkoff, "Society is less interested in the individual than in the position that he occupies." The truth of this is proved almost every day by social incidents and historical evidence. To every social status some symbols and functions of respect are attached. In the modern world, the political sphere in any country can afford many examples which will bear this out. The political platform is forever witnessing the progress and procession of eminent actors who come and go. The ones who go, go for ever and are quickly forgotten and the sympathies earmarked for them are transferred to the newcomers who take their place. It is only a few years ago that hardly anyone outside Egypt was aware of the existence of Col. Nasar whereas today every educated person knows him in his capacity as President of the United Arab Republic. It is only yesterday that Chiang Kai Sheik was regarded as a patriot and great leader but now he is looked upon as a turncoat and an anti-nationalist in Communist China. As long as Stalin continued to be the supreme leader in the Soviet Union he was respected there and in all Communist countries and circles, but the moment he forsook the political arena not only was he forgotten, efforts were made in Russia to remove all traces that may remind people of him. And these are not isolated examples but incidents that happen everyday in the field of politics. Society respects and reveres power. Society retains its interest in an individual only as long as he occupies a high status and wields power; he is forgotten immediately he steps back from the limelight. The respect and honour is conjoined not to the individual but to the status and it is accorded to the individual who occupies it, not to him that did once occupy it.

Social stratification is based on the division of status and the concurring functions between individuals. Status is the medium through which the society manages to determine the kinds of functions to be performed by a particular kind of individual. In this way, the society is not interested as to who occupies a post. Social organisation is maintained through this division of posts. According to Maclver, "It is the sense of status, sustained by economic, political or ecclesiastical power and by distinctive modes of life and cultural expressions corresponding to them which draws class apart from class, gives cohesion to each, and stratifies a whole society."

But from this it is not justified to draw the conclusion that the society is not interested in any manner in the individual. While on the one hand we come across innumerable examples in which the society is interested in the social status of an individual rather than in the individual himself, we also, on the other, find numerous cases in which the interest of the society centres in the specific individual and not in his social status. Is the interest that hundreds of thousands of Indians take in Vinobaji aroused because of some social position that he occupies? And are the robbers and gangsters who have decided to convert afraid of Vinobaji that they revere him and show him respect? What is there in this emaciated old man that people revere and respect him and shower him with their tokens of affectionate respect? Evidently, the people are impressed by his personality, sacrifice and the services that he has rendered to society. Was the respect paid to Sri Aurobindo, Mahatma Gandhi and Swami Ramkrishna Paramhansa stimulated by their social status? Did Jayaprakash Narayan command more regard before he had abandoned politics and the political arena? What post does Bertrand Russell occupy in England that he is respected so much? Ever since he relinquished the prime ministership of England, Eden has disappeared from the public scene but Churchill commanded as great respect even after his retirement as he did in his heyday. All these examples serve to illustrate the fact that the respect that great men win is not due to their social position or status but also by virtue of their personal qualities. The interest shown by the human society in Gandhi, Vivekananda, Gautam Buddha, Christ and Mohammad was not occasioned by their respective social status. The art of the singer captures the hearts of all listeners and enraptures them. The respect that accrues to him is because of his social status. In this way, society takes an interest both in the individual as well as his social status, and besides his social status, improves by virtue of his personal qualities if they prove to be an asset to society. Hence, the assertion made by Ogburn and Nimkoff to the effect that society is more interested in the social status of the individual rather than in his individuality appears to be partial and not representative of the whole truth.

QUESTIONS FOR EXERCISE

1. What is status? How is it determined?
2. Explain the importance of social status.

10

Psychology of Public Opinion

The very title public opinion, suggests that it is the opinion of the public. The public is not a group or a crowd. Public denotes the people of a country. It further refers to the people of the nation or the community. In this way, this conception is more complex and comprehensive than the concept of a group. The members of the public are found to possess 'we' feeling. The public lacks the feature of organisation and is generally dispersed over a large area, but it is not necessary for it to be organised. Besides this general form of public, there is a public related to particular problems such as economic public, political public, etc. These are short period groups. One single individual can be the member of any number of such groups simultaneously. Such a group or public dissolves when the problem for which it was assembled is solved.

WHAT IS PUBLIC?

Public opinion is a term that means the opinion of the public. Hence, before the full implication of the term can be understood, it is necessary that the terms public and opinion should also be understood. In common parlance and in casual conversation, the term 'public' stands misused, being employed to denote community, crowd, nation and in extreme cases even as substitution for the royal 'we'. But a scientific analysis necessitates its distinction from these other terms and its proper definition, so as to obviate the possibilities of its being misconstrued. Similar to the crowd, it, too, is a particular kind of a psychological group. Defining public, Kimball Young has written, "...a non-contiguous and transitory mass of individuals with a common or general interest."[1] It is evident from this

1. Young, K., *Handbook of Social Psychology*, p. 429.

definition that it is not necessary for members of this group to collect together at one place. Physical proximity is not of the essence. The interaction between them, too, is not of direct or perceptible kind. They are scattered over a large area and their group is of a transitory and flimsy kind. But they are knitted or related together by a common interest. This common interest can be political, economic, artistic, moral or related to any other field. This difference in interest and values helps to distinguish between a political public, an economic-minded public, public connected with artistic purpose and a public imbued with morality. A large morass of humanity is involved in a public consequent upon which the power of the public is rather large.

WHAT IS OPINION?

Having considered the concept of public at adequate length, it is now necessary to turn to a definition of the term 'opinion.' In this connection, Kimball Young, in his work, *Handbook of Social Psychology*, has written that "An opinion is a belief somewhat stronger or more intense than a mere notion or impression but less strong than positive knowledge based on complete or adequate knowledge. Opinions are really beliefs about a controversial topic or with respect to the valuative interpretation or moral meaning of certain facts."[2] This particular explanation of the term opinion might lead to a confusion between opinion and belief. Opinion is conjoined to some particular belief but belief and opinion are two different words and it is necessary to distinguish between them. For example, many of the opinions are only formed after considerable discussion on some polemical subject while some beliefs are adopted before any discussion of the subject is held. Secondly, opinion has not the strength and invincibility of belief. Contrarily, belief is stronger than opinion and is hence also relatively more permanent. Yet, it can be said with perfect composure and fidelity that opinion is a particular kind of belief which is formed and which relates to some controversial subject or to the explanation of some facts.

2. Young, K., *Handbook of Social Psychology* (1951), p. 431.

DEFINITION OF PUBLIC OPINION

After analysing the meaning of public and opinion, we may take into consideration some scientific definitions of public opinion. Some of the definitions are the following :

1. Kimball Young's opinion. "Public opinion consists of the opinions held by public at a certain time,"[3] writes Young in this book, *Handbook of Social Psychology.*

2. Cooley's opinion. "Public opinion should be regarded as an organic process and not merely as a state of agreement about some question of the day."[4]

3. Akolkar's view. "Public opinion simply refers to that mass of ideas which people have or express on a given issue,"[5] writes V.V. Akolkar in his book *Social Psychology.*

NATURE OF PUBLIC OPINION

From the foregoing definitions of public opinion, it is evident that in public opinion are assimilated the opinions of individuals concerning various specific problems in addition to their judgements, ideas and notions. Here it is not necessary that every individual should possess identical views and ideas. In fact, public opinion represents the opinion of the majority and the views of the powerful groups. There are always some individuals who are opposed to the public opinion but this does not have the effect of changing the public opinion. It is further not necessary that public opinion should be the opinion of a great many individuals. Actually, as Lowell has indicated, public opinion shows not the preponderance of numerical superiority but the preponderance of influence. Public opinion concerning some subject shows the view-point which is the most powerful. In McDougall's opinion, public opinion is the moral conception of the people.[6] But, as is evident in practice, public opinion is concerned not only with any moral considerations but is also addressed to political and even administrative problems. For example, a democratic government is believed to be the representative of public opinion.

---

3. *Ibid.*, p. 431.
4. Cooley, C.H., *Social Process* (1918), p. 378.
5. Akolkar, V.V., *Social Psychology* (1959), p. 244.
6. Wm. McDougall, *The Group Mind*, pp. 898-99.

CHARACTERISTICS OF PUBLIC OPINION

Ginsberg has prescribed the presence of the following characteristics as essential to an opinion if it is to possess the authority to which public opinion is entitled :[7]

1. Public opinion can be only that opinion which is acceptable to all. In order to be generally accepted, it is not sufficient for it to be the opinion of the majority but it should accord with the interests of the group as well.

2. Public opinion is not the belief of one individual but it is rather the assimilated and combined opinion of all the members of the group.

3. Public opinion is formed by common acceptance by the group.

4. For the public opinion it is necessary that there should be social and cultural unity among the members of the group.

5. In order that public opinion may be formed, the members of the group should possess the facility of exchanging ideas and views.

6. It is indispensable that all members of the group should have the freedom of exchanging views with each other.

7. Only that view is called public opinion which has the firm belief of the public opinion at its back.

PROCESS OF THE FORMATION OF PUBLIC OPINION

The process which results in the formation of public opinion is a very complex process as public opinion is not formed in an instant but is a continuous process. The opinion of the leaders has an important hand in forming public opinion. The process is set in motion when some people draw the attention of other members of the group to some particular problem and stress its importance. These latter individuals then slowly devote their attention to this problem and put forward their respective opinions concerning it. The conclusion that derives from the comparative analysis of opinion so expressed is public opinion. The administration of government also has its influence in this but it is not inevitable that government officials must have a hand in the public opinion. It is the opinion of some

7. Ginsberg, M., *The Psychology of Society* (1951), p. 141.

psychologists that the formation of public opinion is the result of the interaction between individuals in the group. On the other hand, it is contended by some others that the basis or root of public opinion is the unbiased or unprejudiced discussion and argument among the people. It is contended by some other individuals that the elements at the root of the formation of public opinion are of an affective or emotional rather than of an intellectual nature. And these elements are based on mob psychology. Some people have also tried to explain public opinion on the basis of the group mind. In fact, the formation of public opinion is based on the instincts of man. It is not formed through intellectual consideration or on the basis of moral standards. It is further influenced by unconscious desires and complicated and tangled thoughts. It is only because of this that some intelligent leaders turn the public opinion with complete facility. In addition to instincts and motivation, another element that contributes to the formation of public opinion is imitation. When some individuals see other people holding some particular view on some specific problem, they also do the same because they argue to themselves that the opinion must have some element of truth as these people are holding that opinion. In this way, any opinion can become public opinion if it is the opinion of the majority. As has been mentioned earlier, some leaders direct public opinion in the process of its formation but in this directive effort, the greater influence is wielded by the individual who is a specialist on the subject rather than the propagandist. In addition to these elements, the sense of self-respect is also an important constituent of public opinion. Allport has laid great emphasis upon this element. The feelings of self-respect collectively influence the individual and help in the establishment of public opinion. Besides this, common problems and public beliefs are also important constituents of public opinion. The common beliefs or faith towards the public problems is converted into public opinion.

QUESTIONS FOR EXERCISE

1. What is public opinion? Explain its determinants?
2. Describe the characteristics of public opinion.

11

Psychology of Propaganda

In the world of today, propaganda is an important element in the political, economic and social spheres. What is propaganda? It will have to be scientifically defined if it is to be understood. The word 'propaganda,' derives from the Latin *propagare* which means to produce or to spread or to plant the branches in order to grow a new plant. In this way, *propagare* implies production or spreading which is artificial, not natural. Evidently, in its literal meaning, the word 'propaganda' means the artificial propagation or spreading of something. For this reason some individuals look propaganda as something harmful, although it has now been definitely established that propaganda is very essential for the education of the public.

DEFINITION OF PROPAGANDA

It would be useful to glance at some of the definitions of propaganda as such a step would be of help in its understanding. Some of the major definitions are the following :

1. Kimball Young's view. According to Kimball Young, "For our purposes we shall define propaganda as the more or less deliberately planned and systematic use of symbols chiefly through suggestion and related psychological techniques, with a view first to altering and controlling opinions, ideas and values and ultimately to changing overt action along predetermined line."[1]

The above definition of propaganda throws light upon the following important acts :

(a) Propaganda is generally well-thought-out and properly organised.

1. Young, K., *Handbook of Social Psychology* (1951), p. 506.

(b) Propaganda is not done openly and ostentatiously but in symbolic form. For example, when a political party advises the public to vote into office only that person who is the true representative of the public, it means to propagate the idea that only the candidate belonging to its party is the true representative of the people while the other contestants are not.

(c) Propaganda is usually effected through suggestion.

(d) The objective of propaganda is to change or control public opinion. The ultimate or the final aim of propaganda is to convert the action of the public along the desired line by controlling and moulding the ideals and thoughts of the people.

2. Doob's opinion. According to Doob, propaganda is "...a systematic attempt by interested individuals to control the attitudes of groups of individuals through the use of suggestion and consequently to control their action."[2]

The definition points out that propagation of ideals takes place through the medium of suggestion; it is used to control the tendencies of the people; and propaganda is organised or systematic.

In this way, stated briefly, propaganda is a psychological process in which suggestion is systematically employed to influence or to control the ideas, ideals and tendencies of the people indirectly.

KINDS OF PROPAGANDA

The main kinds of propaganda are as follows :

1. Direct and indirect propaganda. From the foregoing definitions it should not be supposed that propaganda is effected only indirectly. In actual fact, propaganda can be both direct and indirect. In direct propaganda the people upon whom it is being used are cognizant of the individual who is doing it and the purpose why he is doing it. For example, the present Indian government is directly propagating the schemes of life insurance, family planning, small savings, etc., besides its many major projects. The people ate fully aware of the fact that this propaganda is governmental and in it, the government points

2. Doob, L.W., *Propaganda : Its Psychology and Technique.*

out the benefits accruing to the public from these schemes and asks the people to adopt them. On the other hand, some propaganda can also be indirect, just as the propaganda against India generated by Pakistan is guided by their intention of taking possession of Kashmir. In indirect propaganda, people are not aware of the objective or purpose of it. For example, it is the practice adopted by many people who resort to propaganda never to reveal their intention which motivates the propaganda. They change the views and ideals of the people in a subtle manner and succeed in forcing them to act in the manner they desire. In wartime many leaders try to arouse the national sentiment and the patriotic fervour in their fellow countrymen, the intention behind such acting being to persuade more and more men to enlist in the army.

2. Other kinds of propaganda. Psychologists have classified propaganda further such as primary and secondary propaganda. Primary propaganda consists in the instigation and excitation of attitudes and prejudices that already exist. To take a common example, the state of tension between the Hindus and Muslims continues from the past into the present. Taking advantage of this, the Azad Kashmir government always excites and tries to force the Muslim population of Kashmir to mutiny and revolt. This is an example of primary propaganda. In secondary propaganda no tendency or mental set is present previously. In it, new tendencies and thoughts are instilled into the people. Some psychologists have also effected distinction between conscious and unconscious propaganda. Conscious propaganda, apparently enough, is done purposely and is preplanned. Unconscious propaganda happens accidentally and is not effected knowingly.

PSYCHOLOGICAL BASIS OF THE APPEAL OF PROPAGANDA

The foregoing description of propaganda throws light upon its various psychological bases and the appeal which it has for the public. Roughly stated, in the background of propaganda are suggestions, motivations, tendencies, beliefs, emotions and feelings. Propaganda is aimed at influencing these factors in the people. These are employed and these are transformed and controlled. If the psychological bases of propaganda are to be properly understood, the relation between these elements and propaganda must be delineated easily.

Propaganda and Suggestion

As has been pointed out earlier, the main basis of propaganda is suggestion or direction. Through the medium of suggestion all kinds of desirable changes can be made in the thoughts and ideals of people. The suggestibility or the power of reacting to a suggestion is not alike in all individuals but even then every individual is influenced by suggestion to some extent. In suggestion, some factors are of particular import. As a general rule, the suggestions or utterances of political leaders, actors and religious saints are respected and imitated. People quote them in their own work. This power of suggestion is because of their prestige. Hence, this is called prestige suggestion. It is proverbially said that the path that the wise and the great tread is the path which ought to be taken. Similarly, the people are also wont to imitate the majority. This is named suggestion of majority. People tend to adopt those activities that are considered good and are indulged in by the majority of individuals. The imitative tendency of human beings is because of their socialisation. The individual who remains unaffected by and indifferent to public opinion and majority is a rare being indeed. In this way, all kinds of practices are propagated in public through the media of the opinions of respected individuals and the suggestions of the majority. For example, much of the propaganda indulged in by Indian National Congress is prefaced by the names of Pt. Nehru and Gandhi.

Propaganda, Motives and Needs

Every activity of the human being is dependent upon his motives and his needs. Without this the human individual cannot be instigated to indulge in any activity at all. That which is not needed, and that which holds no inspiration or motivation cannot be the object of propaganda. Only that can be the object of propagation which is either needed by the public or the need for which is created. For this reason people who are successful in propaganda appeal to the motives of the people. Although the motives and the needs differ from individual to individual, yet in their general form these motives and needs of most individuals concur. To take an example, the desire to be respected in society and to be considered good is an almost universal desire. Almost every individual wants to obtain power. Every individual desires the security of his family and of his own self. And every individual wants to improve and raise his standard of living. Generally speaking, everyone has love for his country and his religion, if any. Everyone stands in perpetual need of food, clothing, occupation, fame and comfort. In propaganda, these needs and motives are aroused and this awakening is exploited by those conducting the propaganda.

Propaganda, Belief and Attitudes

One aim of propaganda is the control and transformation of the beliefs and attitudes of the people. As has been said before, primary propaganda makes use of the existing attitudes while in propaganda of secondary nature, the attitudes are transformed or created anew. In the same way, in propaganda, old beliefs are replaced by new ones, or, at least, an effort is made in this direction. For example, every political party tries to convince the public that it is the true and the only representative of the people and it is the only one which can bring about the true welfare of the people. Everyone speaks of himself as the true representative of the people and wants to create distrust concerning his rivals in the minds of the electors. But in changing beliefs it is essential to be aware of attitudes because otherwise propaganda cannot be effected forcefully. If the public is not at all tendentious in a particular direction, it is of no avail to start propagation in it without any preparation. Before this, the mind of the public should be prepared for it and a tendency towards it created.

Propaganda in Relation to Feelings and Emotions

The things that most easily influence the individual are those that arouse feelings and emotions. It is for this reason that while indulging in propaganda, the people who succeed are those who make progress in creating a favourable attitude towards themselves in the people. According to the need of the moment, they endeavour to excite fear, anger, hope, desire and hatred, etc., in their audience. For example, the communal groups excite the emotions of fear, anger and hatred in their own people with regard to other communities. In attempting to oust the British from the rule of India, different people aroused various emotions in the Indian people and instigated them against the Britishers and propagated the idea of independence of the country among the people. Mahatma Gandhi aroused the emotion of love of the country. The revolutionaries performed the task of spreading hatred and anger towards the British. All kinds of slogans were shouted. The objective of slogans is the excitement of the feelings and emotions of the public. '*Inqalab Zindabad*' is a slogan that aroused the fiend in men when it is heard or uttered. People express their anger by abusing the government in their slogans. The successful leaders control the feelings of the public and turn them into the desired channels. The government tries to win active participation of the people in such movements as prohibition, family planning, life insurance, co-operation, etc., by the display of various kinds of posters and pictures. This method of propaganda, too, is one form of propaganda.

In New York, U.S.A., there is an Institute of Propaganda Analysis. This institute has classified the various methods of propaganda. According to it, the different methods are the following :

1. Name calling. In propagating for somebody, whether in his favour or against him, some means are employed when referring to him. This name-calling in itself is fairly good propaganda, favourable and unfavourable. It is not uncommon, and may serve as a good illustration, for individual of one particular political party to refer to another party by speaking of them, or calling them as traitors.

Some people employ propaganda against another party after giving them communal names.

2. Transfer. In transfer various unrelated facts, ideas or objects are conjoined. For example, many preachers adduce many unrelated facts in favour of their own specific contention.

3. Glittering generalities. There are some words which attract everyone and are acceptable to all. Some words of this kind are world-brotherhood, equality, liberty and fraternity, etc. Propaganda concerning many things is based upon these glittering common conceptions. In the field of international politics, both Russia and America indulge in the propagation of their own views while ostensibly they speak of world peace. The Communist Party uses the slogan of equality and fraternity to further and popularise its own principles. The slogan of world peace and progress of humanity won recognition and consequent employment even by a dictator of the mettle of Hitler.

4. Testimonials. In trying to propagate their own products, thoughts or views, people often solicit and make use of the testimonials of great leaders and renowned individuals. In India, most political parties resort to the age-old cliche that they are adopting the principles of Mahatma Gandhi and are putting them into practice while all others are treading the wrong path, in the election days, the Congress turned to presenting the testimonials issued by Nehruji and Mahatma Gandhiji.

5. Plain folk appeal. In propaganda regular appeal is made to the plain folk concept of the public because the people have a propensity for adopting the folkways. Keeping this idea well focused in their minds, politicians all over the world adopt signs which bear a close relation to common life. For example, the election symbols of the various parties in India are : a pair of bulls for the Congress, a lamp for the Jan Sangh, a cottage for the P.S.P., and the well-known hammer and sickle of the Communists etc. All these implements and objects are very near to folk life.

6. Bandwagon. The influence of the bandwagon is also utilised for the purpose of propaganda. People have a tendency to accept the majority opinion, because majority opinion has the power of suggestion. Hence, every preacher tries to convince the public that it is his opinion that is accepted by the majority. This method is seen in extensive use at the election time. Even though they have received very few votes, the different political parties keep on announcing that they have received many votes and are leading by a wide margin.

7. Card stacking. In this propaganda method, as is evident from its name, facts are twisted and moulded in order to make them appear favourable to one's own view while facts favouring the rival party are by hook or crook proved to be false. In this way, this is a one-sided propaganda. Evidently, this method of propaganda is immoral and misleading. Yet it finds extensive use both in the national as well as the international field. In the national sphere, the government newspapers print news favouring the government policies while the newspapers published by the other political parties print news which are prejudicial to the government's policies, but in both cases the actual news gets transformed because of its modifications to suit the needs of the two rivals. The commonplace fact is brought into prominence while the important fact is made to appear as if of secondary importance. And, the opposition has a peculiar tendency of blaming one particular department for almost everythings that happens to go wrong. Much the same sort of thing happens in the international field also. The Chinese newspapers are persisting in their propaganda against India and are continuing to say that it were the Indians who attacked their soldiers, and the aggression was performed by the Indians who invaded their territory. Similarly, the Pakistan newspapers are also persistently stating that India is making military preparations that threaten the sovereignty and independence of Pakistan.

ESSENTIAL ELEMENTS IN EFFECTIVE PROPAGANDA

Social psychology can do much towards rendering propaganda measures effective. Social psychologists conducted many experiments to discover the means whereby propaganda could be rendered more effective. In all these experiments it was seen consistently that the effect of propaganda is dependent upon the strength of its psychological basis. Kimball Young has defined the following four factors as the psychological basis of propaganda :[3]

1. The object of propaganda as related to the audience.

2. Every element on the basis of which propaganda made more effective and concise.

3. Specific suggestions related to the propaganda and other psychological methods.

4. The effect of propaganda on ideas, viewpoints, values and actions.

The foregoing description of effective propaganda can be condensed into the following seven laws of successful

3. Young, K., *Handbook of Psychology* (1951), pp. 507-08.

propaganda enunciated by Kretch and Crutchfield, based on different experiments conducted by them :[4]

1. Suggestions pertaining to the satiation of some need or motive are easily and promptly accepted. Hence, the orator should base his propaganda on the need and motives of the people.

2. Suggestions offered in indistinct and indeterminate circumstances are accepted more easily than when the suggestions forthcoming pertain to a distinct circumstance. For this reason, the successful orator creates confusing circumstances and then offers suggestions for their solution.

3. The suggestions that concur with the prevailing belief and notions in whatever human group the propaganda is being conducted are the easily acceptable ones.

4. Indirect propaganda is more effective than direct propaganda. People should not come to know of the subject which is being thus propagated among them.

5. The propaganda should have the sanction of society. The suggestions that are given should be in keeping with the general needs of the common people. People should be made to feel that the orator is giving expression to their, and not his own, thoughts.

6. In order to arouse effective excitation, it is necessary that the languages, choice of words, pronunciation and the mode of speech should be such that it may impress the audience at which the propaganda is directed.

7. Propaganda can be countered by contradictory propaganda. The best countering thought or idea can be that which includes the proposal for the most prolonged appeasement of most of the social and economic needs of the people.

Direct and Indirect Media of Propaganda

Of the various media of propaganda, the platform is the most direct. Besides this, the press, radio, cinema, literature, etc., are the indirect media of propaganda. Among the direct

4. Kretch and Crutchfield, *Theory and Problems of Social Psychology*, pp. 357-60.

media of propaganda can be included processions, meetings, slogan shouting, etc. In these methods the orator or the person involved in the propaganda personally appears before the public and informs them of whatever he wants to get off his chest. In this, his physical appearance also influences the audience. In the case of the indirect media, the orator himself is not present before the audience. His ideas and thoughts become known to the public through the medium of literary magazines. His voice can be heard over the radio and he can be seen speaking upon the cinema screen. As a general rule, the direct media or propaganda are more successful than the indirect media. But, on the other hand, indirect media have the added benefit that their propaganda can comprehend a greater number of people, which is not the case with the means of direct propaganda. To take on example, the lecture given over the radio can reach a few million people, whereas the speech delivered from the platform can be heard at most by a few thousand people. In actual fact, the type or means of propaganda depends upon the type and the objects of the propaganda. In case where the actual personality of the speaker is very effective, direct propaganda can be far more beneficial than the indirect means of propaganda. As it generally happens, the presence of a leader and speaker of the calibre of Mr. Nehru is enough to attract a few thousand people to present themselves at his speech. They are influenced not only by what he speaks but also by his actions and his individual personality.

There can be any number of the media of propaganda but only the main ones shall be mentioned here. These media are the following :

(1) Platform, (2) Press, (3) Radio, (4) Television, (5) Cinema, (6) Religion, (7) Education, (8) Literature, (9) Meetings, Processions and Slogans, (10) Use of Force.

1. Platform. The platform is the oldest, and even today, the most important medium of propaganda. In the field of politics, all political parties make use of platform for purpose of propaganda of the party's policies. The contestants contesting the elections try to gain the votes of the electors by speaking from the platform. Not only in India is the platform an important medium of propaganda, but also in such progressive countries as the United States of America, the platform is the main medium of political propaganda. The late president of U.S.A., President Kennedy, made extensive use of this medium in his election campaign. Often, the great leaders are also very good orators. Their speeches have the influence of magic upon the public listening to them. The medium of platform is possessed of some advantages which are not available in the other forms of propaganda. Its greatest advantage arises from the fact, which has been mentioned earlier, that the speaker is personally present in front of the audience. In this he has the opportunity of entrancing and attracting the public by his personal qualities and his personality. The platform exerts much influence from the point of view of communal guidance. Through this medium the speakers often succeed in arousing the desired emotion in the audience and coaxing it to perform the deed that they want it to perform. This particular characteristic is not available in any other medium of propaganda. One main cause of this phenomenon is that the people collect in crowds to listen to a speech. Hence, mob psychology prevails in the audience. People are more influenced by emotions and their prudence and logical mind do not function. For this reason it is not at all difficult to come across incidents where the orator has aroused the public and instigated it so much that the crowd has indulged in worst things from arson to murder. It is not possible to achieve this frenzy of emotion by any other means such as radio, cinema, etc., because the recipient of the inflammatory speech is an individual and not the member of a crowd and hence there is no occasion for blind emulation.

2. Press. The invention of the press led almost to a revolution in the sphere of propaganda. Propaganda effected through the medium of the press comprehends millions of people distributed over great distances. In every country millions of individuals read the newspaper habitually. Thus, the propaganda material published in them is transmitted easily to the public. The ideas expressed in the newspapers are more balanced and logical and it is for this reason that the press is considered the best means of propaganda in the educated society. It is now the regular practice of the leading political parties to have some special papers and magazines of its own. These papers and magazines regularly propagate the views and ideals of the party. Then, there are some government papers also which express and explain the policies and opinions and views of the government and put them before the people.

3. Radio. The most important medium that science has gifted to the field of propaganda is that of the wireless or radio as it is more commonly known. It is an established psychological fact that auditory perception is more effective than visual stimulation. The speech that is heard is more effective and influencing than the speech that is read. This is so because the recipient then hears the voice of the propagandist and in this way is to some extent influenced by his personal contact. It is the accepted thing for the prosperous families today to listen to the radio. There are public radios in the villages and many individuals collect to listen to them. In the towns, there are radios in the betel shops, restaurants and other public places and it is only rarely that the blaring of these instruments does not fall on human ears. In this way, while the press may carry its propaganda only to the educated, the field open to radio includes the uneducated. Its only limitation is in the case of the deaf. Another characteristic of the radio as a medium of propaganda is that its broadcasts are more balanced and acceptable because it is under the control of the government. Propaganda heard over the radio is believed to be more veiled than that heard from the platform or read in the newspaper. Another characteristic of the radio is that one may immediately hear what is going on in a particular place even though one is a thousand miles away from the spot and one feels that he is seeing the incident occur with one's own eyes. The eye-witness account of the Independence Day celebrations in Delhi is broadcast ever the radio. Hearing this account when the listeners hear the Prime Minister speak, they feel as if they are physically witnessing the occasion.

4. Television. Among the various media of propaganda gifted to this sphere by science, the second is the television. The radio succeeds only in carrying the voice of the propagandist to the people but in the case of television this individual can be seen on the television screen alive and kicking. It is evident and need not be pointed out that the propaganda effected over the television will be more comprehensive and more effective than in the case of radio. Recently, in America it happened that while viewing a fight over the television, one person became so excited that he died of heart-failure. In this way, electronic media becomes a direct medium of propaganda.

5. Cinema. Generally speaking, the cinema is a means of recreation but it can also be used for purposes of propaganda. The government uses the cinema to propagate its policies and the plans for the nation's progress and various other programmes. The government has only recently made a film to propagate India's view on the Kashmir issue. Similarly, the government has made many films for propaganda in the public concerning Family planning, Life insurance, Co-operation, Small savings, Prize bonds, etc. In times of war and national crises, the government makes use of the medium of the cinema to propagate knowledge of the actual situation among the people. The medium of the cinema has the advantages of both auditory and visual perception and hence propaganda through it is more accurate and more effective. Compared to the television, the screen of the cinema is bigger and the persons and places seen on the screen appear to be real. Hence, the cinema may arouse and stimulate the feelings, emotions and motives of the people more effectively. In this way the propaganda effected through cinema is more effective in its psychological import. Propaganda through the medium of the cinema has another advantage. The same film for the propagation of the same subject may be simultaneously displayed at hundreds of different places and thus many thousands of people can be influenced at the same time. The main characteristic of the cinema is that by means of it the actual incident can be displayed in all its details without any question of its validity. The films that are made of war and of disturbances are so alive that the members of the audience feel that they are themselves present at the scene and witnessing it in its original form. Hence, they accept it without any reservation and the propaganda through it is completely accepted.

6. Literature. Even though it is considered a defect in literature to possess the tendency for propaganda yet literature has ever been one of the important media of propaganda. Some particular book, just as *The Communist Manifesto* propagates the communist viewpoint. Gandhiji and Vinobaji have written many books aiming at propagating the concept of Sarvodaya. Books such as these are directly aimed at propaganda. Besides them, propagation of thoughts and ideals also takes place through the medium of the various forms of literature, novel, drama, story, poetry, essay and other forms. Almost all the forms of literature have been utilised for the propagation of the communist viewpoint and thought in all countries. Besides political thought, concepts concerning the philosophy of life are also propagated among the masses through the medium of literature. To take a well-known example, a great amount of literature has been created to support the material viewpoint, and it hardly needs to be pointed out that material and empirical concepts and ideals are thereby propagated. When the country is faced with a crisis, the authors and poets of the country propagate the feelings of patriotism and self-sacrifice among the people. Propaganda through the medium of literature has an advantage in as much as it profoundly influences the feelings and experiences of the individual who reads it. No other medium of propaganda can affect this internal and hidden aspect of the human emotions with the same degree of profundity and neither is the influence of any other quite as long lasting as that of literature. Thus literature has proved to be particularly effective in the propaganda of an indirect nature. The reader unconsciously accepts the notions and ideals expressed by the various characters in the books that he reads. In this way, in propaganda through the medium of literature, the personality and the individual skill of the author or the propagandist are of much importance. The greater the degree of indirectness in propaganda through literature, the greater will be its effectiveness.

7. Religion. Religion and education have been used as the media for propaganda since the oldest times. Religion has a very deep influence upon the general public. The ideals or thoughts which possess the sanction of the religious texts or of saints or of great religious men find easy adaptation among the common people. Actually, religious sanction is further backed by divine sanction, or to put it differently, it is believed that God Himself is amenable to these ideals and thoughts. Further, to this is conjoined the popular conceptions of heaven and hell. It is generally believed that an individual attains heaven if he obeys the orders of God whereas he lands in hell and suffers all kinds of privations and troubles if he behaves in contradiction to the wishes of God. Hence, the things that have religious sanction are easily propagated and circulated. Realising this importance of religion many people try to show agreement between their views and the views expressed in the religious texts. One of the main causes of the wide acceptance of the views of Mahatma Gandhi was his religious influence, Had he not been a great soul, a Mahatma, his thoughts could not have found such great popularity in a religious minded country as India.

8. Education. Education is the main medium for the propagation of thoughts, ideals and values. From the very ancient times, the leaders in every race and nation have favoured the idea of imparting national education to the public in order to circulate nationalistic thought among the people. Even if some foreigners want to propagate their own thought in any country, they turn to education for this. The Christian missionaries made comprehensive use of the medium of education in the propagation of their own religion. Nowadays, many governments resort to education to propagate views favouring them among the coming generations. In Germany, Hitler made every effort to change the views of the boys and girls to concur with his own through the medium of education. In communist countries the government everywhere has control over the education and propagates its own ideals among the future generation. The children are taught to think in a particular way. A major characteristic of education as a means of propaganda is that through it only proper and logical facts can be propagated. And because education develops the personality of the individual and increases the degree of prudence in them, it may propagate only those thoughts and notions that are propounded with the help of profound and subtle arguments.

9. Meetings, processions and slogans. Meetings, processions and slogans have their own importance for propaganda concerning the political, economic and religious spheres. Often the economic organisation, labour unions and the unions of various kinds of employees hold meetings to give currency to their views and to circulate them among the public. They take out processions and shout slogans. The special importance of these media of propaganda is that they arouse and stimulate violently the passions and emotions of the people. People participating in meetings and processions behave just like the people in a crowd. They lose much of their prudence and gain in suggestibility. And thus they are easily amenable to being led in favour of or against any particular subject. Slogans are sentences in which the fundamental idea of the propaganda is conveniently condensed. These sentences are so composed as to facilitate their easy memorisation and repetition. The words used in them are such that they easily attract the attention of the audience and affect them emotionally. Slogans are shouted in a state of emotional instability and at the top of the speaker's voice. If slogan-shouting is done collectively, the emotional disturbance spreads rapidly from the epicentre to the people. In the days when the independence movement was at its height, the slogan 'Britishers ! Quit India' was seen deeply affecting the public. Similarly, slogans concerning the Swarajya and Swadeshi were fairly sufficient to propagate the viewpoints in the public.

10. Use of force. Of course, indirect propaganda is more effective than direct propaganda, and hence it does not call for the use of force but even then the use of force has always remained one of the important weapons of propaganda. According to Hadamovsky, force and propaganda have never been completely antagonistic towards each other. The use of force can be a part of propaganda. From the very ancient times, rulers and government resorted to the use of force in order to propagate their own respective views among the public. And in the field of religion, force has been the main weapon of propaganda. The Muslim religious preachers raised the flag of their religion in many countries on the strength of the sword. The Christians also fought wars in the name of religion, and where they did not fight they suppressed the people by other means and propagated their own religion. For example, the Christian missionaries in India loaned money to the Hindus of backward tribes on the condition that they get their religious stock of hair cut. Failing to do this, the Hindus had to return the principal along with the interest! If they accepted the conversion to Christianity, even their loan was wiped out. Dictators such as Hitler, Mussolini and Stalin made extensive use of force in propagating their own ideas and ideals. But all these examples do not prove that the use of force is an appropriate medium of propaganda, nor do they adduce any justification for it. Its greatest defects lie in the fact that in this method something is externally forced upon the people. The people continue to pay respect to it as long as the force is maintained but the moment the force is removed the people want to give it up. Besides this, the use of force for the purpose of propagation leads to the fostering of revolutionary and mutinous ideas within society and a time may come when this force may explode with such violence that it may succeed in destroying the propagandist as well as his propaganda. In history, the people who resorted to the use of force in their campaigns of propaganda are remembered with loathing and disgust. Hence, now the use of force is no longer recognised as an important and appropriate medium of propaganda.

PROPAGANDA PROPHYLAXIS

The counteracting of misleading and deceptive propaganda is an important and serious problem. Consequently, modern governments have started paying attention to it. Many psychologists have experimented upon this problem. The experiments of Biddle and Collier are important. In a general way, the following suggestions can be made for counteracting misleading propaganda and advertisements :

1. Informing the public of the misleading propaganda. In order that misleading propagation should be checked, it is necessary that some social and governmental institutions should constantly carry out research in this direction and should inform the public of its findings. The Propaganda Analysis Institute of New York performs this function. The public can be warned to beware of misleading propaganda through the medium of newspapers, magazines, radio, posters, books and pamphlets.

2. Contradicting propaganda. An important method of counteracting misleading propaganda is contradictory propaganda. For example, if the people can be made to understand thoroughly that there can be no panacea of all ills or that the energy and power lost over many years cannot be recovered in a few hours, the public can be prevented from being deceived by propaganda of this nature. Healthy tendencies and beliefs can be created in different spheres in the public by contradictory behaviour propaganda.

3. Legal prohibition. The government should take strong legal steps to prevent false propagation and threaten the unscrupulous individuals who indulge in such activities. Propaganda of this kind should be declared to be illegal and people who are found indulging in such practices should be punished sternly by the government.

4. Education. Generally, it is the uneducated individual who is likely to be influenced by misleading propaganda. The educated people are not so easily misled. Hence, the most important means to counteracting misleading and deceptive propaganda is education. Through scientific education, the people in the public should be taught to judge everything on the basis of logic and intellect so that they should not be deceived.

5. Economic welfare. Under some economic conditions people are easily misled. For example, it is usually seen that it is the poor who is easily deceived because he is always on the lookout for something which costs less and provides greater utility. Hence the skilled individuals succeeds in making false promises and giving them something spurious in place of the genuine goods. Therefore, some economic improvement is also necessary in order to counteract false propaganda.

6. Social emancipation. There are many social situations that create such superstitions and prejudices that it becomes easy to practise deception even in the field of propaganda. In order to counteract this, some degree of social emancipation is also necessary.

To conclude, it may be said that if misleading and deceptive propaganda is to be counteracted, it is necessary to attack the problem from all angles. The public should be educated. The misleading propaganda should be exposed. The government should sternly punish the miscreants. Propaganda contradicting it should be effected, and all circumstances, whether social or economic, should be eliminated from the society.

QUESTIONS FOR EXERCISE

1. What is propaganda? Explain the psychological basis of its appeal.
2. Write short note on-Propaganda Prophylaxis.

Part III

Psychology in Industry

12

PSYCHOLOGY APPLIED TO INDUSTRY

Psychology is seen to be present in whatever sphere of human life that boasts of human relationships or human endeavour. In the sphere of industry, the relations between the labourers and the owners present a large variety, and one comes across many specimens of behaviour. Industry has many problems, including those of human conduct. For example, cases of labour unrest and dissatisfaction are not uncommon. Many causes culminate in unwillingness on their part to co-operate with the management, and in the desire to coerce the management into paying wages out of all proportion to the work achieved. They indulge in such inflammatory practices as occasional or frequent strikes that lead to factories being closed, ultimately causing loss to the management and equally to the nation. On the other hand, bosses and factory owners are reputedly callous of their unconcern for the welfare of their employees. The least disturbance finds them indulging in lockouts, a process that has disastrous results as the piece-wage employee knows to his detriment. The country loses at the same time. Basically, all these problems are problems of human behaviour, and hence psychology is required to solve them.

DIFFICULTIES IN PRODUCTION

Greater and better quality production in industry requires some very definite prerequisites. Quality of machinery is an undeniable requirement, but it is no less important that it be operated by skilful, and, moreover, willing hands. How can this skill be gauged? There being a vast variety of functions and occupations in a factory, how can one discover the most adequate person for a particular job? Of the many hundreds of individuals who apply for jobs in factories, how is one to select the people who will prove to be the most efficient? For high levels of production, it is essential that the machines should be designed so as to avoid fatigue to the operator as much as is practicable. Lighting should be adequate to avoid inconvenience, accidents and unnecessary strain upon the eyes of the workers. Often, individuals lose their enthusiasm very soon for a routine kind of work? How are their interest and attention to be sustained and recreated? What should be the proper plan of a factory so that accidents are avoided? Psychology can help in the solution of all these problems that face the industry.

PROBLEMS OF DISTRIBUTION

With production the work of industry does not come to an end. It has not concluded. What is equally important is that these produced goods be sold, and sold at profitable rates. If the industry does not meet with success in this direction, all production is worthless, whatever its inherent quality. And for goods to be sold in the market, it is essential that the common buyer be acquainted with the commodity, with its quality. But for anything to happen it is necessary that there should be the necessity for a demand for the commodity, and that the consumer be aware of this need. Here, advertisement pays good dividends and successful advertising is based upon psychological appeal. Evidently, psychology is no less important for the purposes of distribution.

CONDITIONS OF WORK

In industry, the condition under which work is undertaken has an important influence upon the labourer. In healthy conditions, the labourers are healthy, and a general atmosphere of well being and satisfaction pervades the community. If, on the other hand, labourers are required to work in bad conditions, the number of casualties through accidents increases and this leads to dissatisfaction among the labourers. Conditions of work include many tangible and intangible factors such as proper sanitary conditions, arrangements for good air and water, provision of adequate resting places, quiet atmosphere, good climate, proper lighting, and cordial relations between the workers and the bosses with smooth liaison between the two. Guidance at the hands of psychologist brings about the best results in each case. The psychologist must co-operate with the ophthalmic surgeon to decide the best angle of lighting. Colour combinations within the factory premises are known to affect the efficiency of the worker, experiments having revealed that a soothing combination of colour effects improves general efficiency and also reduces the accident rate. And it is for the psychologist to pronounce sentence as to when the machines and general factory premises should be painted.

HUMAN INVOLVEMENTS

Having chosen the right man for the job in a factory is not the end of the problem, as it is necessary, for high levels of production, that the efficiency of the worker be maintained and even improved if his optimum has not been achieved. Labourer is a human being, and not a cog in the wheel. If his talent is to be exploited, it is necessary to keep in view human motives and human psychology. Psychology can easily help to solve all the human problems that crop up in an industry.

FIELD OF INDUSTRIAL PSYCHOLOGY

The foregoing description should have convinced the reader that psychology pervades every aspect of industry, and can do good. Its actual importance for the modern era can be gauged by the knowledge that application of psychology to the field of industry has led to the emergence and development of a separate branch of psychology, known as industrial psychology. In the words of Blum, "Industrial psychology is simply the application or extension of psychological facts and principles to the problems concerning human relations in business and industry." Human relations in industry came into the limelight under extensive investigation after the Industrial Revolution in Europe. Realisation of the magnitude of the problem led to the development of industrial psychology in the twentieth century, a science which tells of the capability and interest of an individual for a particular function. It helps to select the correct person for specialised jobs. It defines the principle whereby proper conditions can be created to achieve the maximum efficiency with the less possible amount of exertion and fatigue. One important aspect of industrial psychology is job analysis. Every factory and mill provides various kinds of work, all of which are analysed by the psychologist who then lays down the qualities that are required of the individual who is to perform it. In a factory, there must be constant supervision of the labourers, work. And industrial psychology effects improvements in the methods of supervision and observation. It helps to maintain an atmosphere in the workhouse which promotes cordial relations between the worker and boss. It puts forward constructive suggestions for improving the efficiency of the average worker, makes occasional tests of their efficiency in order to provide a check on his progress or failure. It has been pointed out earlier, and is fairly evident, that industry today has much need for effective advertisement. And it is industrial psychology that can help in effective and strong advertisement and propaganda. Nowadays, industrial psychology has extended its function to include advice on the manufacture of machinery that can help to minimise fatigue and improve production.

HUMANIST THOUGHT IN INDUSTRY

In the present era, there are many factors promoting the development and increase of humanist thought in the field of industry, reputedly a mechanised giant not amenable to human approaches. No longer is the labourer looked upon in the light of a small cog in the wheel of progress, a mere tool in the massive production machinery. Realisation that industry is to benefit by the happiness and satisfaction of the labour class has dawned, and industrial progress has been allied to labour welfare. This humanisation of industry is a state of human thought for which psychology must be praised. It is due to the prevalence of such enlightened thinking that the capitalist class can be persuaded to think of the welfare of their workers. Stress on the alliance between the physical and mental aspects of human labour is the contribution of psychology. It contends that efficient physical endeavour is not possible in the absence of mental satisfaction. This fact must be kept in mind when improving the methods of working in the factory.

In this manner, industrial psychology is rendering valuable assistance in the entire field of industry. As knowledge of the human individual increases in the domain of psychology, the importance of psychology in the sphere of industry will grow.

PERSONNEL SELECTION

Difficulty in the Selection of Workers

Modern psychology has by now indubitably established that individuals differ from each other in respect of their abilities, qualities of the personality, capabilities and interests. On the other hand, different functions within various industries require particular qualities and abilities in the individuals obliged to perform them. Hence, for this it becomes essential that for a particular function only that person should be retained who possesses the requisite qualities and abilities, a requirement that leads to the problem of selection. This problem has a positive as well as a negative aspect. In its negative aspect the activity of selection consists in sorting out the undesirable individuals from among all those who have applied for appointment to a particular post, while in its positive aspect it consists in selecting one individual from all those who, *prima facie,* seem to qualify for the job. Such selection must take into account the interests, requirements, abilities and attitudes of the applicants.

Why is Personnel Selection Essential?

The main cause of the necessity of personnel selection is the fact of individual difference. Many experiments have led to the establishment of the fact that abilities in individual beings differ considerably as a consequence of hereditary differences. Certain qualities are innate and cannot be improved upon much through training. An individual's attitudes, mental tendency, etc., become fairly evident even in his infancy, and in greater or less degree they remain the same throughout his life. These attitudes have considerable importance for an individual's life. Generally speaking, any work that one can perform best is the one in the direction of which one has a mental tendency. It is not in the mental make-up of every individual to be a successful and skilful engineer, and neither is every man made to be a giant tycoon of business. Some children evince great interest in manual work of a skilled nature and in science, and it is such children who usually develop into good engineers or scientists. All these psychological facts go to prove that the once respected dictum that any individual can be fitted into any job and that training can prepare an individual for any function is wrong. Hence, personnel selection is very much in vogue in every industry in the modern world.

Two Aspects of Personnel Selection

Personnel selection has two aspects, one of which is the analysis of each and every particular independent function in an industry in order to establish the qualities and abilities required of the individual performing it. The second function of this selection is to examine all candidates and determine the qualities and abilities that each of them possesses. The first function is called job analysis while the second aspect is called worker's analysis.

JOB ANALYSIS

Aims of Job Analysis

It has been pointed out before that the main objective of job analysis is selection of personnel. But it can also have other objectives such as improvements in the methods of working, training employees, promotion of employees, obviating accidents and protection of health, etc.

What is Job Analysis?

Defining job analysis Blum has remarked, "A job analysis is an accurate study of the various components of a job. It is concerned not only with an analysis of the duties and conditions of work, but also with the individual qualifications of the worker." It is evident that job analysis will reveal the duties of individuals in a particular job or profession, as also the conditions in which they will be required to work. It will also bring out the qualities required of an individual aspiring to perform some definite function or piece of work. According to J.D. Hackett, in the process of job analysis, the fundamental elements of a job are established and clarified, while simultaneously the abilities desirable in the worker are known, the abilities that will help him to perform his function skilfully. Thus, job analysis has two aspects, one the analysis of duties and conditions of work, and the other the analysis of qualities desired in the worker or employee.

Advantages of Job Analysis

Job analysis confers many advantages. On the basis of 401 essays concerned with job analysis, Zerga pointed out twenty advantages and utilities of job analysis. One is the increase in efficiency, as well as increase in the mutual feelings of workers since everyone is happy to be employed in the job he cherishes. Job analysis can help to determine the salary or wages accruing to the employee for a particular function performed by him. Job analysis helps in the classifications of professions and occupations, it thereby becoming possible to determine the qualities and abilities required for them. Through job analysis it also becomes possible to determine the extent of training necessary for a specific individual to be given for a particular job of work. Job analysis determines the duty of everyone in his own job by determining the responsibility inherent in any kind of work.

Various Components of a Job

Now, the first thing to be mentioned in connection with job analysis is the presence of various components in a job. Headings of information collected in this connection are the following :

1. Identification of the job,
2. Number employed,
3. Statement of duties,
4. Machines used,
5. Analysis of operations,
6. Conditions of work,
7. Pay and incentives,
8. Relation to other allied jobs,
9. Opportunities for transfer and promotion,
10. Time and nature of training,
11. Personal requirements :
    - (a) General — Age, Sex, Nationality, Martial Status,
    - (b) Physical,
    - (c) Educational,
    - (d) Previous experience,
    - (e) General and special abilities,
    - (f) Temperamental and character requirements.

As is evident from the above list, there is extensive collection of data regarding job analysis.

Methods of Job Analysis

Of the many methods employed in job analysis, the main are the following :

1. Individual psychographic method,
2. Questionnaire method,
3. Job psychographic method,
4. Job analysis by text,
5. Motion study method.

These methods will now be described in brief as follows :

1. Individual psychographic method. In this method, the mental peculiarities of an individual successful in a particular kind of job are examined, a list of these peculiarities prepared and this list transcribed in figure form on graph. This provides some standard of judgement in future recruitments for the same job.

2. Questionnaire method. A list of questions is prepared on the basis of the different qualities of personality concerned with the job. This list is then provided to the individuals doing that job, and they are asked to answer these questions. An analysis of the answers received helps to reveal the special qualities necessary for the job, a list of which can now be prepared. This, too, helps in the future selection of candidates for the job in question.

3. Job psychographic method. According to Viteles, there are three things essential to job psychographic method :

(a) Accurate classifications of mental qualities,

(b) valid method of evaluation,

(c) direct examination or analysis by trained examiners.

In this manner, in this method, some specialist analysts study the work, and they evolve a valid and standard method of evaluation. They prepare a very accurate list in which the various mental qualities required for the job are properly and reliably classified. A graph of these qualities is prepared so that selection of candidates for the job may become easier.

4. Job analysis by test. In the test method, some reliable and valid tests are performed on the basis of essential qualities and abilities the candidates are tested for selection and suitability by these tests.

5. Motion study method. Under this method, the speed of an individual worker in performing some job and time consumed therein are both noted. Similar examinations being performed on other individuals doing the same work, the results obtained are compared. Such a study of speed and time helps in job analysis and classification of the workers.

Job analysis can be done by any one or more of these methods, the choice of method being governed by the situation or circumstances.

WORKER'S ANALYSIS

Essential Elements in Worker's Analysis

The second step in personnel selection is that of worker's analysis. In worker's analysis, as is apparent from the term used to denote it, detailed information regarding the applicant's qualities, abilities, experience and other factors is obtained. Roughly speaking, worker's analysis requires information under the following heads :

1. Age,
2. Caste,
3. Sex,
4. Nationality,
5. Physical health and characteristics,
6. Education and training,
7. Experience,
8. Level of intelligence,
9. Mental abilities and their level,
10. Interests and aptitudes,
11. Personality traits.

Having gathered the above information regarding a particular applicant, it becomes, possible to determine the kind of job he is likely to prove proficient in, and the kind of job in which he tends to be a failure. Worker's analysis also reveals the extent and nature of training that a particular individual will require before he can successfully enter a particular profession. Worker's analysis can also help to make a rough estimate for the remuneration that can justifiably be paid to the worker, for the job in which he is expected to excel. Worker's analysis prepares a picture of an individual's personal excellences, by virtue of which it is also called individual analysis.

Methods of Worker's Analysis

Worker's analysis is now a matter of science, so that it has come to use certain specific methods. Broadly speaking, the following are the various methods used in worker's analysis :

1. Application blank,
2. Letters of recommendation,
3. Academic record,
4. Psychological tests,
5. Group tests,
6. Rating,
7. Interview.

It is not essential that all the above methods be used to analyse the abilities of any individual worker, a selection of any one of them being required to meet the need in a particular case. It will be in keeping with the context to glance briefly at these methods :

1. Application blank. Nowadays, the first step in the worker's analysis is the filling in of a blank by the applicant. This application blank can be designed to reveal much information of a varied kind, sometimes being so successful as to reveal the individual's entire background. In the application blank, the individual provides information regarding his age, sex, caste, nationality, earlier or past level of education, training, personal experience, history, etc. What kind of information should be provided in the application blank is determined differently in different professions. Professions that are likely to be influenced by the worker's attitudes, mental inclinations, interests, etc., require that information regarding them should also be provided in the application blank. Many advertisers do not make a detailed report of what the applicant is expected to include in his application; they make a brief mention of a very few things. Application blanks of this kind do not qualify for scientific consideration. An application blank should preferably contain detailed enquiries regarding all important facts and details. Research in this direction can help to form outlines of application blanks for various professions, and according to that outline blanks can be provided to the various applicants and aspirants. Often, evidence is required to substantiate the facts detailed in the application.

2. Letters of recommendation. Letters of recommendation also help in worker's analysis. In this method, the aspirant producer's various recommendations, recommendations from his previous employer, the principal of his school or college, or from some respected stalwarts of society, etc. In these letters, in addition to the natural commendation, some degree of ability is also evidenced, but often these letters are seen to contain many confusing and incorrect pieces of information regarding the individual. One of the simplest ways of misleading the intended employer is to include mention of many qualities that the aspirant does not possess, or to overemphasize the qualities that he is fortunate enough to possess. Are a general rule, such letters of recommendation usually prove to be hindrances rather than helps to the process of job analysis, but if they are valid and justified, reliable and tempered, they can definitely promote job analysis or rather worker's analysis.

3. Academic records. Different professions require different levels of education as an essential qualification. Academic records are evidences of the individual's educational progress and proficiency. These sometimes include cumulative records of the universities.

4. Psychological tests. But the most important and valid method of worker's analysis is that of psychological testing in which the applicant's mental ability, interest, personality and particularly attitude are tested. Results of these tests should be employed with exemplary caution since they can also lead to very serious mistakes.

5. Physical tests. There are some jobs that require physical fitness of various kinds as an essential prerequisite, for example, the eye-sight of a railway guard should be normal and not impaired. And for satisfaction on this point, different physical tests have been devised to suit various professions and their requirements. Nowadays, physical or medical tests have become an essential part of examinations for government jobs.

6. Group tests. There are some professions in which many workers have to work collectively but even if they work individually they are constantly thrown together in the process of their work. Hence in their case, it is essential for them to possess certain group services. Attention is paid to the individual's ability when he is being considered for promotion, over and above the extent of his service. It sometime occurs that an individual's ability and efficiency are so great that he is given promotion by superseding other senior officials. Private business lays much stress on work as well as on ability. The employer stands to gain something if his employees work better and more, so that he is easily enabled to enhance their wages or to give them a greater share in the profits. But in certain occupations, inside and outside the government structure, where the employer himself does not superintend the work, or where, there is no objective or concrete employer himself, or where the employer is of the ingratiating type, promotion depends more on pleasing authority than upon seniority, ability, or results obtained. In professions in which there are no definite laws and rules governing promotion of workers, promotion takes place through the pleasure of those in authority.

From the above description, it is evident that promotion depends upon the following factors :

(1) Seniority,

(2) Ability,

(3) Better and more work,

(4) Kindness of the authority.

Promotion on the Basis of Seniority

In most occupations and services, wages of the employee increase somewhat every year, and thus seniority is a basis of promotions common to almost all occupation. Seniority as a basis of promotions has psychological sanction, as every worker wishes that in view of his greater period of service rendered, he should be given a post above the newcomers. Absence of any definite rules regarding promotion on the grounds of seniority leads to discontent, and people lose interest in work. At the same time, they show no inclination to stick to any one profession. Naturally, the profession as a whole tends to suffer through such vagrancy as every new entrant takes his time in learning the ropes, and if the old ones keep running away, there is much efficiency and effort lost. It is for this reason that in every service, wages improve with seniority, and in most cases promotion also takes place on the same basis. But it is incorrect to consider seniority the sole basis of promotion. Just as the senior individual desires promotion, the more able and efficient also desire promotion and better prospects. If his talent is allowed to lie dormant, and if he has to wait a number of years before he comes into authority, or if he is required to constantly serve under a less efficient man, he is inclined to lose patience and become dissatisfied. His mind wanders out of the periphery of his work, and he feels imposed upon if asked to obey the less able individual who is in authority. And this insubordination leads to defective administration. Hence, where actuality is concerned, ability should also be taken into consideration along with seniority when the question of promotion comes up.

Promotion on the Basis of Ability

The second major basis of promotion is individual ability that takes very young people to the tops of their professions in very short periods of time. And if seniority be the sole basis, then an individual starting at the lowest rung can never reach the top. For this ability and consideration of ability is very essential. Yet, for this reason alone, it is not safe to completely discount seniority, as many occupations place the premium upon experience. Secondly, having put in years of hard and honest service, the employee desires that he be given some token of appreciation for his selfless service, so that if he is not promoted he becomes dissatisfied. And, there can be no general rule regarding the alternate propriety of seniority or ability as the basis of promotion in any individual case, or any single profession. Generally speaking, wages or salary should be commensurate with the years of service put in. But before a key post, or a position that wields very wide authority can be handed to a person, it is essential to inquire into his antecedents and evaluate his abilities.

Promotion on the Basis of Results

Those in authority everywhere, whatever the profession, whatever the service, desire that their subordinates should give off their best. Where private business is concerned, the employer is interested is one thing exclusively, the results in terms of work, both as regards quantity and as regards quality. Hence in such cases, promotion also is dispensed on the basis of results obtained by the individual under review. This particular method of promotion gives very good results in a large majority of cases since it not only satisfies the instincts and interests of those interested in efficiency and ability, but also appears in the form of added inducement to those not so inclined. It leads most people to emulating others, with the result that very good results are achieved all round.

Promotion on the Basis of Kindness or Recommendation

Recommendation or kindness of authorities is perhaps the worst method of promotion. Yet, it is very much in vogue in this enlightened age. In government and semi-government organisations, it is the ingratiating type of individual who figures the highest on lists of promotions as he makes his presence felt by grovelling to the authorities, by entertaining officers, by making judicious presents to them and to members of their families or by benefiting them in other respects. Lacking this effusive sociability, even the most efficient, honest and hardworking individual with a good seniority remains in one position without any hope of progress. Cases of this nature also present very bad examples to other workers, with the result that the best part of their energies are wasted in pleasing the authorities than in working.

Modes of Promotion

The above description of the bases of promotions also reveals the mode of promotion. In fact, an individual has to be selected for promotion in much the same manner in which he is to be selected for appointment. In both cases, much care and understanding should be used in making the selection. What more usually happens is that the care taken in selecting an individual for appointment is far greater than the attention paid to his promotion. And in most cases, promotion is done on the basis of seniority, one of the most prevalent methods. Promoting the individual on the basis of his ability is none the worse. Another good and fairly reliable method of promotion, is the one based upon efficiency and results obtained in previous position. But to promote an individual on one's whim, on recommendation, on one's pleasure, is not at all a good method, instead a thoroughly undesirable one. It is unscientific, unethical and harmful also.

Importance of Promotion

Promotion is an important aspect of every profession. Its propriety is based on the psychological fact that every employee wants promotion and improvement on the basis of efficiency, ability or years of service. Promotion is also an important inducement to the employee to work better and to work more. Promotion gives the worker enthusiasm and confidence, encourages him to produce even better results. Existence of definite rules of promotion induces a sense of security in the employee, as then he can decide on the method he is to follow in order to benefit and gain promotion. Under these conditions, they are not only not discouraged, but are even inclined to try even harder. For this reason, it is essential that in every establishment the rules of promotion be definite and precisely laid down so that there be no case for complaint. Seniority, ability and the quantum of work done form the propriety of promotions. Promotion based on recommendations or personal likes or dislikes, or because of considerations of personal gains is completely improper and unjustified. Such behaviour kills the initiative of other workers and their efficiency falls. Evidently, promotion in any service is as important for the employer as it is for the employee. The employer can use that as a basis for selecting good workers, and thus his work benefits. The worker's inducement to continue his effort is maintained. He is even inclined to improve the quality of his work. But promotion is actually beneficial only when its rules are precise, and are so known to every employee. Its best use can be made only if its basis is correct, proper and scientific.

HUMAN RELATIONS IN INDUSTRY

Inconsiderate Conduct towards Employees

In the older days, the workers in factories were regarded as objects no better than the machines and tools used in it. Behaviour towards them did not qualify to be human. And in many cases, the workers were no better off than slaves. In the days of British India, in the margarine blue factories of the country, many national leaders had to raise their voices in protest against the cruelty meted out to workers under the owners of these factories. In the south, too, owners of factories and mines did not treat their employees at all well. The worker was daunted into submission, and in many occupations the worker was often turned out without prior notice or any compensation. In cases of accident, fatal or incapacitating, the worker and his family were reduced to abject misery and impecunious poverty. When machines were invented, women and children were also added to the labour force, no concessions being made to their delicate condition and ideally exalted position in life. Even when leave was absolutely necessary for women it was not permitted, and pregnant women were often turned out of work. The systems in the factory and working conditions were almost completely deplorable. The owner was concerned solely with his own profit, and the conditions in which work was carried on was not his concern. It was outside the sphere of his thinking to worry about air, light, sanitation, water, etc. that were or were not supplied in adequate quantities. There being no legal bar to the extent of work to be forced out of the labourer, the owners forced the poor workers to work long hours on very small remuneration. Promotion was a term unheard of in that time. Incentives to workers were not required, and equally not tendered. In this way, exploitation was the rule of the day.

Call for Human Behaviour and Decent Conditions

Propagation of socialist and democratic principles caused people to revolt against such conditions. Labour unions were formed at most places. Different professions made their own organisations. In progressive countries labourers and other workers in different professions combined together to voice their desire for better working conditions, and for workers in industries to be treated as human beings should be. Democratic and socialist governments also turned their attention to this problem. Besides this, thinkers and scientists came forward with the suggestion that because of absence of proper human relations in industry, workers were not the only losers, the government and the owners also suffered. This led to the propagation of the thought that efforts should be made to improve working conditions and human relations in industry.

Human Relations in Industrial Administration

In industry, human relations are in evidence in two spheres, in that of administration, and that of welfare. In the field of administration it is the relations between the authority and the worker which are important. A labourer is not a machine, nor a cog in a wheel. He is replete with such human elements as motives, emotions, feelings, hopes, desires and needs. He wants as much as any other that his good work be praised and that his efforts should bring him additional gain. Love and respect are things for which he yearns. Treated like a human being by those in authority above him, his work becomes very much easier and much more pleasurable for him. Various incidents of labour strikes and lockouts were mainly of administrative origin. Administration of a factory involves proper and systematic organisation of the factory, besides human treatment of the workers. It is desirable that a feeling of security be induced in the worker by making precise and definite rules regarding appointment, promotion, etc. within the factory. The position entrusted to the worker should be made permanent. He should be made to know that the road to progress is straight and narrow, and that honesty is very much the best policy. Absence of these conditions is reason enough for the poor worker to feel dissatisfied and to lose his concentration in the work. A worker should be praised for any extraordinary effort that he may put in. He should also be made to benefit in some manner or the other if he does something unusually good. His salaries should be increased, so should his bonus, and he should be given a higher position. Conditions of work should be improved, and the workers of a high calibre be transferred to good places. Such factors being existent, the worker's inspiration in his work continues and so does his enthusiasm. Without these incentives no industry can achieve much good results.

Misunderstandings and differences of opinion between workers and authority are nothing to cause much worry, as they are part and parcel of life, all of them being human and capable of harbouring various kinds of emotions regarding each other. Hence, occasions of conflict are only too natural. Such problems of human relations require careful and tactful handling. If those in authority show laxity of mood, unscrupulous individuals may take undue advantage and turn in bad performances. If on the other hand, the authorities decide to make it rough for the workers, haul them up on every little thing, interfere constantly, offend their respect and threaten them off and on, it would be difficult for the poor workers to maintain their equanimity of mind and work enthusiastically. Actually, the attitude and nature of every worker differ from one to another, but, nevertheless, efforts must be made to maintain cordial relations between them.

Welfare in Industry

At an earlier stage in the development of human thought, the responsibility of an owner was supposed to end once the worker had been remunerated for his efforts on behalf of the owner. Economics as it stands today is more interested in welfare than in financial disposal of obligations. Governments of today are haunted with dreams of the visionary welfare state. Consequently, it is now conceded that besides paying wages to the worker, it is essential to attend to his welfare also. Human services, convenience and pleasures should be available to the worker as to any other individual. Atmosphere at home and in the office or factory should be congenial. They should get adequate opportunities of intellectual, material, moral and economic progress. Factors in their welfare would be the provision of such conveniences as convenient housing, educational and health service facilities, good food and adequate provision for rest and recreation. For female workers it is essential to provide more holidays and rest. Creches and maternity homes should be provided near the working premises for mothers. Special help should be forthcoming to workers when they are ill. Maternity benefit programmes are essential for women workers. Educational facilities should be provided for the children of workers. The future of the workers should also be made secure so that they should be able to concentrate upon their work wholeheartedly. Provident fund benefits, pensions and life insurance schemes are some of the ways in which this can be assured. In this way, it is now believed that the owners should do their best to provide for the integrated development of workers entrusted to their care by society.

Advantages of Welfare Activity

In fact, the mill-owners and industrialists get a certain

percentage of returns on the money that they spend in labour welfare, as this money improves the efficiency, skill and cooperation of the workers. And if in the process of working in a factory, a worker loses his life, or at least his capacity to earn money, it becomes the moral duty of the owner to arrange for the upkeep of his helpless family. Actually, money spent on labour welfare is more in the nature of investment than that of expenditure since whatever is spent ultimately influences the owner favourably. Increase in the labourer's skill means an economy in raw material and increase in production. Scientific selection of workers helps to eliminate the improper exploitation at the hands of middlemen, and this improves the peace and enthusiasm of the workers who work better. In the same manner, technical training of individuals involves an initial expenditure of huge sums of money, but finally it also means considerable additions to their income and profits because a trained individual works better than his untrained counterpart and reduces overall damage. He stands to gain because the trained labourer does better both in quantity and quality of work. An employer does not have to spend much in improving light, ventilation and other facilities on the factory premises, but they have a very great influence upon the health and performance of the workers, with the result that production improves in quality and quantity, percentage of absentees falls, workers do not complain of fatigue, and they less often fall a prey to disease. Healthful conditions of work encourage the workers to attain a peaceful frame of mind and think more kindly and favourably of their employers as they are conscious of the latter's concern for them. This improves their mutual relations, and the workers do not tend to migrate to other jobs very often. Welfare work in respect of prevention of accidents has obviously a very direct advantage for the employer, since he stands to lose just as much as the worker does. He is compelled by law to make some compensation in case of accident, besides which such occurrences lead to unrest among the other workers. If it is a trained worker who is involved in any serious accident, the employer is quite directly hit. Prevention of fire breaking out on the premises is a form of labour welfare that should be right after the employer's own heart, and should concur with his way of thinking. But, it also leads to the welfare of the workers' minds. Efficiency of workers can be increased by providing means and opportunity of rest and refreshment in the factory. Organisation of canteen helps them in getting food at the right time, and they can return to work shortly. It is in such ways as these that the employer stands to derive direct and indirect benefits from schemes of labour welfare.

LABOUR WELFARE

Definition of Labour Welfare

Labour welfare pertains to all such works or schemes that lead to the benefit of labour, but such a general statement does not satisfy the scientific mind. It is a term whose meaning is relative to time and place; as a result it is capable of change. According to the report of the Royal Commission on Labour, "The term 'welfare' as applied to the industrial worker, is one which must necessarily be elastic, bearing a somewhat different interpretation in one country from another, according to the different social customs, the degree of industrialisation and the educational development of the workers." In this manner, the meaning that the term 'labour welfare' will have in any specific country will depend upon the condition of the labourers there. Labour, in general, being uneducated in a country like India, the term will come to include their education also. As defined in the *Encyclopaedia of Social Sciences*, "Labour welfare implies the voluntary efforts of the employers to establish, within the existing industrial system, working and sometimes living conditions of employees beyond what is required by law, the custom of the industry and the condition of the market." Hence, the term labour welfare does not comprehend those activities that are necessitated by the laws of the country, the traditions and customs of industry in that country, or by conditions of the market. Instead, it means the voluntary actions on the part of the employer to improve the lot of his employees. The International Labour Organisation defines labour welfare in these words: "Workers' welfare should be understood as meaning such services, facilities and amenities which may be established in, or in the vicinity of undertaking to enable the persons employed in them to perform their work in healthy, congenial surroundings and provided with amenities conducive to good health and high morale." In this way, the term 'labour welfare' implies schemes and activities that produce conditions that improve the health of the workers as well as those circumstances that improve their morale. It may widely be taken to mean any voluntary action on the part of the employer that benefits the worker in any way. But it does not include any activity that the employer is compelled or coerced into performing, whatever be the benefit accruing to the labour class. Through the medium of labour welfare work, employers and industrialists try to achieve the integral or complete development of their employees.

Labour Welfare Activities

Labour welfare work is believed to be of three kinds :

1. Constitutional legal compulsions regarding the safety and working conditions of workers, etc.

2. Voluntary — Those works that the employer performs for the benefit of workers of his own volition, without any coercion being involved.

3. Mutual — This kind includes the welfare work done by labour unions in cooperation with each other.

Dr. Broughton's View

Dr. Broughton has divided works of labour welfare into two classes : (1) Intra-mural and (2) Extra-mural. The main ones among intra-mural works are :

1. **Scientific selection or appointment.** The scientific selection of workers for the various jobs within the factory.

2. **Industrial training.** Training in various factories for different jobs in the factory.

3. **Arrangement for light, fresh air and water.** The classification comprehends arrangements in the factory for cleanliness, whitewashing, ventilation, drinking water, bathrooms, lavatories, urinals, light, air-conditioning, etc.

4. **Prevention of accidents.** This includes arrangements for protection from dangerous machines, extreme temperatures, fire-fighting, etc.

5. **Other functions.** Such as canteen, provision of rest rooms, refreshment, etc.

Major extra-mural labour welfare functions are the following :

1. Provision of education. This includes adult education, social education, primary education, education of men, women and children, etc.

2. Arrangement of proper housing accommodation.

3. Medical service. This includes rest, cure, paid leave, free treatment, subsidized medical aid, etc.

4. Provision of inexpensive and nourishing food.

5. Facilities of recreation. Clubs, gymnasia, cinema, radio, reading-rooms, libraries, etc.

In addition to the above list, the following activities are also a part of labour welfare service :

(1) Social insurance scheme, (2) provident fund benefits, (3) pension, (4) sickness and maternity benefits, (5) arrangement of maternity homes and creches, (6) provision of co-operative societies, (7) arrangement of cultural programmes, (8) schooling of children.

Advantages to Employers from Intra-mural Welfare Work

In all modern countries, the employers do their best to introduce labour welfare programmes of various kinds because they have come to realise that the money they spend upon labour welfare is not completely lost to them. A very definite percentage of the advantage accruing from it is diverted to them ultimately in the form of increased production or better quality of work rendered by the happy workers. Working in healthy and congenial surroundings, the workers feel contented and delighted in the concern that the employer evinces for them. Cordial relations between employer and employees are thus precipitated, and the workers evince lesser desire to change employment at the least provocation. Prevention of an accident is a direct gain to the employer, even more so when the individual salvaged is a trained person whose training itself would have cost the establishment a packet. Even otherwise, in case of accident, the employer owes it to his conscience to compensate the family of the sufferer in some measure. Other workers in the factory develop a feeling of insecurity if the rate of accidents is high in their establishment. Schemes and plans for prevention of fire or for fire-fighting are a direct gain to the employer, as he would not like to have his factory go up in flames. Skill and efficiency are changing things, and likely to remain in the best condition if the worker is occasionally allowed to rest and refresh himself, either by nourishing himself or by relaxing. Easy availability of good and wholesome food takes a load off the worker's minds, as it is very convenient to eat in a canteen near the premises. In this manner, the owner of a factory stands to gain directly from intra-mural efforts at labour welfare.

Advantages to Owners from Extra-mural Labour Welfare

An owner also gains financially from extra-mural labour welfare activity. Mainly, he benefits in the following ways :

1. Improvement in worker's health. Ordinary arrangements like healthy residences, inexpensive and nourishing food, proper relaxation and refreshment go a long way in maintaining the health of workers. Hence, absenteeism from the factory falls to a minimum, and the per capita output improves. Dissatisfaction is a thing of the past, cordiality and fidelity permeate the very atmosphere, to the delight of the owner.

2. Improvements in worker's efficiency. When education is provided, the worker's efficiency and skill increases, and he can do better work in lesser time. His understanding improves and he is capable of avoiding the inflaming influence of vested interests.

3. Reduction in absenteeism. Prevention of disease and arrangement of medical facilities help to reduce illness or to shorten its influence, as a result of which the number of absentees in the factory decreases, disease being the main cause of it. Social welfare activity helps to induce a healthy outlook in the worker and to maintain a balance in his character which guides him to honest and responsible effort and conduct.

4. Good relations between employer and worker. Provision of such facilities as social insurance, provident fund, pension, gratuity, etc., helps to remove a feeling of insecurity in the worker, as his future becomes secure, and he can rest satisfied with his employer. This improves the relations between the worker and the employer.

5. Reducing worker's dissatisfaction. Healthy recreation facilities and welcome cultural activity help to sublimate the more destructive and undesirable tendencies in the worker's satisfaction. A worker's satisfaction is further increased if his female colleague has the benefit of such facilities as maternity benefits, maternity homes, creches for their children. Being satisfied he is not inclined to strike work, as a result of which the employer gains.

6. Improvement in quantity and quality of production. When these benefits accrue to the workers in a factory, the quantity and quality of production in it improve, a direct benefit to the employer.

7. Employer's moral satisfaction. But the greatest advantage of labour welfare that goes to the employer takes the form of moral satisfaction at having served the cause of humanity. No decent-minded and right-thinking employer can be happy if his employees are poor, ill-fed, badly dressed, uneducated, and unpresentable. Their labour does not bring him any pleasure. Economic improvement and benefit is not the sole basis of labour welfare, even though economic benefit does result from it. Behind it is the sense of humanity, a large heart and a moral or ethical consciousness. Absence of these things leads to exploitation and ultimately to class-struggle.

From the above description it is evident that labour welfare activity benefits the employer no less than his employees, but such activity should be intelligently conceived and generously administered. Planning is a part of every scientific activity but generosity is an essential part of labour welfare because such plans are not based on material considerations but are instead guided by humanitarian principles and view. Finally it can be said that intelligently conceived and generously administered labour welfare activity will ultimately benefit the employer.

Importance of Labour Welfare in India

Compared to other countries, India has much greater need and importance for labour welfare work. Such a condition is caused by certain deficiencies in the Indian labour force, that are not to be found in its counterpart in other countries. It is these defects or deficiencies that increase the importance of labour welfare activity in the country. Briefly, then, the following are the reasons why labour welfare work in India assumes greater importance than in other countries :

1. Lack of labour union. In India, even today the workers are not united into a class. Keeping in view the numbers, labour union movement is still in its infancy. Even in the labour unions that do exist, there is a lack of enlightened leadership, and there is no unity between these unions themselves. Welfare of labourers is a secondary concern, the primary interest being the serving of party and vested interests. In the absence of properly organised labour unions, the workers can neither place their demands effectively before the employer, nor can they think clearly and systematically of their own interest. In other modern progressive countries, workers are strongly organised into labour unions, but as their force is lacking in India, it is essential that the welfare of labourers in the country be efficiently looked after by the employers and the government. This should be treated as a sacred trust till the workers can evolve their own efficient and reliable organisation. This will help the workers stand on their own feet, develop strong unions, think properly of their interests, to progress hand-in-hand, and to take a definite hand in the country's development.

2. Lack of education. As compared with other countries, the percentage of educated workers is very low, most of them being illiterate. Consequently, they are not in a position to receive advanced industrial training, understand the problems in industries, understand their own interests and those of the nation as a whole. This can prove a source of harm not only to the workers but also to the country. Hence labour welfare is required more in India than in other countries. It will help make the workers secure, become industrially efficient and responsible citizens of the country.

3. Problems of absenteeism and migration. Compared to workers in other countries, the Indian labourer is more restless and tendentious towards frequent migration because life in the town does not provide for his needs, and the atmosphere in general does not suit him. Level of wages is far too low to adequately compensate for the high prices of most commodities. Hence, the labourer cannot comfortably settle down in one place. The worker's migratory tendency can be curbed by providing him with adequate housing, improving the conditions in which he is required to work, and other welfare work of a similar nature. This will help the worker establish a home in the town, and he will not have to run frequently to the village for his family. Hence, the problem of absenteeism in factories will be reduced. Recreation and cultural facilities will prevent much indulgence in drug addiction and alcoholism, crime and prostitution and other undesirable activity. Even more than this, the percentage of absentees in factories will fall.

4. Low level of health and nutrition. The Indian worker, as compared with his counterpart in most European countries, is unhealthy and ill-fed. This has reduced his production potential, as compared with the productive capacity of western labourer. Hence he is in very great need of inexpensive nutritive food and good facility in case of hospitalization.

5. Extreme poverty. Another factor is the extreme poverty of the Indian worker. He is unable to provide a healthy living for his family, and a good education for his children. Female labour in the country, as compared with female labour elsewhere, is in even a worse state of health, and adequate protection and assistance are not afforded to it in times of pregnancy and delivery. Hence labour welfare has much to do in this country. The Indian woman labourer will be as happy as other workers in the world when she is given the facilities of maternity benefits, maternity homes and creches for her children. It is essential that the education of boys and girls be provided for. Being poor, the Indian labourer is hardly in any condition to save something for his old age; hence he is in great need of provident fund, pension, gratuity, etc.

6. Lack of training. Percentage of trained workers in India is very low. As compared with other countries, trained personnel in India are hard to come by. Hence it is necessary to have training facilities for such a vast labour force. Possibility of accident increases when the worker is untrained. Hence there should be adequate provision for preventing accidents.

7. Lack of healthy recreation. Healthy recreation is also at a premium in this country, with the result that the workers indulge in crime and activities of irresponsible kind. Their efficiency is further diminished by energy being employed in all kinds of undesirable channels. Hence, it is essential that recreation and enjoyment of a healthy kind be provided.

8. Industrial backwardness of India. From the industrial standpoint, India is far behind other countries. Industrial progress is being aimed at through the medium of five-year plans, but industrial progress is dependent upon the efficiency of the labour force, and labour in India is in a pitiable state. Hence, the labourers are very much in need of all kinds of labour welfare work.

It would have become evident from the above description that labour welfare work in India assumes a much greater importance, as compared with other countries due to a variety of reasons. Labour welfare activity will save the labourer from moral degeneration, reduce the number of incidents of lockouts and strikes in industries, and help achieve success in the country's plans.

STRIKE AND LOCKOUT

Conflict in Industry

If, in some particular profession or occupation, the workers have faith in their employer who thinks considerately of them, their mutual relations remain cordial and occasions of conflict are rare. If workers do not revolt for some reason or the other against conditions of extreme exploitation, and choose to bear their lot gracefully, then also conflict does not occur. On the other hand, if the employer is tactful and chooses to use his diplomacy, there is no reason for a lockout to take place. But these things do not occur very often. What does happen very often is that employers pay no heed to the plight of their employees, even forgetting that the poor chaps are human beings with certain basis needs the fulfilment of which is essential, and that they may revolt against extreme exploitation. In the earlier stages when labourers were not united, the unscrupulous employers could keep them suppressed by tactfully causing dissension among their ranks. But in the present-day conditions in almost every country every big industry has its organised labour unions. Some labour unions are powerful enough to spread over countries, while certain union have political parties to support them in their struggle against exploitation. Many of their leaders are powerful enough to become members of national councils and governments. Wherever any injustice to the labour class occurs, it is brought to their attention so that they can raise a hue and cry over it in the national assemblies and take the matter up with the government concerned; and this activity and representation at the highest level create a notion of power and security in the general ranks of labourers. They are in a position to take the fight into the exploiter's half, and they can resist efforts at exploiting their energies. They organise themselves into a single body if they need to agitate for their demands, they resort to political propaganda, to meetings, processions and ultimately to strikes. Strike is one of the major problems of modern industry.

What is Strike?

Strike is an announcement of non-cooperation with the employer, the first step in it being suspension of all activity, followed by meetings, organised processions, exhibitions in order to elicit the sympathy of the population in general, public representation of their demands carried to the employer through the senior representatives of the labour force. All these activities are adjuncts of a strike. Besides all this, strike nowadays involves the wide propagation of the aims of the strike in the public so that it can be persuaded to side with the labour force. Another aspect of the strike is in informing the government of its objectives and presenting it with a summary of its demands and their justification.

Why do Strikes Occur?

Why do strikes occur at all? Basically, it stems from a distrust of the workers towards their employer. They do not strike, even when required to work in squalid surroundings, so long as they are convinced that the employer is conscious of their needs and is sincerely trying to improve their lot. But when the employer turns a deaf ear to their pleadings and entreaties, when their faith in his sincerity is undermined, they strike work. There is no necessary rule that the demands of striking workers are invariably just and proper. Some strikes take place because the workers are inflamed by some political group that has some end of its own to achieve, are misled by some vested interests or are led to this extreme step as an expression of their disgust. They may choose this method of getting their revenge on the individual. Many workers form the idea that all that the employers possess, their magnificent mansions, their cars, their luxuries, are all the outcome of exploiting workers. This leads to a feeling of jealousy which may find expression through strike even though the general behaviour of the specific employer may be good and the conditions of work normally above reproach. Occasionally, leaders of labour unions also inflame the workers and incite them to strike in order to achieve some personal objective. Most facts are twisted and distorted by the leaders and fed to the poor labourer who swallows it and prepares to strike.

Means of Ending Strikes

In this manner, whether the strike is justified or not, whether its objectives are desirable or not, it originates in a feeling of distrust between the labour force and the employer. This mistrust and lack of confidence are sometimes caused by the employer himself, but whoever is to blame it is essential that conciliation should take place. Even if demands of the striking workers are unjust, they must be heard and attended to. In a strike, the workers conduct themselves in a manner similar to mob behaviour. They lose their power of reasoning. Their emotions are easily aroused, and they become excited over the most insignificant thing. If in such events, the employers choose to behave in an irresponsible manner, the situation can worsen and may lead to setting fire to factories, arson and other destructive activity. But such events and damage can be averted if the workers' demands are given a patient hearing, the workers convinced of the sincerity of their employer, promises of prompt action upon them given, and the inflammatory sources disclosed.

Prevention of Strikes

But prevention is traditionally considered to be better than cure. It is for the employer to avert distrust, or at least to prevent it reaching such proportions that the worker is encouraged to feel justified in striking work. It is for him to try and win the confidence of his staff. Two things are essential for this. The first is that the behaviour towards the workers should be good and understanding, sincere and proper, and secondly attention should be paid to their well-being, improvements in working conditions made and their welfare considered carefully. If these things are done, the workers' trust in their employer becomes unshakeable and strikes become obsolete and unknown activity.

Problem of Lockout

One aspect of the distrust between workers and employer is strike, the other is lockout. In this activity, the office and working premises of the concern under conflict are locked, entry to staff and workers is prohibited. Hundreds and thousands of workers lose their source of income, and are sometimes reduced to such abject poverty that they are on the verge of death because of hunger. The workers lose, but so do the employers. While the machines lie idle, they lose their income, raw material is destroyed in many cases, trade connections are broken because of lack of supply. Secondly, a lockout can incite the workers to violent activity which may cause them to destroy the factory, as their daily bread has been snatched from them. This naturally is no small blow to the employer or his insurance company. The employer has naturally to seek the assistance and protection of the police force, which may be compelled to fire on mobs of unruly workers indulging in destructive activity. If some of them happen to die, the employer is brought into disgrace wherever the incident occurs. Lockouts harm the country's economy even more than they harm the individual owner of the factory. In the modern economic structure in most countries, every industry is dependent upon some other for one or the other thing. Lockouts in one industry can lead to very serious repercussions in other industries which may follow the bad example of the first and resort to lockouts. The worker is not the only class of people dependent upon the functioning of the industry; other classes of shopkeepers and middlemen are also deeply involved. Their earnings also are greatly depleted by such subversive activity. When production of a particular commodity is stopped, its supply drops with the result that it creates an imbalance between the forces of demand and supply in the market so that the prices go up, with much adverse influence upon the poor consumer. In this way, in the modern complex that is a nation's economy, lockout in any one major industry will influence every walk of life in some respect, be it major or minor. In this manner, it can turn into a problem of national magnitude.

Causes of Lockout

A certain concatenation of circumstances may make lockout an inevitable step, but usually it is not justified. It is sometimes used by the employer as an instrument with which to suppress the hapless worker. It may even be an expression of the employer's sadistic bent of mind, as it may give him pleasure to see the worker suffering. Lockouts are sometime thought to be essential in cases where prestige and honour become involved. It may even be used to impress the worker with an employer's power over him. In all such cases, lockouts are completely and beyond doubt unjustified and improper. Its lack of justification lies in the fact that the employer is led to sacrificing the interests of the nation and those of the working force in favour of his own. It should be considered obligatory on the part of the government to intervene, because it becomes a national question. In fact, all incidents of lockouts and strikes can be effectively prevented if the government enacts laws covering labour welfare activity, improvement in their conditions of work, occasional incentives being given to them, security in cases of accidents and old age being provided, and if it ensures their efficient and strict observance.

As has been pointed out earlier, lockouts and strikes are two aspects of the same problem. They stem from mutual distrust between worker and employer, prejudice, in-group feeling, selfish interests and unnecessary self-assertion. All these are psychological in nature, but they do not arise without an antecedent cause. If they are present in weak condition, they do not cause lockouts and strikes. These incidents occur only when these feelings flare up, an occurrence which can certainly be controlled and avoided. The most obvious way of doing so is removing all causes of distrust, prejudice and assertion. For this, on the one hand, an eye should be kept on individuals and groups that encourage them, and on the other hand, welfare work should be undertaken. But for this, cooperation between worker and employers is essential, in addition to government intervention. In the complex economic structure of a nation's economy, lockouts and strikes in any one major industry are likely to assume national importance as every walk of life is influenced in some degree. Hence, their solution should be cooperatively sought after by government, labourers' representatives and their employers.

QUESTIONS FOR EXERCISE

1. "Labour welfare not only keeps industrial peace but also increases production." Discuss this statement on the basis of psychological facts.
2. What is the advantage of establishing human relations in industry?
3. Write short note on Strike and Lockout.
4. What is the role of psychology in industrial organisation? Mention some vital problems of industry which can be solved only by psychology.
5. How would workers be selected in industry? What points should be remembered in this condition?
6. Write short note on Job Analysis.
7. How do you analyse a job? Show how job analysis helps in the selection of fit workers.

13

Psychology of Work and Fatigue

A worker performing his duty in a factory is often faced with many problems that are concerned with his work and the fatigue that it creates. If looked at carefully, it will be evident that the worker cannot work for long at a uniform rate of speed. His tempo of work rises and falls, the former case benefiting the industry and the latter harming it. Hence a study of rise and fall in work is very important. It will thereby become possible to advise not only the employer but also the worker, as in some cases, his remuneration is decided not by the hours he works but by the quantity of work he does. In the present age of industry, industrial psychology has conducted much study on this problem.

COURSE OF WORK

It has been indicated above that the worker does not work uniformly during a course of work. If the worker's performance is graphically represented it will show a work curve which will show his rate of work as varying. In this way, the work curve manifests the rate of working, and it shows that in the beginning work progresses at a rapid pace, but this rapidity is not achieved immediately the work is begun. A high rate of work is attained after the worker has warmed up.

WARMING UP

What does the phrase 'warming up' mean? Most people are aware that when some work is begun, speed in it is picked up after some time. This high rate is due to energy and this energy is warming up, as a high rate of work is not possible without warmth. All workers do not warm up equally fast in all kinds of activity. Different workers require varying periods of time for warming up to different kinds of work to be performed by them. For example, fifteen minutes may suffice to warm up for one kind of work while in some other form of activity the individual worker may have to work for a whole hour before attaining the maximum tempo of work that is characteristic of warming up. Once the worker has warmed up, he works at a very rapid pace. It is for this reason that the phenomenon of warming up has been subjected to a close and scientific scrutiny. It has been observed, for example, that if music is playing while certain work is being done, warming up occurs earlier than when music is not playing. Often labourers are seen singing at work so that they can warm up. Team spirit is another factor that helps in warming up fast. Actually, two basic factors are required for warming up to a piece of work — absence of fatigue from body and mind, and presence of necessary motivation or inspiration. If the body is completely fatigued, then no amount of motivation or incentive will have any effect in warming the individual up. On the other hand, even if the body is not tired, a person will not warm up if there is no motivation involved in his work. Hence, in order to have a worker warmed up, it is essential that he be fresh of mind and body, and that a reason to work at a high rate be present before him, and that he heeds this reason. Fatigue will be studied later, and suggestions for removing it mentioned in the same connection. One major cause of not warming up is boredom or disgust. Ways of reducing boredom in any work will be mentioned later on. Psychologists are still studying ways and means of achieving warming up quickly. These studies should prove of value to both workers and employers.

WORK SPURT

The work curve shows a very high rate of work during the work spurt period. When the worker is working energetically his rate of work is very high. In this period the work curve rises very sharply, but this rise is not maintained over a long stretch of time, as it begins to fall as fatigue sets in. If rate of work is to be maintained at a high level, it is essential that a condition of warming up be continued and fatigue delayed. In this connection, too, many studies are being made.

FATIGUE

In the previous discourse on course of work, work curve,

warming up and work spurt, it has been mentioned time and again that it is essential to delay fatigue, because fatigue delays work and reduces progress. Speed of work falls considerably due to it. The truth of the matter lies in the fact that the proportion in which the worker becomes progressively fatigued, is the proportion in which his work curve takes on a downward trend and progresses in that direction. Work done decreases as fatigue increases. Hence, industrial psychology has made detailed analysis of the causes of fatigue and ways of reducing it.

What is Fatigue?

What is this fatigue? Starch has written that fatigue is the condition of reduced interests and desires. This is a psychological definition of fatigue. According to Freeman, fatigue is a condition in which the organs of the body do not function, and the mind becomes lax. Evidently, fatigue is exclusively neither physical nor mental. This state of laxity, tiredness is a psychophysical condition. It implies the reduced efficiency and capacity of mind or body, or both. A fatigued individual will either not work at all or work less efficiently than otherwise, and is most likely to lie in a recumbent position, in a hapless mood. In the words of Offner, "Fatigue is the reduced capacity of our organism to work properly, that capacity is accompanied with some feeling also which is known as feeling of fatigue." Having worked for many hours, it is natural for the individual to feel fatigued. The time that a particular individual will take in working before encountering the phenomenon of fatigue or exhaustion is another question, but any individual working to his maximum capacity is certain to get tired because his capacity to work is reduced. As capacity to work is reduced, fatigue increases. Briefly, then, fatigue means the decrease in capacity or efficiency.

Characteristics of Fatigue

Fatigue influences both mind and body. As far as the mind is concerned, in a state of fatigue the individual lacks his usual power of thinking, and finds it difficult to concentrate on whatever he has in hand. Sometimes fatigue and exhaustion reach such a state that even emotions cannot burst forth. From the physiological viewpoint, fatigue involves loss of physical efficiency and physical coordination. In a state of fatigue the poisonous element called lactic acid is produced in large quantities in the muscles and nerves. This element is so poisonous and dangerous that very great excess of it can even lead to paralysis, but in the normal course if it increases in quantity in some one part of the body, that part becomes fatigued. Besides lactic acid, carbon dioxide and ammonia are also produced in the body as a result of exhaustion. They, too, are toxic in nature and cause change in the chemical composition of the body. Many psychologists have cooperated in the observation and study of the various parts of the body when in a state of exhaustion and fatigue. Of them, the most important work has been done by Millar and Helmholtz, besides Wundt. Miller restricted his research and study to the condition of nerves during exhaustion. Six years after his effort, in 1850, Helmholtz made a study of the speed of sensation-nerve and motor nerve and observed that when the physique is exhausted, it takes longer for the sensation to travel from organ to the mind and for the motor nerve to take the brain's response to the organ concerned. In the process of his study, Helmholtz evolved an instrument used for measuring contraction of muscles, which was used in 1858 by Wundt. Nowadays the ergograph is used to measure fatigue.

Kinds of Fatigue

Fatigue is of more then one kind, just as efficiency is of more then one kind. Generally, fatigue is believed to take the following four forms :

1. Mental fatigue,
2. Physical fatigue,
3. Nervous fatigue,
4. Boredom.

1. Mental fatigue. Due to persistent mental work or due to excessive strain on the brain, the mind loses its capacity or efficiency. This is mental fatigue. In this manner, in mental fatigue the mind becomes tired or its minute cells and nerves lose their efficiency.

2. Physical fatigue. Physical work leads to decrease in the efficiency of muscles, and this leads to a feeling of fatigue or exhaustion. In this way, physical fatigue is the result of bodily exertion. Mental work in excess of normal capacity leads to an impression of physical ineptitude but in fact this is only mental fatigue. But, as the mind and body are intimately related, exhaustions in the case of either must inevitably influence the other.

3. Nervous fatigue. Man's unconscious mind is very active, but its functioning also involves the expenditure of energy. This, too, leads to an experience of fatigue. In cases of mental conflict, the unconscious mind becomes exhausted, and this causes nervous fatigue.

4. Boredom. Boredom and fatigue are not synonymous. In fatigue the exhaustion is due to the expenditure of energy, but in the case of boredom, the exhaustion is caused when the existing energy in the body is not properly consumed. Causes of fatigue have been an important study for psychologists in the field of psychology. Generally there are many causes of fatigue, one of them being, in some cases the absence of work. But where it is a question of the worker's or labourer's fatigue, it is normally the result of improper method of working or working for long hours without intervening periods of rest. Holling-worth blames long periods of work without rest as the main cause of fatigue. Long hours of work tire the mind as well as the body. But persistent work over a long period of time without any rest cannot be considered to be the sole cause of fatigue. One cause of fatigue is boredom. As has been pointed out before, in much the same manner disinterest, lack of motivation or inspiration, absence of recreation, mental ill-health, physical ailment, etc., can be causes of fatigue. Important among the causes that result in fatigue where industry is concerned are excessive work, interminable work, working without rest, working in wrong manner and absence of sufficient motivation.

Hence, in order to eliminate fatigue, the above causes should be remedied. Industrial psychology makes a study of ways and means of eliminating fatigue also, and such study has resulted in many physical and psychological tools coming to light.

Ways of Eliminating Fatigue

It has been the function of psychology to discover the ways

of removing fatigue and exhaustion, and if possible, of preventing it. The following methods have come to light :

1. Sleep. By far the best method of ending fatigue is sleep. Sleep or repose brings calm and rest to brain cells and body tissue, while all waste matter is excreted. This restores efficiency and freshness to the body.

2. Relaxation. Fatigue can also be reduced by relaxing in a sitting or lying position because the mind or body are freed of tension. Efficiency is thereby regained.

3. Balance of work and rest. As has been mentioned often, excessive work leads to exhaustion of mind or body, but complete jack of work and too much of rest also induce fatigue. This fatigue is the result of boredom. Hence, if fatigue is to be avoided, work is as important as rest. Hence, the best thing is to strike some kind of balance between work and rest.

4. Change in work. In specific physical work, certain distinct parts of the body are strained much more than others. But if the work is changed periodically it is possible to work continuously for longer period. Similarly continuous application to the same kind of mental work does not give our other faculties a chance of expression and we tend to become bored. Hence, change in the nature of work is essential to remove and even to prevent physical as well as nervous fatigue.

5. Recreation. Recreation provides opportunity for our unexpressed capacities to come forward and find manifestation, while at the same time it reduces mental and physical tensions. Hence, recreation is necessary for reducing or preventing fatigue.

6. Change in experiences. Fatigue can also come in because people maintain a very inflexible attitude towards life and always steep themselves in work. Hence, change in experience can also sometimes remove fatigue.

7. Creating interest and motivation in work. Even more important than rest as a cure for fatigue, mental and physical, is the creation of interest and motivation in work. And for this, good work can be rewarded with promotions and bonuses. Such methods prove very efficacious.

The above methods of ending fatigue will prove useful to the large generality of individuals, but every individual can pick a method to suit himself. There can be other methods of removing fatigue, according to interest and nature.

QUESTIONS FOR EXERCISE

1. Explain the psychology of work.
2. What is fatigue? How can it be removed?

14

Efficiency, Time-Motion Study and Therbligs

Importance of Efficiency

Quality and quantity of work, in any factory, industry or office do not depend upon the machines alone. Whatever the quality of mechanical equipment existing in the factory, for a very high level of production it is essential that the individuals operating the machines be experts, and highly qualified. Hence, industrial psychology makes a detailed study of the factors and problems influencing efficiency. Psychologists have also suggested various measures for improving and maintaining the efficiency of working personnel.

What is Efficiency?

What is this efficiency? How can it be discovered or determined? Efficiency is the individual's skill in any specific job, by virtue of which he can perform that function well. Efficiency is not a general quality because no individual can do everything efficiently. He can be highly skilled in only a couple of functions. Different individuals have skill in different kinds of jobs while people who are skilful in the same work differ in the degree of skill that they individually possess. Hence, to say that a particular individual is efficient or skilful amounts to saying nothing in favour of him. His efficiency, or a statement of it, must be qualified by the function in respect of which he is acknowledged to be successful. A skilful person can perform some definite function better and quicker than the average worker. Hence, efficiency is measured or reckoned by quantity of work done, and the time taken in doing it. If mere saving of time is effected, the person cannot be said to be skilful because he must also maintain the quality and quantity of work in that reduced time. Similarly, skill as a quality cannot be attributed to any individual who merely does a lot of work. Evidently, efficiency requires more and better work to be done in less time. If a person possesses all these three qualities, in connection with some definite form of work, more than other individuals doing the same work, he will be said to be more efficient. Evidently, then, efficiency is a relative term. Individuals are efficient as compared to one another. But this efficiency is not affected at all times and between all individuals. Normally, when an individual is said to be efficient, it is implied that he does more work than the average worker in the same unit and does it better in the same time.

Determinants of Efficiency

In order to maintain and improve upon efficiency of individuals, psychologists made a detailed study of the conditions or determinants of efficiency. Efficiency is a psychophysical state in which both mind and body are directly involved. Hence, its determinant can also be roughly divided into the internal and external. External conditions are the following :

1. Rest,
2. Work period,
3. Health,
4. Climate.

Now these various external conditions will be described at some length :

1. Rest. In the foregoing chapter on fatigue, it was mentioned that a person becomes tired if he works without rest, and his skill decreases proportionately : hence it is evident that rest is one essential factor of efficiency. In an experiment Shepard put twelve college students on the chest-waist machine for eight hours, the work then being repeated but with intervening periods of rest. This experiment illustrated that uninterrupted work reduced the worker's efficiency. Watt's experiments showed that work done with adequate provisions for rest led to an increase in efficiency up to 9.3 per cent. Vernon and Bedford studied workers in an electricity plant or power house who worked both with rest and then without rest. They came to the conclusion that work done without rest does not produce very good results. Other experiments have proved that where the work is of a purely mental nature it is best to relax for a period of five minutes after every hour of work, while a ten-minute break is better. Of the entire hours of work in a day, the workers should be given 16.6 per cent as rest.

It must also be kept in mind that providing unnecessary periods of rest has no real benefit, but is instead prone to cause loss. Too long a period of rest leads the worker's mind away from his work completely. Ten minutes are enough under normal conditions. But it is wrong to imagine that lunch time is a period of rest. During the period of rest, the worker must not be given any physical or mental work. Another important thing in this connection is that the time of rest should be predetermined as its uncertainty is harmful because of tension created by it. As it is, the existing tension is not reduced. The time required for rest in a particular form of work is something that cannot be laid down with any severity. There can be no general rule. As a general rule, some rest is required in every form of work, but normally the more tough or difficult work requires longer period of rest.

Rest creates mainly the following benefits :

(a) Production increases in quality and quantity.

(b) Accidents in the industry decrease.

(c) Boredom and disinterest are eliminated.

(d) Relaxation reduces tension and provides comfort.

2. Time of work. Another important determining factor of efficiency is the time of work. If the period of work required from the employee is unnecessarily long it will be natural for the worker to feel exhausted with the result that his efficiency will fall. Many experiments have proved that the labourer should not be compelled to work for more than eight hours. Forty hours in the week is quite sufficient and adequate. As the hours of work increase beyond this, the worker's enthusiasm, efficiency, health, strength and capability, etc., steadily fall, the ultimate outcome of which is harmful for the employer. Hence, the salvation of the employer as well as employed lies in the fact that the hours of work should not be increased beyond well-defined limits.

3. Health. A good health is another requirement of high efficiency. If the worker does not enjoy good health he will be prone to fatigue and low quality in the work done. The importance of health in industry is evident from the development of a new branch of science, the industrial hygiene. It makes a study of all conditions and circumstances that influence the worker's health, and helps in the creation of conditions that will favourably influence it. The advent of industrial hygiene led to improvement in the health of workers as well as in the quality and quantity of work produced by them. According to industrial hygiene, in order to maintain a good standard of health among workers in industrial centres, the following facts should be attended to :

(a) Every industrial centre should be equipped with a good doctor who can immediately attend to a worker should he fall ill.

(b) Special attention must be paid to the prevention of contagious diseases from spreading among workers. Immediately some worker contracts any such disease, he should be quarantined, and put under expert medical care.

(c) As far as possible, alcoholic and other stimulants should not be available to the workers, and even the ones addicted to it should be helped to get rid of their addiction.

(d) Workers should be given essential information on matters of health, and on the prevention of common diseases.

(e) Special attention should be paid to workers physically, mentally or financially backward, and special facilities provided to reduce the degree of backwardness.

4. Climate. Climatic conditions of the place of work also influence efficiency. Many of the important things in this connection have been mentioned in a previous chapter entitled psychology in industry. Modern factories that are scientifically designed have special arrangements for controlled lighting, ventilation, running water, cleanliness, temperature, sound, etc. If this is not done, the health and ultimately the efficiency of the worker suffer.

In addition to the external conditions, efficiency is also affected by some internal conditions, as follows :

1. Motivation,
2. Monotony,
3. Application,
4. Emotional adjustment,
5. Aptitude and personality differences.

1. Motivation. Motivation is intimately concerned with efficiency. If it is lacking, the presence of all physical comfort cannot induce any efficiency. But if it is present, and most other comforts lacking, efficiency is maintained to a fairly large extent. And ways of providing motivation in industry have been studied in a previous chapter, the 16th. For motivated working in industry, it is essential that the needs of the worker be fulfilled, his health be maintained, his future be fairly secure, and that he be promoted and otherwise rewarded adequately for efficient and skilful work. If promotions come as a result of ingratiating behaviour towards the authorities, even the most efficient worker loses motivation. If the people in authority do not behave properly, the worker loses his motivation. All these things have been studied.

2. Boredom. Boredom is another factor that has an adverse effect upon efficiency because in it the mind and body both lose their vigour. Hence, psychologists have conducted many experiments towards discovering the nature of this phenomenon of boredom, and have tried to analyse its causes. The following means can be employed to reduce or prevent boredom in work :

(a) ***Variety in work :*** According to Poffenberger, one cause of boredom is repetition of the same kind of work. It is a matter of common experience that one tires of the same work if persisted in and does not need the endorsement of a psychologist. Hence, if interest in the work is to be maintained, it is necessary that the work presents some variety to the worker. Hence, variety can be used to reduce or even prevent boredom.

(b) ***Rest along with work :*** If there is no adequate arrangement for rest along with work, an individual becomes exhausted, and tends to become bored. Hence, it is desirable to have some definite arrangement for rest along with work, if boredom is to be avoided.

(c) ***Short hours of work :*** If the hours of work are very long, the worker becomes bored and tends to remain fatigued most of the time. Hence, it is essential that the hours of work be not long.

(d) ***Arrangement for recreation :*** Recreation refreshes the individual, hence it is most essential for removing boredom. It is now a common practice to provide the workers with all kinds of equipment with which they can amuse and refresh themselves. It creates novelty as well as a diversion that helps to recreate interest in the worker.

(e) ***Motivation :*** To keep boredom away, motivation in the work of the worker should be maintained by various means. He should not be allowed to work under heavy pressure of any kind. He should be encouraged to develop his own motivation for the work he does.

(f) ***Selection of work according to intelligence, personality and abilities :*** If any work that the individual does, does not conform to his level of intelligence, qualities of his personality, his capacity and special abilities, then he will gradually become increasingly bored. Hence, it is essential that the person chooses his occupation with due regard to his own personality and its complication.

3. Application. Another important and essential internal condition of efficiency is the undisturbed and undivided application of the employee to his work. For this, it is necessary to remove noise and other obstacles or interferences. Sometimes the absence of motivation is another cause of indifference to work. For efficiency it is essential that all internal as well as external diverting factors be removed from the sphere of activity, and the worker encouraged to pursue his work undisturbed and with the fullest application.

4. Emotional adjustment. A study of most accidents reveals that they are caused by inattention, lack of interest, laxity or mental conflict. And all of these factors have emotional maladjustment at their root. Hence, another important condition of efficiency is emotional adjustment. In order to maintain it, generally the conditions of work for the employees should be good. In addition to this, individual guidance should be available to them in order to help them solve some of their personal problems.

5. Characteristic interests and personality traits. Finally, efficiency also depends to a large extent upon the individual's own characteristic interests and personality traits. If his occupation conforms to them, his efficiency is maintained but in case of an adverse choice of trade, his efficiency lies unexploited. Secondly, there is a certain class of individuals in the case of whom it is very difficult to maintain any definite level of efficiency, though efforts can achieve some degree of success in this direction.

From the above account of the various conditions and determining factors of efficiency, it would be apparent that industrial psychology has made considerable headway in its research on this aspect, and that continuous efforts are being made to discover systematic laws. Such an effort can only have the most desirable results for both employer as well as employed.

TIME–MOTION STUDY

Taylor's Studies

Study of time and motion in industrial psychology has revealed many important things regarding efficiency. In 1910 Taylor carried out certain experiments concerning motion. In his study he divided a single function into numerous component parts, and noted the time taken in the performance of each part. After this, he increased their wages and reducing the time taken in the performance of each component task, he studied the results. Following motion study, the latter was time study.

Gilbreth's Studies

But the most important study on this aspect was conducted by Gilbreth. Through a study of time-motion Gilbreth tried to discover the method by means of which a worker can do the greatest amount of work possible in less time than normal. For this, he observed that maximum economy in time could be effected only if all unnecessary activity was eliminated from the function, and only the absolutely essential or inevitable activities were allowed to remain. Conducting experiments of this nature on labourers who haul bricks, Gilbreth concluded that, if all unnecessary movements were excluded, the work normally done in twelve hours could be completed in five, while, instead of moving 120 bricks in an hour it is possible to displace some 350 bricks in the same time. In this study Gilbreth made use of the cyclegraph for studying movements. Stop watches were used to record time. In a time–motion study, all the movements required in any function are divided into the smallest indivisible units. Then, analysis reveals the unnecessary and the necessary activities, the unnecessary or superfluous being eliminated. At a later stage, motion came to be studied with automatic cameras, and with tridimensional cameras even later. Nowadays, besides noting the length, breadth and height, it also records the time. This complete picture is known as the stereo-crono-cyclegraph. With its help it is possible to study all the motions of any one piece of work at the same time.

THERBLIGS

In addition to studying motion, Gilbreth also tried to validate them, and for doing so he determined the symbols of various movements, and he started using those symbols to describe those particular kinds of movements. Gilbreth formed seventeen such symbols of various movements.

These symbols are called therbligs. (This word contains all the letters that Gilbreth's name includes, only their order is reversed.) A simochart is prepared with the help of these therbligs. In the simochart, using the diagrammatic or plotting method, the motions of the various parts of the body are filled in, keeping a definite scale and the due proportion between themselves, and their relative therbligs indicated thereon. The simochart reveals the activity that the specific part of the body has to do for a specific time in performing a specific function.

Advantages of Time-Motion Studies

Time-motion study has proved of immense value to industry. On the one hand, it helps in job analysis, while on the other it helps to discover the method by which a maximum of work can be obtained in the shortest period of time by eliminating all unnecessary movement. Thirdly, studies of this nature also indicate the nature of training to be imparted to trainees intended for certain specific functions. Another benefit deriving from this study is that it helps to fix the value of a particular function, and thereby the salary payable to its performer.

QUESTIONS FOR EXERCISE

1. What is efficiency? What are the factors determining it?
2. Write short notes on :
   (a) Time–Motion Study.
   (b) Therbligs.

15

Morale and Job Satisfaction

What is Morale?

Whatever the industry, production does not depend exclusively upon machines. Machines are driven by the labourers. In addition to the labourers, the factory has clerks, managers and other workers. If the factory is to be run efficiently and profitably, it is essential that all the human elements in the factory should cooperate and work in coordination. It should be an organised affair. And this can be achieved only when all the workers are in a position to be enthusiastic and happy about their work. The attitude that the workers have towards their work in the factory makes a very great difference. It is this individual approach or viewpoint that constitutes their morale.

High Morale and Low Morale

Morale can be high as well as low. The successful industrialists make constant endeavours to maintain a high morale among their working staff because only if this is done can the work in the factory proceed smoothly and efficiently. Production is maintained at a high level and the quality of work done is admirable. On the other hand, once the morale of the factory workers has fallen, the organisation as a whole is constantly faced with problems of all kinds. Sometimes production falls while at others it is the accident rate that goes up alarmingly. Sometimes the workers do not see eye to eye while at others they do so, and strikes are the result. Today, the importance of human relationships has come to be recognised in all industries. A high morale is evidence of the desirable conditions of human relations.

Aspects of Morale

It is evident that morale has a very potent influence upon

social behaviour and conduct. It has, therefore, two aspects — the psychological and the social. In its psychological aspect, morale is constituted by the organisation of industry, and the behaviour or mental tendency of workers towards those in authority above them. In its social aspect, morale is in evidence in the social behaviour of the workers. Accordingly, then, if morale among the workers is high, they exhibit discipline, obedience and communal unity. The lower the tone of this feeling of unity, the lower will be the level of morale.

Influence of Morale upon Attitude towards Authority

Hence, morale has a very explicit influence upon the worker's attitude towards authority. In this connection, Jenkens conducted a very interesting experiment. In it, he took up two groups in one of which the morale was very high and in the other very low. In each group, besides one commander and one officiating officer, there were 17 workers. In order to measure their attitude towards those in authority, each worker was individually and secretly asked to name the officer with whom he would prefer to undertake air travel, and also the name of the officer with whom he would prefer not to undertake any such project. The result of this experiment led to the conclusion that in the case of high morale the attitude towards authority was positive and favourable, while in the case of low morale it is negative and unfavourable. In the group which had a high morale eight workers or soldiers chose the commander as a travelling companion while six of them selected the officiating person as more suitable. On the other hand, in the group with the low morale, no soldier chose to undertake or even prefer an air journey in the company of the commander. Contrary to this, nine soldiers gave evidence of a positive distaste for flying with the officiating individual.

Morale and Mental Condition

One characteristic of a high morale, in addition to the favourable attitude towards those in authority, is that it shuns disappointment or negation. In other words, when the morale is high, disappointment or hopelessness do not exist, and a high level of enthusiasm is maintained. If any problem does rear its head, immediate efforts are made to arrive at a solution. On the other hand, if the morale in a particular group of individuals is low, frustrations and disappointments increase. People lose faith in the future. They are prone to find darkness all around them in which they find themselves groping, to no apparent advantage. Solutions of problems is a far cry, people being more prone to shutting their eyes and looking in the other direction. They exhibit such tendencies as fear.

Morale and Adjustment

In this manner, in conditions of high morale, organisation of the workers is strong, and they can easily adjust to changing circumstances. Usually, they are not conscious of any differences and distinctions among themselves. On the other hand, in the case of low morale adjustment decreases.

Difference in the Morale of Individual Workers

Here, it should be kept in mind that if due to some reason the circumstances in a factory deteriorate temporarily, there is no necessity of the morale of every worker falling. On the other hand, while the general level of morale is high in a unit it is possible for certain individuals to be despondent and depressed. This difference is caused by the existence of individual differences as a result of which all individuals are influenced differently by changes and variations. On the other hand, even among the workers working in the same factory, positions and situations are different. For example, a particular worker may be in the good books of his boss, and this may give him a high morale, while other people may be suffering from low morale as they may not be in the good books of authority. Similarly, the same single occurrence or situation may have the result of improving morale of some people while it may depress others completely. For example, if, in a factory, special benefits are being made available to individuals of a particular group, caste, tribe, religion, this may positively effect their morale while it may have a negative influence on their less fortunate colleagues. It may even be so deep-rooted that they may turn antagonistic towards those in authority and this may cause a further fall in their morale.

Characteristics of a High Morale

From the above description it becomes evident that the following characteristics are evident in the case of high morale :

1. Positive or favourable attitude towards those in authority,
2. Self-induced obedience,
3. Positive feeling of respect and confidence for authorities,
4. Collective administration, unity and adjustment,
5. Rejection of frustration and a sense of enthusiasm,
6. Mental peace and satisfaction,
7. Productivity and system in work.

Requirement for a High Level of Morale

Normal Meyer has laid much stress on team spirit in morale. Morale is maintained intact if there is team spirit, and the following things are required for maintaining a high level of team spirit :

1. Application to work. This assimilates the essence of enthusiasm and powerful motives, as a result of which the person moves consistently in the direction of predetermined objectives.

2. Avoid diversion from work. This is a quantity of existent morale. In a state of this kind, people are not easily diverted from their tasks even when faced with failure.

3. Sense of cooperation. If a sense of cooperation within a community is present, people do not think in individual terms but in collective terms, and cooperate with each other as they identify personal success with the success of the community.

Characteristics of a Low Morale

Contrary to high morale, the following characteristics are in evidence in the case of low morale :

1. Antagonistic attitude towards those in authority,
2. Lack of obedience or forced obedience,
3. Feelings of hatred, jealousy, doubt, disrespect, lack of confidence towards those in authority,
4. Disappointment, unenthusiastic insipidity,
5. Lack of collective administration and unity, belief in lone effort,
6. Mental turmoil and unhappiness,
7. Lack of system and productivity in work,

8. Tendency to circulate all kinds of rumours,
9. Poisoning minds of others towards authority behind its back,
10. Lack of application to work,
11. Mutual conflicts and non-cooperation.

Methods of Measuring Morale

In order to discover the level of morale in a worker in any industry, it is necessary to observe the above-mentioned characteristics in him. Nowadays, morale is measured by the use of many scientific methods that reveal not only the level of morale as it exists, but also the causes whereby it has come into existence. They can then be remedied and a high morale be restored. The main methods are the following :

1. Common worker's opinion analysis. One very popularly used method of measuring the morale is the common worker's opinion analysis method in which the opinions of the average worker are collected and analysed. For this certain scientific questionnaires are prepared. These reveal the worker's opinions regarding the various aspects of the industry as well as towards the authorities. The worker does not have to reveal his name in answering these questionnaires. This has the initial advantage of assuring the worker of secrecy regarding his views. When the questionnaires are received back after having been fielded and duly completed by the workers, it becomes possible to see the various scores on which the workers have complained. If some particular object or subject is a matter of complaint in a large majority of cases, efforts can be made to rectify it. Success in this method depends upon the degree to which the questionnaire is scientific, and upon the degree of truth in the worker's responses.

2. Interview of departed workers. In this method, those individuals are directly interviewed who have departed from the unit in question for various reasons. One main advantage of this method is that it reveals the reasons whereby the workers feel compelled to seek jobs elsewhere, so that future desertion on the part of present employees can be discouraged. Another feature of this method is that having left the employment of a particular concern or unit he feels free to give expression to his frank views on any and every aspect of the business. Another advantage of this method is that the views of departed employees cannot result in any harm to the administration or to those in authority. There can be no doubt that some workers may have grievances against the administration or their job that has no relation whatsoever with actual and real conditions. But if many workers leave their jobs on the same pretext, then, evidently, it is necessary to put an end to the source of complaint in order to maintain a high level of morale. In this manner, this method has proved extraordinarily useful in measuring the existing level of morale, and suggesting methods for improvements. It also locates the causes of falling morale. If, however, most of the departed employees speak well and favourably of the work and the administration of the factory or business house, then there is every reason to believe that morale is at a high level.

3. Attitude measurement. As has been pointed out earlier, morale is an expression of the worker's attitude towards their work, the authorities and general administration or organisation. Hence, the workers' attitude can be known in order to evaluate their morale. For example, if the answers to the following queries were supplied by workers, their attitudes in these respects could be known :

1. I work in the company under compulsion.
2. The authorities in the company believe in the policy of paying as little wages as can practicably be paid.
3. If I can get the same salary in a different company, I am prepared to resign from my present position.
4. I have no respect for or faith in those in authority above me.
5. The conditions of work in which I work cannot be said to be good by any standards.
6. I find no freedom, pleasure or satisfaction in my work.

The worker's attitudes can be discovered by requiring him to mark the above queries right or wrong.

If most of the workers mark the above observations as correct, then obviously the level of morale is notoriously low. Other statements of a similar nature can be distributed among the workers in the form of a printed form or brochure and they can be required to mark them right or wrong according to their own inclination, so that the level of morale can be discovered as well as their attitudes towards various aspects of their occupation. Much importance in this method is attached to the choice of statements, which should be selected scientifically, as this makes the whole process much easier. The statements should be precise and exact so that the workers should be able to express their opinions clearly and categorically; vagueness must be avoided on both sides. This method is especially efficacious in the case of workers of a clerical class. Even uneducated and illiterate workers can make a mark on the statements. As this method also does not require of the worker that he reveals his name, he can fearlessly and without fear of bias or prejudice give expression to his frank opinion. Various statements are evaluated previously, and the scoring can be done accordingly. This gives the whole method a certain air of validity and accuracy. Once the answers have been received, the median of the various scores can be taken to gauge the attitude of the individual worker. If most of the answers are adverse it is concluded that morale is low, following which efforts are made to discover the causes that help it to be low, and remedies are suggested and in some cases actually applied. Generally speaking, every industry can formulate its own list of statements, but among the most important of the kind is that prepared by Arbauk and Bergon. Thurston and Chiev have made a detailed analysis of these statements.

4. Sociological method. Nowadays, particularly in the case of group studies, the sociological method is very prevalent. Moreover, a method for measuring the morale, can be used to discover characteristics of the worker's group organisation whereby the level of morale can be discovered. In the Jenken's experiment described earlier, only one aspect of the group organisation is included. Accordingly, the worker is given a questionnaire containing certain questions intended to throw light on the characteristics of group organisation. For example, the workers are asked to name and enumerate the individuals with whom they would like to work, or under whom they would prefer to work, or in which sort of company do they prefer to spend their time or have anything to do with. If the answers of many individuals to this question seem to speak favourably of any one individual, and the answers seem to show respect, love and confidence for the individual, it is fairly evident that he is capable of becoming a good administrator. If he is already in the administrative cadre, then it evinces a high level of morale in the workers, for respect and confidence in authority is a sign of high morale. But if he is not so situated, then the answers seem to show lack of confidence in the existing administration, a lack of confidence that can be rectified by promoting the desired individual into the administrative block, or otherwise by advising the existing administrative group to mend its ways and adopt others more calculated to win the confidence and respect of their subordinates. In this manner, it is evident that no method can help in realising the condition of morale in any unit, and in discovering the means of improving existing morale.

Essential Requirements for High Morale

Having studied the methods by which morale can be measured and evaluated, it is better to make a study of the elements that determine it. These elements are roughly divided into the following classes :

1. Physical requirements. This classification includes those physical conditions that influence morale, such as conditions of work, post, pay increases, methods of salary payment, conduct of inspector or authority, etc.

2. Mental requirements. These include such elements as praise, knowledge of success, fulfilment of cooperative needs, patience, forbearance, freedom, unity, feeling of equality, motivation, self-confidence and other psychological elements.

Physical Requirements for High Morale

1. Conditions of work. As has been evident from the account of morale all through, the conditions of work have an important influence upon it. If the conditions of work favour the worker and create interest in the work, morale is likely to be high. On the contrary, if the conditions of work are not favourable and serve to distract the interest of the worker, morale is likely to fall. Conditions of work, being a comprehensive term, it includes both physical and mental or psychological conditions. These will be described under mental and physical requirements. A fairly extensive description of them has already been given in a previous chapter, that on psychology in industry. Various researches have led to the belief that physical conditions of work have an important influence upon morale in the workers. As Tindall and Cair have proved on the basis of their experimentation, good conditions of work help to maintain a very high morale. In this connection, Cair his pointed out the influence of music on the mental condition of workers. Kulier's experiment seems to indicate that in bad conditions of work morale tends to fall because the worker evinces signs of worry, distaste, irritability, anxiety, sleeplessness, laziness, lethargy, etc.

2. Position and promotion. Studying the morale of various individuals in various positions of different companies, Arbock came to the conclusion that the attitude of foremen is better than that of clerks while that of clerks is more favourable than is the case with other classes of workers. This study reveals that the morale of individuals is also susceptible to such influences as the post that he is holding. The main psychological fact at the root of this phenomenon is that if the individual in question does not get a position that concurs with his psychological bent of mind, his enthusiasm begins to wane, and he loses confidence in those who are in authority above him. Hence, if morale is to be kept high in any and every industry, it is essential that posts be allotted in accordance with the ability and labour of the individuals, and that these posts be improved from time to time. Much the same phenomena come to light in a study of promotion in a previous chapter.

3. Increase in salary. It is a psychological fact that workers are primarily concerned with their salary or wages. Shepard has stressed the fact that if the worker's wages are reassessed from time to time and appropriate changes are made, the morale tends to occupy a high level. On the contrary, if the wages remain stationary for a long time, and there is no advancement, the workers' enthusiasm is dampened, and they tend to heap blame on their officers. Increase in pay should be made dependent upon hard work and other qualities. If increase in pay depends upon the personal idiosyncrasy of the individual in power, most people become cynical as they do not like to cringe before such a person. Secondly, even the ingratiating types who win increases in pay and promotions through subservience rarely have a high morale. Hence, for pay increase to have a favourable influence upon morale, it is essential that the basis of increase be proper and the same for everyone.

4. Method of distributing salaries. Morale is also influenced by the method of distributing salary no less than by increase in it. All studies to date on the subject have not led to any conclusive idea as to which method is definitely the best. Some methods are of, course, better than certain others. Various methods will be examined briefly here :

(a) ***Share of profits :*** Under this method, the workers in companies and factories are given bonuses and share of profits from time to time. The following facts need to be mentioned in connection with this method :

(i) This method engenders dissatisfaction in the better and more efficient workers because they find that other less efficient and skilful than themselves are deriving the same benefits without actually deserving them.

(ii) In this method, the worker is never sure of his actual income in the near future because neither the quantity of profit is shared nor the time of its distribution is certain.

Despite the above clear difficulties and drawbacks, this method has been found to meet with the approval of approximately one-third workers. Besides, this method is also rather simple, as a consequence of which it is one of the most, widely used today.

(b) ***Remuneration according to work*** **:** In this method, the worker is reimbursed according to the quantity of material he produces. The research made by Mathewson on this subject has made it abundantly clear that the method can succeed only if the worker is confident that the rate of payment will not fall, because he usually expects that if he works more he will earn more but also thereby create a reason for the company reducing the rate of payment. Fear of this kind guides them to reduce their rate of working.

It is evident that if the worker can be convinced of the stability of payment rates, the piece wages method is superior to the bonus method, but it requires that the following facts can be kept in mind :

(i) Attention should be concerned not only on quantity but also on quality.

(ii) In paying the worker, it should be made abundantly clear to him that he is being paid according to a certain definite rate for a specific kind of work so that no doubt lingers in his mind and compels him to work slower.

(iii) In connection with remuneration, the rates should be constant and there should be no fear of the rate of payment being reduced.

If the above facts are kept in mind, and the appropriate arrangements made, the morale of the worker can be kept high through the piece wages method, because it is by this method that the worker is constantly inspired to work more and to produce better results. It is also very good from the point of view of creating good incentives.

5. Ability to profit. Among the physical requirements, another is the possibility and opportunity of progress in any concern. If the workers in a company are being paid dividends out of its profits, then it should be equally distributed. In another words, all workers should be given the opportunity to progress and earn high wages, without any discrimination. If this is not done, most of them tend to turn against the authorities in their company, while at the same time a feeling of jealousy for those who have progressed is engendered in the unfortunate ones. This destroys not only collective organisation and administrative efficiency, but also faith and belief in the authorities. Hence, the rules governing promotions and increase in salary should be equally applicable to all, and they should be clearly understood by all of them. No one should be given a chance to complain on these grounds.

Psychological Requirement for High Morale

Having completed a cursory study of the physical requirements of morale, a detailed study of its psychological requirements will now be made :

1. Praise. It is a matter of general psychological knowledge that praise of good work and effort helps to infuse further enthusiasm and energy in the worker.

Studies conducted by such eminent psychologists as Thorndike and Hurlock, evinced that praise of a workers' effort helps to increase his motivation. In fact, the influence of the reward and punishment scheme on work is fairly evident and widely known. Any work that derives punishment for the perpetrator is shunned by him in future, while he desires to repeat any work that results in reward. Praise is a psychological reward. Praise by individuals for whom we have respect and in whose judgement we have faith matters a lot to us. If the authorities in the factory or office praise all good effort, then morale becomes high among the workers. On the other hand, if good work and hard labour go unpraised or unnoticed, enthusiasm wanes in the worker, as he feels that he is not being valued according to his merits. This fact is one of the important reasons why work in an impersonal psychological organisation like government office is rarely of a high order of efficiency. Direct praise or blame is rarely forthcoming, except from very conscientious individuals in authority.

2. Knowledge of success. Some other experiments have brought to light the fact that if the worker is aware of the degree of success he is achieving in his work, his interest and enthusiasm in it are maintained, and so is the high level of morale. In very big factories where the individual worker does no more than make only a very small cog in a very big wheel and is not aware of the effect of his own effort towards the completed wheel, boredom and disinterest are likely to set in very early. What is here implied is not the knowledge of the mere result. Result of work can be bad as well as good. Knowledge of failure can only serve to lower the morale, but if the worker is again encouraged to think in terms of success, morale can be regained. As a general rule, success ensures a high morale. Success is the reward of effort. And reward is a favourable element in the creation and maintenance of morale. Colstaad's studies showed that the morale of workers in shops that have a very big turnover with large profits is much higher and better than that of workers employed in smaller organisations with a smaller turnover and lesser profits. This evidence is rooted in the psychological fact that success increases an individual's confidence in himself and he comes to realise his own importance. His social prestige increases, and in order to maintain all these privileges intact, he is driven to work with even greater energy and resolve.

3. Fulfilment of collective needs. Man works not only to meet the needs of his body, such needs as food and clothing, but also to satisfy certain other collective psychological requirements. He is also desirous of meeting others, giving vent to his feelings and emotions, thoughts and beliefs, exhibiting himself, knowing himself and winning social prestige and recognition. Any kind of work that affords all these advantages to the worker is almost certain to create a very high morale in him, but if all these things are not made available to him, morale is likely to fall, if it was ever high. Hence, in maintaining the morale of their workers, the organisers and authorities should keep in mind the fact that the worker's collective needs be also fulfilled and satisfied.

4. Forbearance and good behaviour of authorities. Workers attach much importance to the behaviour of inspectors, managers and others in authority, towards them. If conduct towards them is not all that can be desired, general morale is likely to suffer. If the worker is constantly interrupted and scolded over his work, he loses all respect for the officer. Actually, the only course of keeping workers contented that is open to the officers and authorities is that of good and considerate behaviour towards them. In such circumstances, the workers are inclined to pay little attention to other conditions around them and are enthusiastic enough to do anything that is likely to benefit their factory organisation. This is due to an identity of interests that is felt by the worker. A sense of possession invades him. On the contrary, the worker's self-respect is injured if the authority above him behaves in an irresponsible manner towards him. In fact, a position of authority does not require occupational skill so much as it requires the qualities of leadership and organisation, a skill in diplomacy. A leader plays an important part in maintaining the morale of a group of people. In company offices and factories, the leaders are none other than managers and authorities, and it is good for them to have a good knowledge of human psychology. Their behaviour towards the worker should be such that it should easily adjust in the collective organisation. Tolerance is an important quality in leaders. Tolerance only adds to the respect that is forthcoming; it does not detract from it. But tolerance does not imply that the officer or leader should calmly overlook the mistakes of his subordinates. What is important is that due importance be given to all things brought to his notice. It is hardly proper to be constantly wrangling over small and inconsequential matters. But to overlook a thing of great magnitude is again a serious fault that should not be allowed to go uncorrected. Those in authority should be possessed of democratic qualities. Studies conducted in the Iowa University of the United States of America and by Lipik have revealed that group working under a democratic leader is completely organised. In such a group, the workers continue with their duties even during the leader's absence. They have favourable mental attitudes towards the leader and other fellow workers. Contrary to this, morale in the group that works under an authoritarian or autocratic leader is usually low, work being continued in his presence because of fear but being suspended in his absence. They entertain feelings of jealousy and hatred for such a leader. In this manner, it is evident that for maintaining a high level of morale among workers, there is great importance attached to tolerant and considerate behaviour on the part of officers.

5. Freedom of workers. In whichever company or factory a worker loses his identity to the extent of being reduced to the level of a small cog in the huge wheel, he is dissatisfied with his work because it appears heavy and insipid to him. Hence, in order to maintain the worker's morale at a high level it is essential that he be given the maximum degree of freedom that his function and position allow. He should also not be prevented from meeting other fellow workers, in particular those individuals who are in authority. It helps in creating a more intimate and knowledgeable atmosphere, in which he can tell his troubles to the proverbial daddy. But giving freedom does not imply that discipline should be done away with. Independence within the framework of laws is the most desirable state of affairs.

6. Sense of organisation and identity or equality. It has been pointed out earlier that collective or group organisation is indicative of high morale. Hence, it is essential that a sense of organisation and unity should circulate freely among the workers. Psychologists, among them May and Wright, concluded from their examinations and study that in order to maintain a high morale among workers in industries it is essential that the workers have in themselves a feeling of being organised and united or equal. The workers should be able to identify themselves with their factory or office or organisation, and think of its interests as if they were their own. If this is achieved, even the most difficult times can be successfully seen through by making a collective effort. Increase in the feeling of unity and identity can be facilitated by many things such as a definite name of the company or organisation, a definite dress and a common badge. Besides these, certain group objectives can be set up, the achievement of which involves organised and collective effort on the part of the workers. Exerting oneself along with many others, straining for the same objectives serves to lessen tension, increase mutual goodwill and promote organisation. Workers should be made to realise that they are important and responsible members of the industry. They should also be equipped with knowledge of the various parts of the industry, so that they can come to look upon it as their own industry. Some mill-owners are under the impression that their interest lies in keeping the workers quarrelling among themselves. As a policy this may have some immediate benefits but in the long run this is a very harmful policy because lack of collective organisation in workers lowers their morale, and this finally has an adverse influence upon the quality and quantity of work done by the workers.

JOB SATISFACTION

The importance of job satisfaction is fairly evident from a description of the importance of maintaining morale in any industry. If a worker is not satisfied with his work, then both the quantity and quality of his output will suffer. If his job satisfaction increases then there is an improvement in both the quality and quantity of production. Factories in which the workers are satisfied with their officers are also characterised by a high morale. The following things are generally important for creating job satisfaction :

1. Attending to and solving problems. It is desirable that the complaints of the workers be heard patiently and the problems solved as far as possible. Factories in which the workers' demands are not heeded suffer because the workers lose confidence in the management and become frustrated.

2. Satisfactory future. Every worker is definitely concerned about his future prospects. If the factory rules clearly lay down the conditions of promotions and advancement, and if the worker gets the expected promotion and improvement in pay scales at the right time, he feels satisfied and becomes confident of his future. If on the other hand, the worker feels that even good work will not be rewarded, he becomes frustrated and slack in his work.

3. Testing the worker's ability and progress. Every worker, whether in a factory or an office, desires that he should be paid according to his ability. If he has undergone some new training or has increased his ability to work in some way, he should be compensated for his better ability through a raise in salary. Organisations in which the management keeps an eye on the ability and progress of its workers normally have a high degree of job satisfaction among their workers. It is necessary that the management should give the worker some opportunity of progressing higher and higher. If, on the other hand, the organisation does not pay any attention to the abilities and increased efficiency of its staff, it suffers in the long run because the workers lose interest in their job and do not often try to improve their level of efficiency. This happens because they feel that an increase in qualifications of efficiency is not related to progress or promotion.

4. Respect for creative suggestions. Generally speaking, the worker working under a particular set of conditions is best qualified to say how and where improvements can be made. If workers are encouraged to suggest ways and means of improving the condition of work, they often come up with very valuable ideas. This helps in increasing job satisfaction because when the worker is praised for giving a good practical idea he tends to pay more attention to his work in order to win more praise. If such suggestions are neglected then the worker feels dissatisfied since apparently there can be no improvement in the conditions in which he works.

5. Creative analysis or evaluation of the work. In every organisation the manager or the supervisor has to offer criticism of the work performed by the worker because he must point out the worker's mistakes and try to eliminate them. If this criticism is offered in a cordial and friendly way, more as suggestion than as criticism, then the worker feels gratified and pays attention to it. His job satisfaction is also thereby maintained. But if the worker is abused or bitterly criticised for his mistakes, he loses his peace of mind.

6. Increase in wages. Rules governing increase in salary should be clear and explicit and should be acted upon impartially and as and when these are due, because any delay in this matter would send wrong signals. If the worker gets the anticipated increase in salary at the right time, he feels satisfied with his job. If this does not happen, dissatisfaction is the result. Increase in salary is, in fact, the most important factor in job satisfaction.

7. Praise for good performance. If workers are not praised for exceptional performance in their work, they lose interest in it and as a result, the organisation suffers. Even if they do good work, they still remain dissatisfied and disgruntled. Generally, the worker prefers to work well and remain occupied than merely to pass the time allotted to him. If he is also encouraged in his work by an occasional word of praise and respect, he is further motivated to maintain a high level of efficiency and in fact to improve it. If he is not praised for his work, his enthusiasm and zeal immediately fall.

8. Promotion according to ability. In every organisation some people are always being retired after completion of their tenure while younger people are promoted to take their places. If promotion is based upon the ability of the worker then the worker's mental satisfaction is maintained. If, on the other hand, promotion depends upon other factors such as casteism, personal favour, etc., then the worker's interest in his work declines.

9. Proper quantum of work. If job satisfaction is to be maintained, it is essential that the quantity of work does not exceed the individual's ability to complete it. If he has to work more than he comfortably can for a long time, the worker is bound to become disgusted, depressed and tired.

10. Equal wages for equal work. Labour unions in almost every industry are now demanding that there should be equal pay for equal work. In any factory or office, a worker must be paid as much as other workers are being paid in other organisations for similar work. The worker feels satisfied if this equality is maintained. If it is not, then the worker loses his satisfaction.

11. Freedom to seek help in solving problems. Very often the worker is faced by problems in his work that he cannot solve alone. In such a case he should be free to seek help and guidance from other workers or even from the managers.

12. Absence of unnecessary intervention and criticism. No individual wants to sacrifice his self respect. If the worker is unnecessarily shown disrespect or abused, he quickly becomes dissatisfied. Hence he should be protected from useless interruptions and criticism.

13. Satisfactory hours of work. The hours of work in any factory or office should be convenient and so arranged as to offer the least possible inconvenience to the largest number of employees. If this is not looked into, the workers become dissatisfied.

14. Availability of leave and rest. In every industrial organisation the workers should be given the proper amount of rest and holidays on festivals and other occasions of social celebrations. Nowadays it is thought necessary to give a half holiday every fifteen days in addition to the weekly holiday. Rest given on festivals and on occasions of general celebration is in addition to this. Besides, the worker is also permitted to take leave for medical or other private reasons. Female workers are allowed fairly long leave during pregnancy. It is generally seen that workers feel satisfied if the management in any organisation follows a liberal policy towards leave for workers.

It is evident from the above description of factors influencing job satisfaction that it necessitates the creation of certain conditions of work. Different factors may be of importance in different situations. Increase in wages is a common factor which is important everywhere. Promotion is another factor which plays an important role in maintaining or destroying job satisfaction. Apart from this, the other factors may be more or less important, depending upon the situation. For example, an organisation in which the worker's educational degrees have great importance should also see to it that the worker is promoted when he adds to his qualifications. On the other hand, in an organisation in which training or paper qualifications have no value, this question will not arise at all. Finally, it can be said that job satisfaction depends on all those factors which influence morale.

QUESTIONS FOR EXERCISE

1. What is the nature of morale in industry? Discuss the determinants of morale.
2. What steps would you suggest for building morale in a large scale sugar factory in rural area?
3. What is job satisfaction? Explain the facts creating it.

16

Psychology of Advertisement

What is Advertisement?

If you ask a person as to what is the medicine for headache, he will name Aspro even though he may have never used it, because he has heard the name of this patent medicine so many times that it spontaneously comes to the forefront of the mind as soon as headache is mentioned. Not many persons use Dalda in India but how many are there who do not know it? These days whenever an educated person goes out to purchase cloth he checks the mark of 'Sanforized' on it. All this is due to advertisement. Advertisement introduces things to persons. It points out to the special characteristics of commodities. In the words of Husband, "Advertisement may be defined as publicity which calls attention to the existence and merits of certain foods and services."[1]

IMPORTANCE OF ADVERTISEMENT

One finds a lot of competition in the present day economic field. The problem of selling is not solved by mere manufacturing. To illustrate, suppose a firm manufactures a particular type of soap. Now, unless the buyers come to know about the existence of this particular brand of soap how can they buy it? Again, even the knowledge of its existence is not sufficient to boost its sale. They should know its peculiarities and qualities. But the problem does not end here. Even when the buyer is told of the qualities of soap, it is not necessary that he may come to believe them. And even if he believes it still he may have no desire to buy it. This shows the importance of advertisement. These days advertisement has become a

1. Husband, R.W., *Applied Psychology* (Rev. ed.), Harper and Brothers, New York (1949), p. 467.

science and even an art. In progressive countries constant researches are being conducted in the field of advertisement. After a thing is advertised, the results of advertisement are checked. This shows the results of special types of advertisement on the buyers of particular things. Very interesting facts have been discovered by this research. For example, it has been found that advertisements through moving things, animals and human beings are more impressive than through motionless things and animals respectively. In fact, success in the sale of anything depends on success in its advertisement.

AIMS OF ADVERTISEMENT

The following are the main aims of advertisement :

1. Drawing attention. The first and foremost aim of advertisement is to draw the attention of the persons towards a particular thing or service. In the cities, on big railway junctions and on busy squares, one finds advertisement of different things in bold letters. At one place one finds the word USHA in red light, at another place there is TATA in moving light. Bare names in capital words are written in very sizable signboards. These advertisements do not describe the qualities of the objects they advertise. They only introduce these names to the public. Electric bulbs are used to draw attention. Big signboards draw more attention than smaller ones. Figures, colours, headings, form, light, etc., all the different items of advertisement aim at drawing the attention.

2. Creating interest. Generally speaking only that object draws attention which is interesting. Why do you find the pictures of film actresses in the advertisement of Lux toilet soap? Why are pictures of women displayed in posters advertising *bidis*? Have you ever seen the day-by-day of Rexona soap? What is the secret of the success of advertisement? The answer is that it lies in creating interest. The aim of displaying women's pictures in the advertisement of things is to create interest in them. Most men take interest in beautiful women. A successful advertiser takes cognizance of the interest of the buyers because interest and attention are closely related.

3. Creating belief. As has been pointed out earlier, mere knowledge of the existence of a thing or mere introduction with its qualities is not sufficient for its being sold. The main problem is to create belief among the buyers that it has these particular types of qualities. This can be done in a variety of ways. One way is to seek recommendations from eminent leaders, film actors and actresses, etc. Certificates from eminent physicians are helpful in the advertisement of medicines. Sometimes the number of commodities sold is advertised to create faith in their quality, *e.g.*, 50,000 copies of such and such books have been sold.

4. Remembering. Advertisement should influence memory because a person does not need a thing while he reads its advertisement. The advertisement should be such that when he needs it he should be able to recall its name and the name of the firm manufacturing it.

5. Creating a desire to buy. In the end, the main purpose of the advertisement is to create a desire among persons to buy it. It is hence that advertisers check the influence of advertisement on sale. The success of an advertisement is correlated to the success in sales. Though the advertisement is attractive and interesting these do not constitute its aim. Its main aim is to boost the sales of a commodity. All else is mere means to achieve this end.

PSYCHOLOGICAL BASES OF THE APPEAL OF ADVERTISEMENT

In the words of Blum, "The core of all advertising is suggestion."[2] Advertisement aims at suggesting buying of a particular thing; advertisement is a science of drawing attention. Some traits attract more attention than others. Much progress has been made in the art of advertisement by the discovery of internal and external determinants of attention. In order to understand the importance of attention as the psychological basis of advertisement, it shall be relevant to describe briefly the internal and external determinants of attention.

CONDITIONS OF ATTENTION

As a selective act of the mind, attention depends upon several conditions. These conditions may be of two types — external or objective and internal or subjective. External or

2. Blum, M.L., *Industrial Psychology and its Social Foundations*, Harper and Bros., New York (1944), p. 448.

objective conditions are related with the environment. In the environment or surroundings of the individual there are several stimuli, but he does not attend to all of them at the same time, because some stimuli are stronger than others. The factors making these stimuli stronger than others are known as external determinants of attention. Besides the external conditions, the mental conditions, culture and heredity also influence attention. Owing to these internal conditions, some objects attract our attention more than others. These are internal determinants of attention. The methods of achieving attention are based upon these external and internal determinants of attention.

External Determinants of Attention

The following are the most important external determinants of attention :

1. Nature of stimulus. Nature of stimulus means its type, *i.e.*, whether it is visual, gustatory, auditory, olfactory or tactual stimulus. It has been found by experiments that in comparison with other sensations, colour and sound attract more attention. Among the pictures, the pictures of human beings attract more attention than those of animals or objects. Among the pictures of human beings those of beautiful women attract more attention. Besides these, the coloured pictures attract more attention than colourless ones. All these factors are important in advertisement. In the auditory stimulus, the melodious voice attracts more attention than other voices.

2. Intensity of the stimulus. The intensity of the stimulus is a helpful condition in attention. In comparison with the weak stimuli, the intense stimulus attracts more attention of the organism. High sound, excessive pressure and acute pain attract our attention. In the market there is always some buzzing sound and yet the pedestrians hear the horn of the motor car, since the sound of the horn is louder than other sounds. But it is not always necessary that one should attend to the intensity of the stimulus. Sometimes while walking on the road, calling of our name attracts so much attention that we fail to hear even the loud sound of the motor horn. As a matter of fact, the attraction of the attention does not depend on any single factor, but on several factors interconnected with one another. Hence, it can be said that other things being the same, the more intense stimulus will attract more attention.

3. Size of the stimulus. In the visual stimuli, the size of the stimulus is also a determinant of attention. As a general rule, the bigger size attracts more attention, but a small advertisement on a very wide background also attracts attention. Thus the attraction of an object does not depend upon its size alone, but also on its background. To illustrate, a big black spot on a black face will not attract so much attention as a very small black spot on a white face.

4. Location of the stimulus. The location of the stimulus also affects attention. In the visual stimuli, the most effective location is just in front of the eyes. The role of different pages in the newspaper or the magazine and the different places on the same page, is important in advertisement. It has been found by experiments that advertisements given on the front page or on the upper half of any page attract more attention.

5. Contrast of the stimulus. The contrast to the stimulus is also an important determinant of attention, *e.g.*, the presence of a woman among men and that of a man among women definitely attracts more attention.

6. Change of the stimulus. Attention cannot be concentrated for a long time on some particular object. Hence, the change of the stimulus also affects attention. Attention is sustained by change of the stimulus. The advertisers change their advertisements from time to time lest it may cease to be attractive.

7. Isolation of the stimulus. A man sitting alone in some corner of the park hotel or club attracts more attention than others. A student sitting alone at the far corner of the class is seen first. Thus isolation is an important external determinant of attention. This fact is based upon the reason that the isolated individual is not mixed with other individuals and hence seen separately in his own background. By experiments in advertisement it has been found that only the fact of isolation attracts 30 per cent more attention. In the *British Journal of Educational psychology,* D.E. Berlyne points out the following principles based upon experiments :

(a) In comparison with the unchanged stimulus, the stimulus changed in the near past has more possibility of attracting attention.

(b) The effect of the change goes on diminishing with the passage of time.

(c) Whenever stimuli are changed together and in which one is left unchanged, the effect of change is not noticeable.

(d) If change goes on in the changed stimuli, the process of attention is rather permanent and strong.

The modes of change also influence the process of attention. If there is a change absolutely it attracts more attention. While studying one does not hear the sound of the clock or that of electric fan but if either of these suddenly stops, one cannot fail to attend to it. Man becomes used to regular changes and does not pay much attention to them. But if some irregular change or any sudden change occurs, it at once draws attention.

8. Duration of the stimulus. As a general rule, the stimulus having more duration attracts more attention. Thus duration of the stimulus is an important determinant of the attention. But sometimes the smallest flashing of a movement attracts more attention than the bigger stimuli, *e.g.*, a sudden flash of light for several seconds will attract more attention in a dark night than the continuous burning lamp.

9. Repetition of the stimulus. Along with duration, repetition of the stimulus is also an important determinant of attention. It is a commonplace observation that when the teacher has also to attract the attention of students towards a particular phenomenon, he repeats it several times. But sometimes, man ceases to attend to a phenomenon simply because it is repeated many times, *e.g.*, if a man says some things about himself, we take interest in it once or twice, but if we find that he always repeats the same thing, we cease to pay attention to it.

10. Movement in the stimulus. In comparison with the static, the moving stimuli attract more attention. The position of a stimulus changes due to movements. An object lying in some corner of the room will not attract our attention, but even if there is some illusion of movement in it, we cannot help attending to it. The influence of movement in stimulus is widely used by the shopkeepers and businessmen, who advertise through moving electric lights.

Internal Determinants of Attention

The conditions of attention as described so far are the external determinants of attention. They can also be called external laws of attention. The presence of these conditions in the environments is helpful for attention. Besides these, internal conditions are also helpful in drawing attention. These conditions are related with motives. As a matter of fact, the influence of external conditions depends on these internal conditions to a very great extent. The hungry man will attend to the form and stimuli of the food. A man with full belly will not attend to food, however nice it might appear. In the advertisements those demonstrating the naked organs of the woman have maximum power of attention. Those interested in cinema look to the advertisements of cinema at first sight. It is difficult to describe all the internal conditions helpful in attention. Hence, only the most important will be enumerated here :

1. Interest. Innate and acquired interests draw the individual's attention to particular objects. Doctors, engineers, professors, all attend to the objects of their own interest. Even among the professors, an object attracting the attention of a professor of Geology, need not attract the attention of a professor of Philosophy as well. Thus the innumerable differences in interests create innumerable determinants of attention in different men. The stimuli influencing innate tendencies attract more attention than those influencing acquired interest.

2. Basic drives. The basic drives and impulses of the individual are also important in drawing its attention. The animal attends to particular stimulus when driven by the basic drives of hunger, thirst, sex, etc., *e.g.*, a normal man motivated by sex will naturally attend to the individuals of opposite sex. We all know it by experience that when hungry we many attend to even a distasteful object, but while our belly is full, we may not attend to even the most tasteful food. Among the motives, fear has got definite influence upon attention. All men who fear snake will attend to all things resembling the snake. Like fear, curiosity also influences attention. We attend to even the smallest details of the object towards which we have curiosity.

Innate need also is very important in attention. The influence of sexual need in attention is very much exploited in advertisements. Normally, the sexual need in human beings can be easily evoked. Hunger, thirst, etc. are felt occasionally and the means to satisfy them are also readily available, but neither the sexual need is ever fully satisfied nor the means of satisfying it are available to all the persons all the time. Hence, most of the advertisements draw attention by stimulating the sexual need in human beings.

3. Mental Set. Mental set is one of the most important internal determinants of attention. Mental set means the tendency or bent of the whole mind. A man will attend to those objects towards which his mind is set. In the days of examinations, the mental set of the students is generally towards the examination and hence even the smallest thing concerning the examination will attract their attention.

4. Aim. Aim also influences attention. Every man has some immediate and some ultimate aims *e.g.*, the immediate aim of the student is to pass the examination while the ultimate aim may be to get a job to earn a living or anything else. The man whose aim is not to pass the examination will be concerned with textbooks or notes etc., but one who has the aim to pass the examination will at once attend to them.

5. Meaning. In comparison with meaningless things, meaningful things and talks attract more attention. A man will not attend to a thing which has no meaning for him. Men do not like to hear meaningless talk. If some persons are talking in Tamil, the Punjabi will not like to hear it since for him it has no meaning.

6. Habit. Habit is also an important determinant of attention. If a man is habituated to rising early and winding his clock early in the morning, he must attend to the clock as soon as he gets up. It has been rightly pointed out that man learns as to which object he should attend and which he should not and thus develops habits of attending and not attending to things. Thus habit has two aspects in relation to attention. On the one side, men develop a habit of attending to necessary and desirable things and on the other side they develop the habit of not attending to unnecessary and undesirable things. Both these kind of habits help man in his daily routine.

7. Disposition and temperament. Both disposition and temperament are important internal determinants of attention *e.g.*, a man having a religious disposition and spiritual temperament will attend to religious matters, while another person having a sexual disposition and criminal temperament will attend to matters concerning sex or crimes etc. William James has rightly pointed out that it is our tendency to take interest in particular things. Our innate disposition and mental development determine that which, among the crowd of sensations, should attract our attention.

8. Past experience. Past experience also affects attention. If we know it by our past experience that a particular person is sincere to us, we shall pay attention to whatever he advises us. If we know by experience that he is not sincere to us, we shall not attend even to his most serious advice.

9. Emotion. Emotion is also an important determinant of attention. It is a matter of everyday experience that we attend to even the smallest fault of a person whom we hate while we do not attend even to the greatest blunder of a person whom we love. A mother seldom finds fault with her child. The lovers find the whole world singing and dancing and immersed in romance.

10. Social motives. Social motives are important determinants of attention. In advertisements the human figures attract more attention than figures of animals and things. The reason is that man is guided by his social motives. News about altruism, bravery and saving other's life by putting oneself in danger, attract our attention because we praise these qualities. Men attend to things concerning their duties for social motives.

Besides the conditions described above, many other factors influence attention. Heredity, education and training have a wide influence on attention. The family, school, club, class and society of which an individual is a member, do have some influence on his attention. The physical condition, desire, purpose of the person concerned also affect his attention. Thus all the factors influencing the personality of a man affect his attention as well. As a matter of fact, it is difficult to describe all direct and indirect determinants of attention. The description given here, however, includes the most important of such factors.

ADVERTISEMENT AND MEMORY

Memory has got much importance in the psychological basis of advertisement. The advertisement should be such that those who hear, read or see it may remember it. It is then alone that they will buy it when needed. The thing should be named such as also exhibits its function. This leads to the association of name with function, so that it is recalled whenever that particular function is needed. Examples of some such names are Nahan soap, Sina machine, Sulekha ink, etc. There is much difficulty in the advertisement of things which bear difficult names that cannot be remembered easily. Sometimes the fact of the relation of advertisement with memory is misused. For example, when a particular trade mark becomes famous, some unscrupulous persons give a similar name to their products. Names such as Sunlight and Lifebuoy followed after Sunlight and Lifebuoy soaps became well known.

ADVERTISEMENT AND SUGGESTION

As has been pointed out earlier, the main psychological basis of advertisement is suggestion. The meaning of suggestion is to motivate a person to do a particular kind of work. Some advertisements directly ask for the purchase of particular things. Recommendations of film actors and actresses are used as suggestion in some other advertisements. You must have seen recommendations of many beautiful film actresses for the skin care from Lux soap. Such advertisements involve prestige suggestion. Advertisers of vegetable oil often present certificates of its being harmless. Such advertisements suggest for the purchase of particular things.

ADVERTISEMENT AND ATTITUDE

Attitude is also a very important psychological element in the basis of advertisement. It is a permanent organisation of motivational, emotional, perceptual and cognitive processes in a person towards objects surrounding him. Advertisement cannot be effective unless attitude is favourable. For example, in every free country one finds pro-nation attitude among people. Hence, things can be advertised in the name of Swadeshi.

While closing our discussion over the psychological basis of advertisement, it will be relevant to analyse different elements of its psychological appeal. An advertisement consists of illustration, colour, headline, text or copy, trade mark or trade name and layout or arrangement of the advertisement. All these must have psychological appeal in order to make advertisement affective. Some important points in this connection will be pointed out here :

1. Illustration. Illustrations in an advertisement should be real and interesting. If they are only real they will attract less attention. If they are only interesting, they will not motivate purchase.

2. Colour. Colours plays an important role in advertisement, but its success depends on right choice of suitable colours. In different seasons different colours are agreeable. Distinction of age and sex also has considerable bearing on this issue. As a general rule while blue colour appeals to men, red appeals to women. Again, while dark colours are favoured by the young, the aged favour light colours. In summer blue and green colours are more agreeable while in winter red and black may be more useful for advertisement.

3. Headline. Generally every advertisement bears a headline. The headline has two aims — on the one hand it creates interest in the advertisement, on the other hand it motivates persons to buy a particular thing. Therefore, firstly, the headline should be such as can be easily remembered. Secondly, it should lead to the desire to read the entire text of the advertisement. Thirdly, it should be brief and attractive. Life Insurance Corporation of India has given many much advertisements.

4. Text or copy. An advertisement contains a text or copy to give information regarding the object and its utility. This requires much precaution. Generally, indirect text is more appealing. Sometimes manufacturers of cloth, rubber and paper advertise the story of cloth, rubber and paper respectively. This is interesting and also advertises the commodity indirectly. Text should be brief. It should tell the truth, create faith and the motive to purchase the thing advertised.

5. Trade mark or trade name. Generally every manufacturer has a certain trade mark or trade name, *e.g.*, Tata, Bata, Lipton, Brook Bond, Kodak, etc. Gradually, these trade marks become popular and things are bought by trade name. Sometimes, however, a trade mark becomes so much popular that it no more represents a particular manufacturer but becomes a synonym for particular thing. For example, the word Bata is used for shoes. Some manufacturers only advertise their trade name or trade mark.

6. Layout. In the end, the above-mentioned items in an advertisement should be organised in a proper layout. In a good layout sufficient space is left bare. The illustration which has to be emphasised should be very clear. If an advertisement is on the whole page, it need not have any border. If it is less than a page it may have border. The illustration, colour and background should be sufficiently matching. Generally, plain advertisements are better. If many things are huddled up together, the onlooker may not remember any of them.

While advertising, care should be taken to consider the sex, age, class, education and economic level of the persons for whom the advertisement is prepared, for all these factors make difference in the interest, disposition, motivation and attention of the persons concerned. For example, persons belonging to lower and middle-income group are more attracted to such advertisement as promise to give things in less expenses, whereas such advertisements will not appeal to rich persons because they do not pay so much attention to price as to quality and novelty of a thing. Arguments may be advanced in the text of the advertisement meant for educated buyers whereas they are useless in the case of uneducated persons. Advertisements for young men and women should be interesting and attractive. Women are more influenced by suggestion and less by reasoning. Thus, the effectiveness of advertisement depends on the strength of its appeal to the particular class of persons who are supposed to buy that particular thing. Practical success of an advertisement depends upon the psychological insight of the advertiser.

QUESTIONS FOR EXERCISE

1. What is advertisement? Analyse bases of its appeal.
2. Write short note on Psychology of Advertisement.

Bibliography

Akolkar, V., *Social Psychology,* Asia Publishing House.

Anastasi, A., *Psychological Testing,* Macmillan.

Bell, J.E., *Projective Techniques,* Longmans Green.

Bellak, L., *The T.A.T. and C.A.T., in Clinical Use,* Grune and Stratton, New York.

Bernard, H.W., *Mental Hygiene for Classroom Teachers,* McGraw Hill.

Bhatia, C.M., *Mental Testing and National Reconstruction,* Hind Kitabs.

Bhatia C.M., *Performance Test of Intelligence,* Oxford University Press.

Bingham, W.V.D., *Aptitude and Aptitude Testing,* Harper and Brothers.

Blum, M.L., *Industrial Psychology and its Social Foundations,* Harper and Brothers, New York.

Blum and Balansky, *Counselling and Psychology,* Prentice Hall.

Brown, J.E., *The Psychodynamics of Abnormal Behaviour,* McGraw Hill Book Co., New York.

Burt, H.E., *Applied Psychology,* Prentice Hall.

Gray, J.S., *Psychology Applied to Human Affairs,* McGraw Hill Book Co., New York.

Grifith, C.R., *An Introduction to Applied Psychology,* Macmillan Co., New York.

Husband, R.W., *Applied Psychology,* Harper and Brothers, New York.

Maier, N.R.F., *Psychology in Industry,* Houghton Mifflin.

Murrey, H.A., *Explorations in Personality in India : A Symposium,* Bombay.

Nanavati and Vakil, *Group Prejudices in India : A Symposium,* Bombay.

Shafer and Shoben, *The Psychology of Adjustment*, Houghton Mifflin.

Sherif, M. and Sherif, C.W., *An Outline of Social Psychology*, Harper and Brothers, New York.

Verson, P.E., *Structure of Human Abilities*, John Willey.